First World War

and Army of Occupation

War Diary

France, Belgium and Germany

9 DIVISION
Headquarters, Branches and Services
Royal Army Ordnance Corps
Deputy Assistant Director Ordnance Services
and Royal Army Veterinary Corps
Assistant Director Veterinary Services
9 May 1915 - 24 October 1919

WO95/1750

The Naval & Military Press Ltd
www.nmarchive.com
Published in association with The National Archives

Published by

The Naval & Military Press Ltd

Unit 10 Ridgewood Industrial Park,

Uckfield, East Sussex,

TN22 5QE England

Tel: +44 (0) 1825 749494

www.naval-military-press.com

www.nmarchive.com

This diary has been reprinted in facsimile from the original. Any imperfections are inevitably reproduced and the quality may fall short of modern type and cartographic standards.

Contents

Document type	Place/Title	Date From	Date To
Heading	9th Division D.A.D.O.S. Aug 1915-1919 Apr		
Heading	War Diary D.A.D.O.S. 9th Division August September 1915		
Heading	9th Division H.Q. 9th Div: D.A.D.O.S. Vols 4 And 5 August 1 to Sep 15		
Heading	War Diary of D.A.D.O.S. 9th Division. From 1-8-15 to 30-9-15		
Heading	War Diary of D.A.D.O.S. 9th Div. From 1.8.15 to 30-9.15		
War Diary	Bethune	01/08/1915	15/08/1915
War Diary	Fillers	16/08/1915	30/08/1915
War Diary	Bethune	31/08/1915	30/09/1915
Heading	War Diary D.A.D.O.S. 9th Division October 1915		
Heading	H.Q. 9th Div. D.A.D.O.S. Vol: 6 Oct 15.		
Heading	War Diary of D.A.D.O.S. 9th Division. From 1/10/15 to 30/10/15		
War Diary	Bethune	01/10/1915	02/10/1915
War Diary	Poperinghe	03/10/1915	30/10/1915
Heading	War Diary D.A.D.O.S. 9th Division November 1915		
Heading	H.Q. 9th Div: D.A.D.O. Vol 7 Nov 15		
Heading	War Diary of D.A.D.O.S. 9th Division. From 1/11/15 to 30/11/15		
War Diary	Poperinghe	01/11/1915	30/11/1915
Heading	War Diary D.A.D.O.S. 9th Division December 1915		
Heading	D.A.D.O.S. 9th Div: Vol: 8		
Heading	War Diary of D.A.D.O.S. 9th Division. From 1.12.15. to 31.12.15		
War Diary	Poperinghe	01/12/1915	20/12/1915
War Diary	Merris	21/12/1915	31/12/1915
Heading	D.A.D.O.S. 9th Div: Vol: 9 Jan 16		
Heading	War Diary of D.A.D.O.S. 9th Division. From 1 Jany 1916 to 31 Jany 1916		
War Diary	Merris	01/01/1916	25/01/1916
War Diary	Nippe	26/01/1916	31/01/1916
Heading	War Diary of D.A.D.O.S. 9th Division. From 1.2.16 to 29.2.16		
War Diary	Nippe	01/02/1916	13/02/1916
War Diary	Steenwerck	14/02/1916	29/02/1916
Heading	D A D O S 9th Div Vol 11		
Heading	War Diary of D.A.D.O.S. 9th Division. From 1.3.16 to 31.3.16		
War Diary	Steenwerck	01/03/1916	31/03/1916
Heading	War Diary of D.A.D.O.S. 9th Division. From 1-4-16 to 30-4-16		
War Diary	Steenwerck	01/04/1916	30/04/1916
Heading	War Diary D.A.D.O.S. 9th Divn. From 1-5-16 to 31-5-16		
War Diary	Steenwerck	01/05/1916	29/05/1916
War Diary	Merris	30/05/1916	30/05/1916
War Diary	Enguinegatte	31/05/1916	01/06/1916

Heading	War Diary D.A.D.O.S. 9th Divn. 1/6/16 to 30/6/16		
War Diary	Enguinegatte	01/06/1916	15/06/1916
War Diary	Ailly	16/06/1916	19/06/1916
War Diary	Corbie	20/06/1916	30/06/1916
Heading	War Diary of D.A.D.O.S. 9th (Scottish) Division. From July 1st 1916 to 31st 1916		
War Diary	Corbie	01/07/1916	03/07/1916
War Diary	Grovetown	04/07/1916	22/07/1916
War Diary	Molancourt	23/07/1916	23/07/1916
War Diary	Port Reay	24/07/1916	25/07/1916
War Diary	Bruay	26/07/1916	31/07/1916
Heading	War Diary of D.A.D.O.S. 9th Division. From 1.8.16 to 31.8.16		
War Diary	Bruay	01/08/1916	13/08/1916
War Diary	Estree Cauchie	14/08/1916	31/08/1916
Heading	War Diary D.A.D.O.S. 9th Dn. From 1st Sept. 1916 to 31st Sept 1916		
War Diary	Estree Cauchie	01/09/1916	30/09/1916
Heading	War Diary D.A.D.O.S. 9th Division 1-10-16 31-10-16		
War Diary	Field	28/09/1916	31/09/1916
War Diary	Field	01/09/1916	28/09/1916
Heading	War Diary D.A.D.O.S. 9th Dn 1-11-16 to 31-11-16		
War Diary	Field	01/11/1916	30/11/1916
Heading	War Diary D.A.D.O.S. 9th Dn From 1-12-16 to 31-12-16		
War Diary	Field	01/12/1916	31/12/1916
Heading	War Diary D.A.D.O.S. 9th (Scottish) Divn From 1st Jany 1917 to 31st Jany 1917		
War Diary	Duisans	01/01/1917	31/01/1917
Heading	War Diary of D.A.D.O.S. 9th Division. From 1-2-17 to 28-2-17		
War Diary	Field	01/02/1917	28/02/1917
Heading	War Diary D.A.D.O.S. 9th Dn. From 1st March 1917 to 31st March		
War Diary	Field	01/03/1917	31/03/1917
Heading	War Diary D.A.D.O.S. 9th Dn From 1.4.17 to 30.4.17		
War Diary	Field	01/04/1917	30/04/1917
Heading	War Diary D.A.D.O.S. 9th (Scottish) Divn From 1st May 1917 to 31 May 1917		
War Diary	Field	01/05/1917	31/05/1917
Heading	War Diary D.A.D.O.S. 9th Divn. From 1st June 1917 to 30 June 1917		
War Diary	Field	01/06/1917	30/06/1917
Heading	War Diary D.A.D.O.S. 9th Dn. From 1st July 1917 to 31st July 1917		
War Diary	Tincques	01/07/1917	09/07/1917
War Diary	Warlus	10/07/1917	27/07/1917
War Diary	Bus	28/07/1917	31/07/1917
Heading	War Diary D.A.D.O.S. 9th Dn. From 1st August 1917 to 31st August 1917		
War Diary	Field	01/08/1917	06/08/1917
War Diary	Field Bus.	07/08/1917	29/08/1917
War Diary	Achiet	30/08/1917	31/08/1917
Heading	War Diary D.A.D.O.S. 9th Dn. From 1st Sept 1917 to 30th Setp 1917		
War Diary	Achiet Le Grand	01/09/1917	11/09/1917

War Diary	Brandhoek	12/09/1917	22/09/1917
War Diary	Winnizeele	23/09/1917	26/09/1917
War Diary	Arneke	27/09/1917	30/09/1917
Heading	War Diary D.A.D.O.S. 9th Dn. From 1st October 1917 to 31st October 1917		
War Diary	Amcke	01/10/1917	11/10/1917
War Diary	Border Camp	12/10/1917	31/10/1917
Heading	War Diary D.A.D.O.S. 9th Division From 1st Nov 1917 to 30 Nov 1917		
War Diary	Field	01/11/1917	30/11/1917
Heading	War Diary D.A.D.O.S. 9th Dn. From 1st December 1917 to 31st December 1917		
War Diary	Field	01/12/1917	31/12/1917
Heading	War Diary D.A.D.O.S. 9th Division 1st Jany 1918 to 31 Jany 1918		
War Diary	Field	01/01/1918	31/01/1918
Heading	War Diary D.A.D.O.S. 9th Dn. From 1st Feb 1918 to 28th Feb 1918		
War Diary	Field	01/02/1918	28/02/1918
Heading	War Diary D.A.D.O.S. 9th (Scottish) Division From 1st March 1918 to 31st 1918		
War Diary	Field	01/03/1918	31/03/1918
Heading	War Diary D.A.D.O.S. 9th Dn. From 1st April 1918 to 31st April		
War Diary	Field	01/04/1918	30/04/1918
Heading	War Diary D.A.D.O.S. 9th Dn. From 1st May 1918 to 31st May 1918		
War Diary	Field	01/05/1918	31/05/1918
Heading	War Diary D.A.D.O.S. 9th Dn. From 1st June 1918 30th June 1918		
War Diary	Field	01/06/1918	30/06/1918
Heading	War Diary D.A.D.O.S. 9th Dn. From 1st July 1918 to 30th July 1918		
War Diary	Field	01/07/1918	31/07/1918
Heading	War Diary D.A.D.O.S. 9th Divn. From 1-8-1918 to 31-8-1918		
War Diary	Field	01/08/1918	31/08/1918
Heading	War Diary D.A.D.O.S. 9th Divn. From 1-9-18 to 31-9-18		
War Diary	Field	01/09/1918	30/09/1918
Heading	War Diary D.A.D.O.S. 9th Division From 1-12-18 to 31-10-18.		
War Diary	Field	01/10/1918	31/10/1918
Heading	War Diary D.A.D.O.S. 9th Dn From 1-11-18 to 31-11-18		
War Diary	Field	01/11/1918	30/11/1918
Heading	War Diary D.A.D.O.S. 9th Dn. From 1st Dec 1918 to 31st Dec 1918		
War Diary	Field	01/12/1918	24/12/1918
War Diary	Ohligs	25/12/1918	31/12/1918
Heading	Confidential War Diary D.A.D.O.S. 9th Divn From 1st Jany 1919 to 31st Jany 1919		
War Diary	Ohligs Germany	01/01/1919	31/01/1919
Heading	War Diary D.A.D.O.S. 9th Divn. From 1-2-19 to 28-2-19		
War Diary	Ohligs Germany	01/02/1919	28/02/1919

Heading	War Diary D.A.D.O.S. Lowland Divn From 1st March 1919 to 31st March 1919		
War Diary	Ohligs Germany	01/03/1919	08/03/1919
War Diary	Ohligs	09/03/1919	31/03/1919
War Diary	Ohligs Germany	01/04/1919	30/04/1919
Heading	9th Division Asst Dir. Vety Services May 1915-1919 Oct		
Heading	War Diary A.D.V.S. 9th Division May 1915		
Heading	A.D.V.S. 9th Division Vol I, 9-27.5.15		
War Diary	Bordon	09/05/1915	09/05/1915
War Diary	Southampton	09/05/1915	09/05/1915
War Diary	Le Havre	10/05/1915	10/05/1915
War Diary	Corques	11/05/1915	16/05/1915
War Diary	Le Nippe	17/05/1915	17/05/1915
War Diary	Nippe	17/05/1915	27/05/1915
Heading	War Diary A.D.V.S. 9th Division June 1915		
Heading	A.D.I.S. 9th Div. Vol: 2 June 15		
War Diary		04/06/1915	28/06/1915
War Diary	Neippe	05/06/1915	05/06/1915
War Diary	Busnes	05/06/1915	25/06/1915
War Diary	Lilliers	25/06/1915	28/06/1915
War Diary	Locon	28/06/1915	28/06/1915
Heading	War Diary A.D.V.S. 9th Division July 1915		
Heading	9th Division Headquarters 9th Division A.D.V.S. Vol III 1-26-7-15		
War Diary	Locon	01/07/1915	26/07/1915
Heading	War Diary A.D.V.S. 9th Division August September October 1915		
Heading	9th Division H.Q. 9th Division A.D.V.S. Vols 4, 5, 6 Aug Sept & Oct. 15 a.v.d.		
War Diary		06/08/1915	31/08/1915
War Diary		01/09/1915	30/09/1915
War Diary		01/10/1915	29/10/1915
Miscellaneous	D A & Q M G 9th Scottish Division.	09/09/1915	09/09/1915
Miscellaneous	C 21st Mobile Vety Section	12/09/1915	12/09/1915
Miscellaneous	All Brigades	21/09/1915	21/09/1915
Miscellaneous	V.O. Fram	21/09/1915	21/09/1915
Heading	War Diary A.D.V.S. 9th Division November 1915		
Heading	H.Q. 9th Div: A.D.V.S. Vol: 7 Nov 15		
War Diary	V Corps 2nd army area	05/11/1915	30/11/1915
Heading	War Diary A.D.V.S. 9th Division December 1915		
Heading	A.D.V.S. 9th Divn Vol: 8		
War Diary		03/12/1915	31/12/1915
Heading	A.D.V.S. 9th Div: Vol: 9		
War Diary		02/01/1916	31/05/1916
Heading	A.V.G. Section P G.S.Essex Base		
War Diary	In the Field	01/06/1916	30/06/1916
War Diary	Fourth Army Area	01/07/1916	25/07/1916
War Diary	First Army Area IV Corps Bruay	31/07/1916	31/07/1916
War Diary	First Army Area	04/08/1916	31/08/1916
War Diary	IV Corps Area First Army	01/09/1916	31/10/1916
Miscellaneous	Officer in charge, A.G. Section, Base.	12/12/1916	12/12/1916
War Diary	VI Corps Third Army Area	02/11/1916	31/01/1917
Miscellaneous	Officer i/c. A.G. Office, Base.	07/02/1917	07/02/1917
War Diary	VI Corps Area Third Army.	03/02/1917	23/02/1917

War Diary	HLR 9th (Scottish) Division XVII Corps Area Third Army	02/03/1917	31/03/1917
War Diary	XVII Corps Area Third Army	05/04/1917	31/05/1917
War Diary	XVII Corps Third Army	02/06/1917	16/07/1917
War Diary	In the Field	17/07/1917	30/08/1917
War Diary	IV Corps Third Army Area	01/08/1917	27/08/1917
War Diary	In the Field	06/10/1917	31/01/1918
Heading	9th Division They to attach War Diary for February 1918		
War Diary	In the Field	01/02/1918	31/12/1918
War Diary	Germany	01/01/1919	31/01/1919
War Diary	In the Field	01/02/1919	18/02/1919
War Diary	Ohligs	19/02/1919	19/03/1919
War Diary	Ohligs Germany	20/03/1919	31/03/1919
War Diary	Ohligs	01/04/1919	23/05/1919
War Diary	Krum	24/05/1919	31/05/1919
War Diary	Ohligs	01/05/1919	30/06/1919
War Diary	Germany	01/07/1919	31/07/1919
War Diary	Harff	01/08/1919	24/10/1919

9TH DIVISION

D. A. D. O. S.

AUG 1915 - ~~DEC 1918~~ 1919 APR

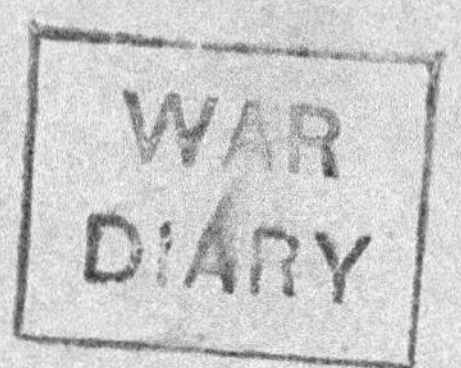

D. A..D. O. S.

9th Division

AUGUST SEPTEMBER

1915

121
7198

9th Division

HQ. 9th Div: D.A.D.O.S.

DEOS

Vols 4 and 5

August & Sept 15

Confidential

War Diary

of

D.A.D.O.S.

9th Division.

From:- 1-8-15.

To :- 30-9-15.

Army Form C. 2118.

Instructions regarding War Diaries and Intelligence Summaries are contained in F. S. Regs., Part II. and the Staff Manual respectively. Title pages will be prepared in manuscript.

WAR DIARY
or
~~INTELLIGENCE SUMMARY.~~
(Erase heading not required.)

Place	Date	Hour	Summary of Events and Information	Remarks and references to Appendices
			Confidential War Diary of D.A.D.O.S. 9th Div. From 1. 8. 15 To 30-9. 15	

Instructions regarding War Diaries and Intelligence Summaries are contained in F. S. Regs., Part II. and the Staff Manual respectively. Title pages will be prepared in manuscript.

WAR DIARY
or
INTELLIGENCE SUMMARY.
(Erase heading not required.)

Army Form C. 2118.

Place	Date	Hour	Summary of Events and Information	Remarks and references to Appendices
	August			
Bethune	1		First Issue of Battle sights at rate of 4 per Bn. made. ISH	
"	6		First consignment of Satchels for carrying Tube Pattern smoke Helmet, indented for 13.7.15, received ISH	
"	7		Local purchase of hand Syringes for use in Trenches made. These issued at rate of 2 per Bn. ISH	
"	8		Pte. Marsh A.O.C. taken on strength to replace Pte. Dean A.O.C invalided to Base ISH	
"	10		One Lattery Lens sight issued to H.Q. of 26th 27th 28th Infty Bdes ISH	
"	11		Second Issue of Smoke Helmets commenced ISH	
"	15		Instructions received from Divisional H.Q. to Indent for materials to open Divisional Shoemakers Shop. ISH	
Lillers	16		Division moved to Busnes for rest. Ordnance Store moved from Bethune to Lillers ISH	
"	20		One Lattery Lens sight received + issued to 26th Infty. Bde ISH	
"	21		Issue commenced of "Helmets Flannelette with glass eyepieces to Infantry Units. ISH	

Instructions regarding War Diaries and Intelligence Summaries are contained in F. S. Regs., Part II. and the Staff Manual respectively. Title pages will be prepared in manuscript.

WAR DIARY

or

INTELLIGENCE SUMMARY.

(Erase heading not required.)

Army Form C. 2118.

Place	Date	Hour	Summary of Events and Information	Remarks and references to Appendices
Lilliers	August 22		One Ulster Pattern sight received & issued to 28th Infty Bde. JSW	
			First issue of Phosphorescent Night Sights made to Infantry Units JSW	
"	27		Instructions received to Indent for 24 Cases Vickers .303 inch	
"	28		gun. Two per 12 Infty Bns. Hitherto only in possession of 2 per Bn. JSW	
			Instructed to purchase ~~[illegible]~~ Pliers for use with hand grenades	
"	30		as unable to obtain locally, wired Ordnance Paris. JSW	
Bethune	31		Moved from Lilliers back to Bethune to same Store as previously.	
			Wired Base for 16 Vermorel Sprayers to replace Unserviceable JSW	

J S Brogden Major

DADOS 9th Div.

1577 Wt. W10791/1773 500,000 1/15 D. D. & L. A.D.S.S./Forms/C. 2118.

Instructions regarding War Diaries and Intelligence Summaries are contained in F. S. Regs., Part II. and the Staff Manual respectively. Title pages will be prepared in manuscript.

WAR DIARY
or
INTELLIGENCE SUMMARY.
(Erase heading not required.)

Army Form C. 2118.

Place	Date	Hour	Summary of Events and Information	Remarks and references to Appendices
Bethune	September 1		Second Issue of Phosphorescent Night Sights. I.S.H.	
"	2		First Issue of Stabbing Knives received from 1st Corps. Local manufacture of casualty screens for Infty for purpose of indicating captured enemy trenches. I.S.H.	
"	3		Pliers received from Paris and issued at rate of 20 per Infty Bn. I.S.H.	
"	4		Bethune Shelled I.S.H.	
"	6		Periscopes No 5 coming up from Base in lieu of No 14 for issue to Artillery I.S.H.	
"	7		Wired Base for one Ordnance Q.F. 4.5 in. How. to replace one damaged in action "C" Battery 53 Brigade I.S.H.	
"	8		One periscope Harp shaped issued to each Artillery Brigade H.Q. for report. Blankets one per man demanded for Division. I.S.H.	
"	9		One ordnance Q.F. 4.5 in How. demanded on 7th Inst. received and issued to C/53. Battery I.S.H.	
"	11		Hastened issue of Vermoral Sprayers demanded on 31st Ulto. I.S.H.	
"	13		Smoke Helmets, tube pattern being issued to Artillery. I.S.H.	

1577 Wt. W10791/1773 500,000 1/15 D. D. & L. A.D.S.S./Forms/C. 2118.

Army Form C. 2118.

Instructions regarding War Diaries and Intelligence Summaries are contained in F. S. Regs., Part II. and the Staff Manual respectively. Title pages will be prepared in manuscript.

WAR DIARY
or
INTELLIGENCE SUMMARY.
(Erase heading not required.)

Place	Date	Hour	Summary of Events and Information	Remarks and references to Appendices
Bethune	September 14		Received first consignment of Blankets 3400. ISW	
"	15		Issue of Ulster Pattern sight one each to H.Q. 26th & 28th Infty Bdes.	
"	16		Third issue of Phosphorescent night sights. ISW	
"	17		Commenced issue of Lewis Machine Guns ~~to~~ Infty. Bns at rate of 4 per Bn ISW	
"	18		D.D.O.S. First Army inspected Store. Indented on Base for 20 Two horse limbered wagons, transport for Lewis Machine Guns. Complete Turnouts. ISW	
"	19		Notification received of approval of issue of Stoves Loyers. Indented for 50. Wired O.O. railhead to reconsign blankets to Base as Division going into action & could not receive them. ISW	
"	21		Periscopes No 19 received from Base for issue to Artillery in lieu of No 14. ISW	
"	22		Issue made of Salvus Breathing apparatus to H.Q. 26, 27 & 28 Brigades & Motor Machine Gun Battery. First Issue to H.Q. 26 & 28 Brigades of 5 Pistols illuminating 1½ in ISW	

Army Form C. 2118.

Instructions regarding War Diaries and Intelligence Summaries are contained in F. S. Regs., Part II. and the Staff Manual respectively. Title pages will be prepared in manuscript.

WAR DIARY
or
INTELLIGENCE SUMMARY.
(Erase heading not required.)

Place	Date	Hour	Summary of Events and Information	Remarks and references to Appendices
	September			
Bethune	24		Original issue of Satchels for Smoke Helmets completed. JSB	
"	25		Attack by Division on German lines. Ordnance Lorries lent A.D.M.S. to bring in wounded. Further issue of Phosphorescent night sights. JSB	
"	26		"Tried" Horse for 1 Ord. Q.F. 18 Pr. to replace damaged gun. Indent for 30 Vermorel Sprayers to replace similar quantity destroyed by Shell fire. JSB	
"	27		Instructed by AA & QMG to demand complete refit of clothing except boots for 7000 Infantry coming out of action in anticipation of requirements. Redemanded Blankets. Tried Horse for one Ord. Q.F. 18 Pr. C/57 to replace gun damaged in action. General commanding Division killed in action.	
"	28		Division relieved & returned to Bethune	
"	29		Part of clothing indented for on 27th Inst found to be in excess of requirements. Returned to Base.	
"	30		Demand for Blankets cancelled. Issue to be made by 5th Corps	

J S Brogden Major
DADOS 9th Div.

WAR DIARY

D. A. D. O. S.

9th DIVISION

OCTOBER 1915

121
7518

H.Q. 9th Div: D.A.D.O.S.

Vol: 6

Oct 15.

4

DEoS

Army Form C. 2118.

Instructions regarding War Diaries and Intelligence Summaries are contained in F. S. Regs., Part II. and the Staff Manual respectively. Title pages will be prepared in manuscript.

WAR DIARY
or
INTELLIGENCE SUMMARY.
(Erase heading not required.)

Place	Date	Hour	Summary of Events and Information	Remarks and references to Appendices
			Confidential War Diary of D.A.D.O.S. 9th Division From 1/10/15 to 31/10/15	

1577 Wt. W10791/1773 500,000 1/15 D. D. & L. A.D.S.S./Forms/C. 2118.

Army Form C. 2118.

WAR DIARY
or
~~INTELLIGENCE SUMMARY.~~
(Erase heading not required.)

Instructions regarding War Diaries and Intelligence Summaries are contained in F. S. Regs., Part II. and the Staff Manual respectively. Title pages will be prepared in manuscript.

Place	Date	Hour	Summary of Events and Information	Remarks and references to Appendices
	Oct			
Bethune	1		28th Infantry Bde. left for Poperinghe ISW	
"	2		Bethune shelled ISW	
Poperinghe	3		Left Bethune for Poperinghe. Ordnance Store in Rue de Casern. Base removed to Calais for clothing &c. Havre deals with Sections 14–18 except 16 B. ISW	
"	4		Poperinghe shelled. ISW	
"	11		Sent to Hazebrouck for Sniperscopes, Rifle Batteries &c. from 2nd Army Workshops. Indent sent for Satchels for Smoke Helmets to complete ISW	
"	12		Demand on 5th Corps for 500 Tube Pattern Smoke Helmets for Reinforcements. Special Bulk demand for Winter Clothes sent. Improved pattern Steel Helmets now approved for issue. Salvus ~~breathing~~ breathing sets returned to Store ISW	
"	13		West Bomb Thrower issued to Grenade School ISW	
"	14		Issued to H.Q. 28th Infty. Bde. Stores from 2nd Army Workshops drawn on 11th Inst.	ISW
"	15		Indent on Calais for 36 Salvus breathing sets to complete to Establishment	ISW
"	16		Belgian artillery transferred to 28th Div. ISW	
"	18		Clothing for Bathing Establishment wired for. ISW	
"	19		Notified by D.D.O.S. that 6000 undercoats fur have been ordered for Division for use in Trenches HB	

Army Form C. 2118.

Instructions regarding War Diaries and Intelligence Summaries are contained in F. S. Regs., Part II. and the Staff Manual respectively. Title pages will be prepared in manuscript.

WAR DIARY
or
~~INTELLIGENCE SUMMARY~~.
(Erase heading not required.)

Place	Date	Hour	Summary of Events and Information	Remarks and references to Appendices
Poperinghe	Oct. 20		Received 10 Vermoral Sprayers from Base leaving balance of 6 still due. Demanded from Base 1000 Smoke Helmets Flannelette for Reinforcements. JSW	
"	21		Wired Base for 12500 Undercoats fur to complete to 18500 for Division. Also demanded 400 Braziers as first supply. JSW	
"	22		Notified from 5th Corps to draw smoke helmets demanded. JSW	
"	23		1000 Smoke Helmets received. Satchels again hastened from base. 6000 Undercoats fur. received & issued at rate of 480 per Bn. + 240 to Pioneers. JSW	
"	24		Shelled early in the morning. First consignment of Braziers (200) received from Base. 75 Sets Tent bottoms issued Canada Huts. JSW	
"	25		1500 T.P. Smoke Helmets demanded from Corps. JSW	
"	26		The 1500 Smoke Helmets demanded 25th received. Further issue of Tent Bottoms to Canada Huts. JSW	
"	27		Inspection of 5th Corps by H. M. The King. JSW	
"	28		Demand on 5th Corps for 1000 T.P. Smoke Helmets. JSW	
"	29		Issue of 50 Sets Tent Bottoms to 7th Seaforths. JSW	
"	30		Issue made of Knob Kerries at rate of 52 to each Infty Bde. & 10 to Pioneers & Received 1000 Prs Gum Boots Thigh. JSW	

J. S. Brogden Major
DADOS 9th Div.

1577 Wt. W10791/1773 500,000 1/15 D. D. & L. A.D.S.S./Forms/C. 2118.

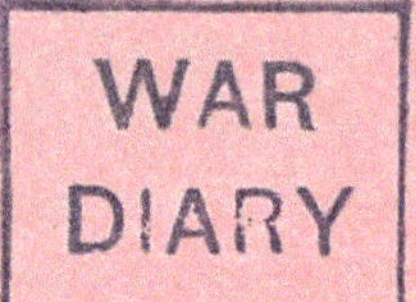

D. A. D. O. S.

9th DIVISION

NOVE?BER I9I5

H.Q. 9th Div.
Vol 7
121/7624
K
Nov 15

Confidential

War Diary of DADOS 9th Division

From 1/11/15

To 30/11/15

Army Form C. 2118.

WAR DIARY
or
~~INTELLIGENCE SUMMARY.~~
(Erase heading not required.)

Instructions regarding War Diaries and Intelligence Summaries are contained in F. S. Regs., Part II. and the Staff Manual respectively. Title pages will be prepared in manuscript.

Place	Date Nov	Hour	Summary of Events and Information	Remarks and references to Appendices
Poperinghe	1		First issue of "Boots Gum Thigh" made to Infantry Bns. ISK	
"	2		Further consignment of Braziers received from Base leaving 50 still due to complete. ISK	
"	3		Demanded Shirts, socks & drawers for new Divisional Bathing Establishment. Hastened issue of Drawers short for Highland Battalions, demanded 21.10.15. Boots G.S. or Shoepack issued 9 prs. per Infty Bn. 24 per Battery Artillery ISK	
"	4		Received first consignment of vests woollen demanded 12.10.15 ISK	
"	5		Further consignment of Leather Jerkins received. ISK	
"	7		Received visit from D.D.O.S 2nd Army ISK	
"	8		Demanded 1000 Smoke Helmets, Tube pattern from 5th Corps to replace unserviceable & for issue to reinforcements. ISK	
"	9		Further supply of Undercoats fur & Leather Jerkins received from Base. Further issue of Gum Boots Thigh to Infty Bns. Wired Base for one Gun, Vickers to replace one destroyed by shell fire, belonging to 7th Seaforths. ISK	
"	10		Demanded Blankets G.S. as second issue to Labour Bn. R.E. under authority D.D.O.S 2nd Army. Notified by 5th Corps that Smoke Helmets demanded 8/11/15 may be drawn. 2nd Army ask if large Braziers will meet requirements in lieu of small to complete balance of 50 accepted. Further issue of Gum Boots Thigh to Infty Bns. ISK	

Army Form C. 2118.

Instructions regarding War Diaries and Intelligence Summaries are contained in F. S. Regs., Part II. and the Staff Manual respectively. Title pages will be prepared in manuscript.

WAR DIARY

or

~~INTELLIGENCE SUMMARY.~~

(Erase heading not required.)

Place	Date Nov	Hour	Summary of Events and Information	Remarks and references to Appendices
Poperinghe	11		Received Gun Vickers for 7th Seaforths Indented for 9th Inst & issued same. ISB.	
"	13		Wired Base asking why mounted services should not receive Leather Jerkins & is anything bas being issued in lieu. Hastened Indent for Goggles anti gas. ISB	
"	14		Demanded Frost nails under authority DDOS 2nd Army. Registered 10,000th Indent since arrival overseas. May 7/15. Blankets received for Labour Bn. ISB	
"	15		First consignment of Goggles anti gas received ISB	
"	17–24		On leave to England. ISB	
"	26		First Snow. Notified by 5 Corps OO that a further 2000 Gum Boots Thigh are available. First consignment of 2nd Tube Helmet received from Base. ISB	
"	27.		2000 Gum Boots Thigh drawn from 5th Corps. Issue of 2nd Blanket continued. ISB	
"	28		Hard Frost. 16 Lewis Machine Guns received from Base. ISB	
"	29.		Further 36 Lewis Machine Guns to complete to 4 per Bn received ISB	
"	30		Notified by DDOS 2nd Army that A/Sub Conductor Bradford is to proceed to England for Duty ISB	

I S Brogden Major
DADOS 9th Div
1/12/15

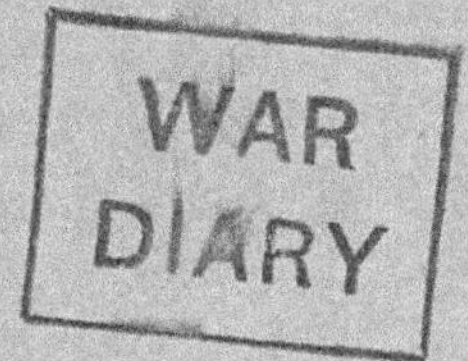

~~XXXXXXXXXX~~

D. A. D. O. S.

9th DIVISION

DECEMBER 1915

D.A.D.O.S. 9th Div:
Vol: 8

121
7931

Army Form C. 2118

WAR DIARY
or
~~INTELLIGENCE SUMMARY~~
(Erase heading not required.)

Instructions regarding War Diaries and Intelligence Summaries are contained in F. S. Regs., Part II. and the Staff Manual respectively. Title Pages will be prepared in manuscript.

Place	Date	Hour	Summary of Events and Information	Remarks and references to Appendices
			Confidential War Diary of D.A.D.O.S. 9th Division From 1. 12. 15 To 31. 12. 15	

1875 Wt. W593/826 1,000,000 4/15 J.B.C. & A. A.D.S.S./Forms/C. 2118.

Army Form C. 2118

Instructions regarding War Diaries and Intelligence Summaries are contained in F. S. Regs., Part II. and the Staff Manual respectively. Title Pages will be prepared in manuscript.

WAR DIARY
or
INTELLIGENCE SUMMARY
(Erase heading not required.)

Place	Date	Hour	Summary of Events and Information	Remarks and references to Appendices
Poperinghe	1/12/15		Further issues of Lewis machine guns to Infantry Units of this Division. 2 pm. Station shelled. G.H.	
	2/12/15			
	3/12/15		Actg: Sub:Cond! Bradford A.O.C. left for England G.H.	
	4/12/15		First consignment of Shirts Flannel G.S. arrived, for issue in lieu of vests woollen. G.H.	
	5/12/15			
	6/12/15		Further consignment received & issue made of Phosphorescent night lights to Infantry Bgdes. G.H.	
	7/12/15		Rec? 1500 Gum Boots Thigh from 5th Corps. G.H.	
	8/12/15		Issue made of Gum Boots Thigh to Infantry Bat. G.H.	
	9/12/15			
	10/12/15			
	11/12/15		Private Sweeney A.O.C. storeman, reported for duty. G.H.	
	12/12/15		Receipt & issue begun of Body Bands 18000. G.H.	
	13/12/15		Lt. G. Hyde. A.O.D. reported for duty. D.D.O.S. 2nd Army visited Store. G.H.	

1875 Wt. W593/826 1,000,000 4/15 J.B.C. & A. A.D.S.S./Forms/C. 2118.

Instructions regarding War Diaries and Intelligence Summaries are contained in F. S. Regs., Part II. and the Staff Manual respectively. Title Pages will be prepared in manuscript.

WAR DIARY
or
~~INTELLIGENCE SUMMARY~~
(Erase heading not required.)

Army Form C. 2118

Place	Date	Hour	Summary of Events and Information	Remarks and references to Appendices
Poperinghe	14/12/15			
	15/12/15		Went to Merris with Maj: Brogden, & inspected accomodation for offices & dump. [initials]	
	16/12/15			
	17/12/15		Wired Base to stop sending supplies during changing of area. [initials]	
	18/12/15		Major Brogden sent to Hospital at Hazebrouck. Visited H.Q. 2nd Army re dummy Cartridges for Div'l practice. [initials]	
	19/12/15		Poperinghe heavily shelled, and bombarded by aeroplanes between 10 am. & noon. Shelling continued at intervals all day. Visited Merris to arrange exchange of Smoke helmets. [initials]	
	20/12/15		Left Poperinghe. Office in working order at Merris 4 p.m. Stores all in, with exception of blankets by 10 p.m. [initials]	
Merris	21/12/15		Blankets fetched from Poperinghe [initials]	
	22/12/15		~~Issues begin again~~ Arranged with H.Q. for issue to troops of 2nd Blanket Store received from Base. [initials]	
	23/12/15		Most of Units excepting R.F.A. drew blankets & stores. Arranged a new system for regulating traffic. 100 steel helmets arrived. Also 10 baths & 2 heaters. Visited railhead & spoke R.O.O. at Hazebrouck Garage. Col: Dymock came on inspection duties. [initials]	

1875 Wt. W593/826 1,000,000 4/15 J.B.C. & A. A.D.S.S./Forms/C. 2118.

Army Form C. 2118

WAR DIARY
or
INTELLIGENCE SUMMARY
(Erase heading not required.)

Instructions regarding War Diaries and Intelligence Summaries are contained in F. S. Regs., Part II. and the Staff Manual respectively. Title Pages will be prepared in manuscript.

Place	Date	Hour	Summary of Events and Information	Remarks and references to Appendices
Merris	24/12/15		Called at Hospital, Hazebrouck for Maj: Brogden & took him to HQ. 2nd Army - an Visited Railhead & interviewed L/Cpl White whom DDOS (X) had enquired about & found that he had been previously been acting there for 50th Divn who were in the area before 9th Divn. GH	
	25/12/15			
	26/12/15		Received 9 bootplates for distribution on trial & report. 3 issued to each Field Coy. 10 Grenade carriers for distribution by Div. HQ. received from HQ 2nd A. Received 24,000 dummy cartridges, issued 4000 to each Inf: Brig: and 1800 to R. Engineers - GH	
	27/12/15		Called on Lt Reidy RA HQ. Bollezeele to arrange issue of stores to Brigades of RFA whilst in that area. 100 prs: of Shoepacks & Boots F.S. recd. Issued remainder of dummy cartridges. GH	
	28/12/15		LP of 16 Hurricane Lamps - Major Brogden left for GHQ for instructions. GH	
	29/12/15		Visited HQ 27th Inf. Brig: Outtersteene, & HQ 26th Brig: Bailleul - also 8th Black Watch - Number of aeroplanes to be seen east of Bailleul - LP 20 Hurricane Lamps for 27th Inf Brig: Maj: Brogden left Divn for duty GHQ. Troops. GH	
	30/12/15		Outstanding leather jerkins & undercoats for recd from Base - 1st receipt of steel helmets towards 1 per. of. issue. 100 issued to 12th Royl: Scots. Asked Base to arrange equally in turn to Brigades. GH	

1875 Wt. W593/826 1,000,000 4/15 J.B.C. & A. A.D.S.S./Forms/C. 2118.

Army Form C. 2118

Instructions regarding War Diaries and Intelligence Summaries are contained in F. S. Regs., Part II. and the Staff Manual respectively. Title Pages will be prepared in manuscript.

WAR DIARY

or

~~INTELLIGENCE SUMMARY~~

(Erase heading not required.)

Place	Date	Hour	Summary of Events and Information	Remarks and references to Appendices
Merris.	31/12/15		Twenty five extinguishers rec'd from Base. [initials]	

[signature] Lt
D.A.D.O.S. 9th Div. 1/1/16

1875 Wt. W593/826 1,000,000 4/15 J.B.C. & A. A.D.S.S./Forms/C. 2118.

D.A.D.O.S. 9th Div:

Vol: 9

Jan '16

Instructions regarding War Diaries and Intelligence Summaries are contained in F. S. Regs., Part II. and the Staff Manual respectively. Title Pages will be prepared in manuscript.

WAR DIARY
or
~~INTELLIGENCE~~ SUMMARY
(Erase heading not required.)

Army Form C. 2118

Place	Date	Hour	Summary of Events and Information	Remarks and references to Appendices
			Confidential War Diary of D.A.D.O.S. 9th Division From 1 Jany 1916 To 31 " 1916	

1875 Wt. W593/826 1,000,000 4/15 J.B.C. & A. A.D.S.S./Forms/C. 2118.

Instructions regarding War Diaries and Intelligence Summaries are contained in F. S. Regs., Part II. and the Staff Manual respectively. Title Pages will be prepared in manuscript.

WAR DIARY
or
~~INTELLIGENCE~~ SUMMARY
(Erase heading not required.)

Army Form C. 2118

Place	Date	Hour	Summary of Events and Information	Remarks and references to Appendices
Meteren	1/1/16		Visited H.Q. 28th Inf: Bgde: re new Machine Gun Coy: No difficulty in obtaining their Ordnance Stores. Two electric cartridge signalling lamps received. A.A.&Q.M.G. called with D.A.D.M.G. [initials]	
	2/1/16		Received 950 pairs Gum Boots Thigh. Nosebags 1000 deficient from Base & urgently required [initials]	
	3/1/16		Ordered 1000 nosebags. Wired base for 1000 sets underclothing for Divl Bath. Purchased 5 wringers for Divl Baths. [initials]	
	4/1/16		Received 340 Lanterns Tent Folding. [initials]	
	5/1/16			
	6/1/16		Called at Grenade School ref. quick release straps for Grenade Carriers, and recommended [illegible]. Visited H.Q. 27th Inf Bgde. [initials]	
	7/1/16		Visited H.Q. 2nd Army ref: machine gun returns, & drill Smoke Helmets. [initials]	
	8/1/16		Arranged with A.D.O.S. 2nd Corps ref: 95 horse rugs in bad condition dumped at store - to be washed at 21st Divl Bath. [initials]	
	9/1/16		A.D.O.S. 2nd Corps called. [initials]	
	10/1/16		Receipt of Lumbermans boots & socks. 333 prs of each. 100 steel helmets recd for 28th Inf Bgde. Visited Nieppe to see about dump. 3 German planes flew over dropping bombs locally doing no damage. Bombs also dropped at Hazebrouck and St Omer. S.C. Swift arrived to relieve S.C. Honey [initials]	

1875 Wt. W593/826 1,000,000 4/15 J.B.C. & A. A.D.S.S./Forms/C. 2118.

Army Form C. 2118

Instructions regarding War Diaries and Intelligence Summaries are contained in F. S. Regs., Part II. and the Staff Manual respectively. Title Pages will be prepared in manuscript.

WAR DIARY
or
~~INTELLIGENCE~~ SUMMARY
(Erase heading not required.)

Place	Date	Hour	Summary of Events and Information	Remarks and references to Appendices
Merris	11/1/16		Canvas buckets for Mills grenades recd (10) Div: H.Q. arranged for dist: 3 to each Inf: Brig + 1 to Grenade School GH	
	12/1/16		Visited Railhead. GH	
	13/1/16		A.D.O.S. 2nd Corps called. Enquired of 2nd Army re supply of syrens for alarm signals in trenches GH	
	14/1/16		5 rifles with telescopic sights recd which completed Div. on scale of 4 per regt. Gas test in Div: by C.A. 2nd Army GH	
	15/1/16		Recd 100 steel helmets from Base for 6th K.O.S.B. also machine gun parts for M.G. Coys of 26th + 28th Inf Bgdes: A.D.O.S. 2nd Corps called. Furnished report on Sub. Of Swept to D.D.O.S. 2nd Army. Indents recd: to replace smoke helmets used in test. GH	
	16/1/16			
	17/1/16		50 steel helmets recd (6th K.O.S.B.) Wrote Base requesting these should be Divided equally as far as possible between Inf. Brigades. Recd up to full allotment of Primus Stoves (50) + Fire ext: 40. Visited R'head GH	
	18/1/16		Order recd re telescopic rifles from H.Q. Army. To be handed to Sch: of Sniping + distributed according to orders Army H.Q.	
	19/1/16		—	
	20/1/16		—	

1875 Wt. W593/826 1,000,000 4/15 J.B.C. & A. A.D.S.S./Forms/C. 2118.

Instructions regarding War Diaries and Intelligence Summaries are contained in F. S. Regs., Part II. and the Staff Manual respectively. Title Pages will be prepared in manuscript.

WAR DIARY
or
~~INTELLIGENCE~~ SUMMARY
(Erase heading not required.)

Army Form C. 2118

Place	Date	Hour	Summary of Events and Information	Remarks and references to Appendices
Merris	21/1/16		Visited Ordnance 25th Divn Nieppe & arranged transport of Ordnance Stores. GH	
	22/1/16		First supply of Special tube helmets for R.A. recd 6 battys: completed 1 each. GH	
			Visited H.Q. 2nd Army.	
	23/1/16		Advised by Army H.Q. that increase of Vermorel Sprayers up to 100 per Divn is author-ized. Wired Base accordingly for 50. Khaki badges for Bomb throwers.	
	24/1/16		Visited Ordnance 25th Divn GH	
	25/1/16		Moved to Nieppe arriving at 3 pm. GH	
Nieppe	26/1/16		Visited Div. H.Q. at Merris. ADOS 2nd Corps called. Nieppe shelled between 1 & 1.30 pm 8 shells 5 "duds". One horse killed. GH	
	27/1/16		Visited railhead. 19 tons stores from Base. Divl H.Q. moved in. 400 steel helmets recd. GH	
	28/1/16		ADOS called. GH	
	29/1/16		Nieppe shelled 3.30 pm. 3 shells. 7 horses killed & 3 injured. Several H.Q. [illegible] injured. Instruments for Divl Band arrived. GH	
	30/1/16			
	31/1/16		4290 P.H. smoke helmets recd & issued 26th & 27th Inf. Brigades. GH	

Graham [illegible] Lt
DADOS. 9th Divn
2/2/16

1875 Wt. W593/826 1,000,000 4/15 J.B.C. & A. A.D.S.S./Forms/C. 2118.

Instructions regarding War Diaries and Intelligence Summaries are contained in F. S. Regs., Part II. and the Staff Manual respectively. Title Pages will be prepared in manuscript.

WAR DIARY
or
INTELLIGENCE SUMMARY
(Erase heading not required.)

Army Form C. 2118

Place	Date	Hour	Summary of Events and Information	Remarks and references to Appendices
			Confidential War Diary of D.A.D.O.S. 9th Division from 1.2.16 to 29.2.16	

1875 Wt. W593/826 1,000,000 4/15 J.B.C. & A. A.D.S.S./Forms/C. 2118.

Army Form C. 2118

WAR DIARY
or
INTELLIGENCE SUMMARY
(Erase heading not required.)

Instructions regarding War Diaries and Intelligence Summaries are contained in F. S. Regs., Part II. and the Staff Manual respectively. Title Pages will be prepared in manuscript.

Place	Date	Hour	Summary of Events and Information	Remarks and references to Appendices
Nieppe	1/2/16		Lt. Morgan A.O.D. arrived for instruction in Divisional work. – [initials]	
	2/2/16		Placed order for Grenade Carriers 3000. Four G.S. wagons received for 9th Seaforth (Pioneers) to replace limbered. [initials]	
	3rd		Sub Cond. Honey left 9th Div. for duty with H.Q. Troops. – [initials]	
	4th		Pte. Edmundson A.O.C. reported for duty in instructing men in repair of Gumboots thigh. – [initials]	
	4th		50 Steel helmets recd. from Base. 1000 P pat. smoke helmets for replacements received. Arranged for Glasgow Yeomanry to be issued with proportion of Steel helmets as they are going into trenches. [initials]	
	5th		Visited 26th Brigade H.Q. Ploegsteert – also H.Q. 10th Gordons with Col. Spurrow. Visited Divisional Baths re demands for soap soda. [initials]	
	6th		Visited 26 Machine Gun Coy's lines – Discovered horses feeding off ground – Reprimanded Corporal in charge & instructed him to draw 30 nosebags immediately from Ordnance. Examined his Indent Book which showed none as due. Visited Recreation Room at Le Romarin as requested by H.Q. [initials]	
	7th		Inspected Salvage Coy. dump, collected rifles. [initials]	
	8th		Visited Railhead. – Pte. Edmundson left for duty with 25th Div. after having instructed 18 men sent from Brigades. [initials]	

1875 Wt. W593/826 1,000,000 4/15 J.B.C. & A. A.D.S.S./Forms/C. 2118.

Instructions regarding War Diaries and Intelligence Summaries are contained in F. S. Regs., Part II. and the Staff Manual respectively. Title Pages will be prepared in manuscript.

WAR DIARY
or
INTELLIGENCE SUMMARY
(Erase heading not required.)

Army Form C. 2118

Place	Date	Hour	Summary of Events and Information	Remarks and references to Appendices
Nieppe	9/2/16		Nieppe shelled. 13 shells in all, one or two failed to explode. RA cook killed. 3 wounded. G.A.	
	10th		Visited 2nd Army H.Q. reference question of netting for screening. One shell 9 pm. 200 steel helmets from Base. G.A.	
	11th		Bought canvas for use at Grenade School. Visited Kuilhuis G.A.	
	12th		Received orders to remove to Steenwerck. Visited there to look for suitable place for dump. Col Crawley S.S.O. assisted in finding a good barn. G.A.	
	13th		Moved to Steenwerck. 14,000 P.H. smoke helmets received from Base. Found receipt of such a quantity a source of inconvenience when not previously advised. G.A.	
Steenwerck	14th		Considerable aeroplane activity. G.A.	
	15th		Arranged with C.R.A. to repair road into dump. G.A.	
	16th		Col: Dymock called. 2 Stromboss horns recd. G.A.	
	17th			
	18th		3 more Stromboss Horns recd. Cpl Hawkes arrived from Woolwich for instruction G.A.	

1875 Wt. W593/826 1,000,000 4/15 J.B.C. & A. A.D.S.S./Forms/C. 2118.

Instructions regarding War Diaries and Intelligence Summaries are contained in F. S. Regs., Part II. and the Staff Manual respectively. Title Pages will be prepared in manuscript.

WAR DIARY
or
INTELLIGENCE SUMMARY
(Erase heading not required.)

Army Form C. 2118

Place	Date	Hour	Summary of Events and Information	Remarks and references to Appendices
Steenwerck	19/2/16		Many enemy aeroplanes about. 8 Protractors 8" received – also 200 steel helmets. FA	
	20th		3 more Strombos horns recd. Air raid Bailleul, several killed and wounded – 200 steel helmets recd. FA	
	21st		Air raid on Hazebrouck – 8 bombs – Periscope Note recd, also 2 Strombos horns. FA	
	22nd		Snow. Ordered 24 white capuchons for patrols – made in two hours. FA	
	23rd			
	24th		Recd 40 footplates – 45 Lattey lens sights 9 Strombos horns. FA	
	25th		Recd 100 steel helmets. 6 Pistols illuminating. FA	
	26th		Had 24 more cloaks for patrols made. FA	
	27th		Lt Morgan left for instruction with 17th Divn. FA	
	28th			
	29th		4 Lattey lens sights recd. FA	

Graham [illegible] Capt
DADOS 9th Divn

1875 Wt. W593/826 1,000,000 4/15 J.B.C. & A. A.D.S.S./Forms/C. 2118.

DADOS
9th DW
Vol II E

Instructions regarding War Diaries and Intelligence Summaries are contained in F. S. Regs., Part II. and the Staff Manual respectively. Title Pages will be prepared in manuscript.

WAR DIARY
or
INTELLIGENCE SUMMARY
(Erase heading not required.)

Army Form C. 2118

Place	Date	Hour	Summary of Events and Information	Remarks and references to Appendices
			Confidential	
			War Diary of	
			D.A.D.O.S. 9th Division	
			From 1 : 3 : 16	
			To 31 : 3 : 16	

1875 Wt. W593/826 1,000,000 4/15 J.B.C. & A. A.D.S.S./Forms/C. 2118.

Army Form C. 2118

Instructions regarding War Diaries and Intelligence Summaries are contained in F. S. Regs., Part II. and the Staff Manual respectively. Title Pages will be prepared in manuscript.

WAR DIARY
or
INTELLIGENCE SUMMARY
(Erase heading not required.)

Place	Date	Hour	Summary of Events and Information	Remarks and references to Appendices
Steenwoorde	1/3/16		Recd O.O. 2nd Corps Tps. 30 Vermorel Sprayers – Visited 8th Gordons, 5th Camerons, 9th Scot Rifles 7th Seaforths inspecting stores &c. G.H.	
	2/3/16			
	3/3/16		Recd 12th Strombos horns – one ·470 bore rifle with 9 rds: ammn for special purpose, issued to 26th Bgde: G.H.	
	4/3/16		Recd 10 hooks limber. 2 Mtgs: disappearing, + 1 compressed air hooter – 2nd in. 8th Gordons seemed to think that under present conditions binoculars were an excessive issue to battalions – G.H.	
	5/3/16		500 Trench helmets recd which to date is largest single receipt of these – The supply is slow, + continual requests for more received – G.H.	
	6th		ADVS reports that R.A. units are complaining of shortage of nose bags and haynets – On looking up records I find that there is no ground for the complaints – G.H.	
	7th		Recd indent from 28th Bgde for special ammn G.H.	
	8th		Col: Gardyne 8th Gordons, called and was shown working of Ordnance stores – appeared much interested + pleased G.H.	
	9th		Coloured screens for R.A. required – Referred matter to A.D.O.S. Corps – Visited Railhead – G.H.	

1875 Wt. W593/826 1,000,000 4/15 J.B.C. & A. A.D.S.S./Forms/C. 2118.

Instructions regarding War Diaries and Intelligence Summaries are contained in F. S. Regs., Part II. and the Staff Manual respectively. Title Pages will be prepared in manuscript.

WAR DIARY
or
INTELLIGENCE SUMMARY
(Erase heading not required.)

Army Form C. 2118

Place	Date	Hour	Summary of Events and Information	Remarks and references to Appendices
Oosthoek [illegible]	10/3/16		Visited Railhead – ADOS Corps. – TH	
	11th		Col. McHardy (AA&QMG) visited store ~~expressed~~ himself well satisfied with the work & arrangement. – TH	
	12th		4 Rifle battys: recd. from Base – they were [illegible] issued to 24th Divn. TH	
	13th		ADOS called – Discussed operations in event of move. – Recd. 29 Pistols 1½" 4 light mounting. TH	
	14th		Recd. 500 steel helmets. 6 Pistols 1½" 50 Footplates. TH	
	15th		Recd. 5 more Food Containers – these do not seem to be very popular, and are not, I think, generally used by the Troops. TH	
	16th		Discussion re return of Winter Clothing at HQ. Divn. [illegible] to visit all Brigade HQ. to discuss with them. – TH	
	17th		Recd. 152 Tower Respirators. Visited HQ. 2nd Army. TH	
	18th / 19th		Recd. 450 Steel Helmets. Visited various RA. horse lines – which I find generally display considerable lack of care with nosebags and haynets – Spoke A.D.V.S. regarding this. – TH	

1875 Wt. W593/826 1,000,000 4/15 J.B.C. & A. A.D.S.S./Forms/C. 2118.

Instructions regarding War Diaries and Intelligence Summaries are contained in F. S. Regs., Part II. and the Staff Manual respectively. Title Pages will be prepared in manuscript.

WAR DIARY
or
INTELLIGENCE SUMMARY
(Erase heading not required.)

Army Form C. 2118

Place	Date	Hour	Summary of Events and Information	Remarks and references to Appendices
Steenwerck	20/3/16		Visited QM stores of 4 units - Recd Footplates 50 Mats protecting 29 - [initials]	
	21/3/16		Visited more R.A. horselines - G.O.C. (Genl Furse) visited store - and was apparently much interested in the method employed in receiving & issuing stores to Division. He expressed himself as being much pleased - [initials]	
	22nd		Recd 48 Tower Respirators - [initials]	
	23rd			
	24th		Recd 300 Steel Helmets. Question of covers for these discussed at HQ Divn. Sample recd from Army HQ was much too heavy & cumbersome. [initials]	
	25th		Visited HQ 26th 27th 28th Inf: Bgdes: Discussed return of Winter Clothing - Arranged dates for receiving at A.O.D. [illegible] - [initials]	
	26th		Visited HQ 50th 51st 52nd Bgdes R.A. & discussed as above with them - [initials]	
	27th			
	28th		Recd Pistols 1½" .7 [initials]	
	29th		Visited Divl Baths Nieppe ref. to demands for underclothing [initials]	
	30th			
	31st		Arranged for additional help for Winter Clothing.	

[signature] Capt
DADOS 9th Divn

Instructions regarding War Diaries and Intelligence Summaries are contained in F. S. Regs., Part II. and the Staff Manual respectively. Title Pages will be prepared in manuscript.

WAR DIARY
or
INTELLIGENCE SUMMARY
(Erase heading not required.)

Army Form C. 2118

D A D O S
9 D W
Vol 12

Place	Date	Hour	Summary of Events and Information	Remarks and references to Appendices
			Confidential War Diary of D.A.D.O.S. 9th Division From 1-4-16 To 30-4-16	

1875 Wt. W593/826 1,000,000 4/15 J.B.C. & A. A.D.S.S./Forms/C. 2118.

Army Form C. 2118

Instructions regarding War Diaries and Intelligence Summaries are contained in F. S. Regs., Part II. and the Staff Manual respectively. Title Pages will be prepared in manuscript.

WAR DIARY
or
~~INTELLIGENCE~~ SUMMARY
(Erase heading not required.)

Place	Date	Hour	Summary of Events and Information	Remarks and references to Appendices
Steenwerck	1/4/16	—	Recd from Base shields for bombers – 15 single 15 double [initials]	
	2/4/16	—	Winter Clothing being returned – and in good condition – [initials]	
	3/4/16	—	ADOS called – Transfer of 26 Lewis Guns ordered from 9th Div: to Canadians – [initials]	
	4/4/16	—	Visited Railhead – & School of Sniping re rifles with Tel: sights. Saw several steel plates which 'armour piercing' bullets had failed to do much damage.	
	5th	—		
	6th		Round of visits to Qm. stores – Most of these seem to be run satisfactorily – No complaints of shortage of stores –	
	7th	—	Recd 162 Tower respirators –	
	8th		Food Containers not reqd as being returned to Base – Disposal reported from Corps HQ	
	9th			
	10th		Nearly all undercoats put or in – Drafts seem to be supplied with them from Base which causes odd ments to be returned –	
	11th			
	12th		Recd Div. Res. of 19500 smoke helmets.	
	13th		Advised DAG. re return of 2nd group winter Clothing –	
	14th		Visited 9th Scot: Rif: regarding mountings for Lewis Guns – New mounting said to be very satisfactory, being light, & does not impede the portability of gun.	
	15th		Gum Boots being retd: Bomb dropped on Steenwerck at 11pm no damage.	
	16th			
	17th		Visited Railhead – ADOS. Corps & DDOS. 2nd Army.	
	18th		Question raised by 9th Scot. Rif re head dress – Tam o Shanter & Balmorals. Referred matter to Corps HQ. Issued Corn paste – leave stopped.	

1875 Wt. W593/826 1,000,000 4/15 J.B.C. & A. A.D.S.S./Forms/C. 2118.

Army Form C. 2118

Instructions regarding War Diaries and Intelligence Summaries are contained in F. S. Regs., Part II. and the Staff Manual respectively. Title Pages will be prepared in manuscript.

WAR DIARY
or
INTELLIGENCE SUMMARY
(Erase heading not required.)

Place	Date	Hour	Summary of Events and Information	Remarks and references to Appendices
Steenwerck	19/4/16		Recd from Base 27 Dials Traversing ·303" M.G. also 7 Rings yard scale B.F. 18 pr: 27 " Elevating " 7 Straps [illegible] Nos 80–85 [illegible]. 27 Levels spirit Mk. IV. [initials]	
	20th			
	21st			
	22nd			
	23rd		South Africans arrived – 2 regts. (2nd & 3rd) & part of another (1st). Visited their HQ. Issued "Drill" smoke helmets. [initials]	
	24th		Visited S.A. Bde: HQ. also Regtl HQ. Issued P.H. smoke helmets to all of 2nd & 3rd. [initials]	
	25th		Reissued 1295 P.H.G. helmets recd yesterday. – Recd 3000 steel helmets. [initials]	
	26th	—	Visited QM. stores of S.A. regts: Gas alarm during night. Ordered lorry to be loaded with smoke helmets & to be kept in readiness. [initials]	
	27th		Recd 898 covers for steel helmets. Call for 30 cylinders [illegible] lorry. [initials]	
	28th		Obtained sanction to draw 20 cylinders from Heavy Mobile Workshops. [initials]	
	29th		Visited A.D.O.S. Corps – Demands for S.H. continue abnormal. Gas expert condemns many. [initials]	
	30th			

[signature] Capt
DADOS 9th Div.

1875 Wt. W593/826 1,000,000 4/15 J.B.C. & A. A.D.S.S./Forms/C. 2118.

Instructions regarding War Diaries and Intelligence Summaries are contained in F. S. Regs., Part II. and the Staff Manual respectively. Title Pages will be prepared in manuscript.

WAR DIARY
or
INTELLIGENCE SUMMARY
(Erase heading not required.)

Army Form C. 2118

D A D O S
9th Div

Place	Date	Hour	Summary of Events and Information	Remarks and references to Appendices
			Confidential War Diary D.A.D.O.S. 9th Divn From 1 - 5 - 16 To 31 - 5 - 16	Vol 13. May

1875 Wt. W593/826 1,000,000 4/15 J.B.C. & A. A.D.S.S./Forms/C. 2118.

Instructions regarding War Diaries and Intelligence Summaries are contained in F. S. Regs., Part II. and the Staff Manual respectively. Title Pages will be prepared in manuscript.

WAR DIARY
or
~~INTELLIGENCE~~ SUMMARY
(Erase heading not required.)

Army Form C. 2118

Place	Date	Hour	Summary of Events and Information	Remarks and references to Appendices
Steenwerck	1/5/16		Round of visits to QM's stores – Inspected state of 1914 patt. equipment & found that it was still in good condition, although a little saggy & untidy looking – [initials]	
	2		Return of blankets by units of the Divn: begins, weather good – [initials]	
	3		Recd one Jarrason telescope for Div! RA Visited HQ. 2nd Army & ADOS Corps. [initials]	
	4		Recd 250 overall suits from Base – Visited other QM stores re equipt. [initials]	
	5		Recd set of equipment patt 08 for SA Bgde 625. Visited HQ. SA Bgde: Pont Nieppe with ADMS [initials]	
	6		Recd 10 handcarts for Trench mortars. Arranged with OO 2nd Corps Troops to take duty for me when on leave. [initials]	
	7			
	8		Went on leave [initials]	
	9		4th Btt SA arrived 396 Tower Respirts received. [initials]	
	10		More web-equipment recd for SA. [initials]	
	11		Recd 2 Spirit Levels M! Mk IV [initials]	
	12		Recd 1163 Box Respirators, & 6 Bicycles for RA. [initials]	
	13		Further supply of bicycles for RA (4) [initials]	
	14			
	15			
	16		Reported for duty again after leave [initials]	

1875 Wt. W593/826 1,000,000 4/15 J.B.C. & A. A.D.S.S./Forms/C. 2118.

Instructions regarding War Diaries and Intelligence Summaries are contained in F. S. Regs., Part II. and the Staff Manual respectively. Title Pages will be prepared in manuscript.

WAR DIARY
or
INTELLIGENCE SUMMARY
(Erase heading not required.)

Army Form C. 2118

Place	Date	Hour	Summary of Events and Information	Remarks and references to Appendices
Steenwerck	17/5/16			
	18		Visited Hq. RA. ref: changes visited Div. Column with Staff Capt: & arranged about indents under new formation of B.A.C. GA	
	19		Showed two officers under instr. at Div. Hq. our system of working Ordnance stores GA	
	20		Visited Hq. FA. Bde: re badges and titles. Considerable shelling of the Billet today – This place has been shelled more recently than hitherto GA	
	21		Visited Divl. Baths at Pont Nieppe ref: return of underclothing – Also visited Qm stores 8th Black Watch & 7th Seaforths – GA	
	22		Visited DDOS 2nd Army	
	23		Inspected new area for suitable store – Found one in central situation at Enguinegatte – Distance away from here about 25 miles. GA	
	24		Recd 3000 steel helmets – Withdrew 36 bicycles from Cyclist Coy: for distribn to RA. Recd 39 disting marks in 3 patterns from Base. GA	
	25		Recd 5 No. 9 Periscopes GA	
	26		Recd 13 Lewis Guns from Base – Visited Cyclist Coy re state of bicycles GA	
	27		Recd 3 Lewis Guns from 2nd Canadians, also 4 3" Trench Mortars. GA	
	28		Stopped receipt of stores from Base in anticipation of move, & made arrangements with incoming Divn (41st) re taking over certain stores GA	

1875 Wt. W593/826 1,000,000 4/15 J.B.C. & A. A.D.S.S./Forms/C. 2118.

Instructions regarding War Diaries and Intelligence Summaries are contained in F. S. Regs., Part II. and the Staff Manual respectively. Title Pages will be prepared in manuscript.

WAR DIARY
or
INTELLIGENCE SUMMARY
(Erase heading not required.)

Army Form C. 2118

Place	Date	Hour	Summary of Events and Information	Remarks and references to Appendices
Steenwerck	29/5/16			
Merris	30/5/16		Moved in on our way to Training Area. Did not unload lorries.	
Enguinegatte	31st		Continued journey to Enguinegatte via Hazebrouck & Aire. Reopened office & store.	
"	1/6			

[illegible] Capt. D.A.D.O.S. 9th Divn
1/6/16

1875 Wt. W593/826 1,000,000 4/15 J.B.C. & A. A.D.S.S./Forms/C. 2118.

Instructions regarding War Diaries and Intelligence Summaries are contained in F. S. Regs., Part II. and the Staff Manual respectively. Title pages will be prepared in manuscript.

WAR DIARY
or
INTELLIGENCE SUMMARY.
(Erase heading not required.)

Army Form C. 2118.

DADOS
9th Div

Place	Date	Hour	Summary of Events and Information	Remarks and references to Appendices
			Confidential War Diary DADOS. 9th Div. 1/6/16 to 30/6/16	Vol 14 June

1577 Wt. W10791/1773 500,000 1/15 D. D. & L. A.D.S.S./Forms/C. 2118.

Instructions regarding War Diaries and Intelligence Summaries are contained in F. S. Regs., Part II. and the Staff Manual respectively. Title pages will be prepared in manuscript.

WAR DIARY
or
~~INTELLIGENCE~~ SUMMARY.

(Erase heading not required.)

Army Form C. 2118.

Place	Date	Hour	Summary of Events and Information	Remarks and references to Appendices
Erquinghem	1/6/16		16 Tons general stores rec'd from Base also 2300 steel helmets which almost completes Divn GA	
	2		9 Tons stores rec'd Railhead 15 miles away at Steenbecque – GA	
	3		Visited railhead – also Divl Supply Col: ref. lorries GA	
	4		Visited H.Q. R.A. ref: Trench Mortars – Sent 4 Tm. to Adv. W'shops Hazebrouck GA	
	5		Went round 27 Bgde area. Decided that stores had better be sent to units instead of their drawing from here. GA	
	6		Visited R.A. H.Q. also R'head & Hazebrouck for purchases GA	
	7		Made round of visits to S.A. Qm. stores – Demands from these units very heavy & suggest waste. Spoke about matter to D.H.Q. GA	
	8		Accumulation of stores now distributed – The transport of Divl: Res: of Smoke Helmets is great inconvenience – All available lorries needed for other services, & difficulty experienced in obtaining sufficient transport. Decided to send S.H. per train from Lillers to near Amiens. GA	
	9			
	10		Visited H.Q. 26th Bde: & S.A. Fld: Amb: GA	
	11		Made arrangements with R.T.O. Lillers to dump Smoke Helmets at Station GA	
	12		Orders to move came earlier than expected – Various Divl arrangements cancelled in consequence – Weather bad, raining & windy – District exposed GA Stopped stores from Base	
	13			

Instructions regarding War Diaries and Intelligence Summaries are contained in F. S. Regs., Part II. and the Staff Manual respectively. Title pages will be prepared in manuscript.

WAR DIARY
or
INTELLIGENCE SUMMARY.
(Erase heading not required.)

Army Form C. 2118.

Place	Date	Hour	Summary of Events and Information	Remarks and references to Appendices
Enguinegatte	14/6/16			
	15		Went to Vaux sur Somme with Divl. A.G. Arranged for Ordnance Store at Ailly – Place crowded with other Divns & store difficult to find – Railhead Longpré 17 miles away GA	
Ailly	16		Lorries with stores arrived from Enguinegatte after trek of 50 miles without mishap. GA	
	17		Drew Smoke Helmets from Longeau & sent on to advanced store at Corbie to await our arrival there GA	
	18		A few units near at hand drew stores – The Divn: widely scattered – issues do not go on with much speed – Stay here only 2 days – GA	
	19		Moved from Ailly to Corbie 17 miles – R'head now at Heilly 4 miles away GA	
Corbie	20		Arrangements made to issue from Supply refilling point on Canal at Sailly – R'head train comes in at 3.30 am where my lorries park. GA	
	21		Great activity all over district in view of approaching offensive – Roads teeming with motor lorries – & towns full of soldiers French & English GA	
	22		Visited Bray with DADOS & arranged to pitch tent with a few stores at forward area – the store consisting of a few smoke helmets & grenade carriers, coloured patches &c. Hastened Base for Steel Helmets. GA	
	23		Visited DADOS 30th Divn.	
	24		DAG decided to withdraw packs from men – ADOS suggests drawing & taking to store there – taken. Arranging for coloured patches &c GA	

1577 Wt. W10791/1773 500,000 1/15 D. D. & L. A.D.S.S./Forms/C. 2118.

Instructions regarding War Diaries and Intelligence Summaries are contained in F. S. Regs., Part II. and the Staff Manual respectively. Title pages will be prepared in manuscript.

WAR DIARY
or
~~INTELLIGENCE~~ SUMMARY.
(Erase heading not required.)

Army Form C. 2118.

Place	Date	Hour	Summary of Events and Information	Remarks and references to Appendices
Corbie	25/6			
	26		Visited HQ 27 Inf: Bde: at Chipilly, refilling point Sailly – arranged with O.C. Train to fix up shelter. [initials]	
	27		A Sub Cdr Williams left Div: after doing excellent work for 8th Corps Tps. A Sub Cdr McGaffney of 4A Bde takes his place – [initials]	
	28		Stores here cramped for room – the impossibility of being mobile with only 4 lorries becomes more & more noticeable – DAG compel me to hold so much reserve stock such as grenade carriers of which I have 11000 [initials]	
	29		Went to Grovetown near Bray to select site for dump. No shelter of any kind – Arranged with ADOS for tarpaulins [initials]	
	30		Moved some stores to Grovetown – [initials]	

[signature] Capt
DADOS 9th Div 1/7/16

1577 Wt. W10791/1773 500,000 1/15 D. D. & L. A.D.S.S./Forms/C. 2118.

9 July — Army Form C. 2118.

9 Div DADOS

Vol 15

Instructions regarding War Diaries and Intelligence Summaries are contained in F. S. Regs., Part II. and the Staff Manual respectively. Title pages will be prepared in manuscript.

WAR DIARY
or
INTELLIGENCE SUMMARY.
(Erase heading not required.)

Place	Date	Hour	Summary of Events and Information	Remarks and references to Appendices
			Confidential War Diary of D.A.D.O.S. 9th (Scottish) Division from July 1st 1916 to " 31st 1916	

1577 Wt. W10791/1773 500,000 1/15 D. D. & L. A.D.S.S./Forms/C. 2118.

Army Form C. 2118

Instructions regarding War Diaries and Intelligence Summaries are contained in F. S. Regs., Part II. and the Staff Manual respectively. Title Pages will be prepared in manuscript.

WAR DIARY
or
INTELLIGENCE SUMMARY
(Erase heading not required.)

Place	Date	Hour	Summary of Events and Information	Remarks and references to Appendices
	JULY			
Corbie	1		Moved some stores to Grovetown where store is proposed to be made. Arranged with 9th Seaforths for assistance in erecting temporary shelters for accomodation – Drew tarpaulins from O.O. XV Corps for this purpose – Left two men in charge.	
			Visited new D.H.Q. in dug-outs at Grovetown	
	2		Completed move of stores & office to Grovetown.	
	3			
Grovetown	4		Visited 28 M.[?] Coy. ref: Collars for Stokes Mortars said to have been handed in to D.O.M. with [struck out] mortars. These cannot be traced anywhere. Visited D.O.M. XIII & XV Corps trying to trace without effect	
	5			
	6			
	7		Demanded 3 Lewis Guns for 11th Royal Scots to replace those destroyed by shellfire. The salvage from battlefield being returned in great quantities. A few haversacks were found to contain live bombs. Boxes of grenades returned also. I have asked D.H.Q. to arrange that as far as possible these latter stores shall not be sent to Ordnance. Three German Field Guns recd. captured by 12th Royal Scots. 1 machine gun captured by 6th K.O.S.B. & 2 Trench Mortars by D.O.M. (returning [?])	
	8			

1875 Wt. W593/826 1,000,000 4/15 J.B.C. & A. A.D.S.S./Forms/C. 2118.

Instructions regarding War Diaries and Intelligence Summaries are contained in F. S. Regs., Part II. and the Staff Manual respectively. Title Pages will be prepared in manuscript.

WAR DIARY
or
INTELLIGENCE SUMMARY
(Erase heading not required.)

Army Form C. 2118.

Place	Date	Hour	Summary of Events and Information	Remarks and references to Appendices
Grovetown	July 9		One Vickers & two tripods demanded for 27th Bgde: M.G. Co: to replace destroyed by shell-fire. DHQ have arranged that no live bombs or grenades shall be sent to Ordnance but to Divl Amm: Dump. One is struck by the absence of moveable parts in captured guns – No breech mechanism in the field guns & no dial sights	
	10		Another Vickers demanded by 27th Bgde. to replace – One damaged Vickers MG recd beyond local repair dispatched to base – Drew 6 tarpaulins from O.O. XIII C.T. for Rd. Ammn Dump. Consignment of wire cutters recd from Salisbury Coy: Inn. 27/1 reports 27 shell jackets & 38 Tantalus carriers destroyed – Have asked ADOS. if these shell jackets can be replaced. Wired for gun carriage 18 pr: for B 51 – [initials] Drew 644 steel helmets from Dressing Station	
	11		Visited ADOS ref gun carr: 18 pr: No dial sight reqd for this carriage. Returned to base via Amm. Rlhead 1 box German ammn for T.M. Recd 27 tents C.S. in lieu of shelters, & 16 tarpaulins from Corps Tps. Recd one wooden wire-bound trench mortar or canister thrower – bore about 12", with 10 rounds ammn for same – Two Vickers & 1 Lewis gun recd for 27th M.G. Coy. & 9th Royal Scots respectively – [initials]	
	12		Visited ADOS ref: position of railhead – Stores continuing to arrive at Mericourt although Grovetown is official r'head. Drew 100 steel helmets from Dressing Station. Recd 1 German Field gun from 9th Seaforths.	

1875 Wt. W593/826 1,000,000 4/15 J.B.C. & A. A.D.S.S./Forms/C. 2118.

Instructions regarding War Diaries and Intelligence Summaries are contained in F. S. Regs., Part II. and the Staff Manual respectively. Title Pages will be prepared in manuscript.

WAR DIARY
or
INTELLIGENCE SUMMARY
(Erase heading not required.)

Army Form C. 2118

Place	Date	Hour	Summary of Events and Information	Remarks and references to Appendices
Grovetown	July 13		Recd instructions from DHQ reference to forthcoming action by 9th Division. Obtained 9 Signalling Sheets from Amiens, issued 1 to 4th SA1 for Battn head qrs. [initials]	
	14		Visited ADOS XIII Corps. Obtained 250 steel helmets from Dressing Sta. [illegible] from 189 Magazines for Lewis Gun for KOSB. [initials]	
	15		Wire recd from 1st DWS stating important stores awaiting there & asking how to send. Wired reply.	
			Obtained 550 steel helmets from D.S. Drew 1 No. 32 [illegible] from XIII Corps. Asked Supply Col. to remove Corporal in charge of my lorries. Arranged that men on duty with lorries when not actually engaged on work therewith should assist in stores if required. [initials]	
	16		Visited Corps Ord ref springs 18 pr. 300 more steel helmets from D.S. Recd & issued 1 Vickers MG to 27th MG Coy. [initials]	
	17		Sent car to Hazebrouck for detonators from 2nd Army Workshops. Visited 27th Bde Transport Lines. Issued 3 tarpaulins to 27th Bde. [initials]	
	18		3 Stokes mortars recd from 27th Bde & desp. to H.M. Workshops Beauval. Visited DHQ. at B Copse with Col. Crawley. Fetched signalling [illegible] from Amiens, also [illegible] patches	

1875 Wt. W593/826 1,000,000 4/15 J.B.C. & A. A.D.S.S./Forms/C. 2118.

Army Form C. 2118

Instructions regarding War Diaries and Intelligence Summaries are contained in F. S. Regs., Part II. and the Staff Manual respectively. Title Pages will be prepared in manuscript.

WAR DIARY
or
INTELLIGENCE SUMMARY
(Erase heading not required.)

Place	Date	Hour	Summary of Events and Information	Remarks and references to Appendices
Grovetown	July 18 contd		Received 3 Stokes mortars from A.M. Workshops at Beauval. Recd 72 Landcarts for Lewis Guns. Issued 100 shelters and 5 G.S. tents + 1 tarpaulin to S.A. Bgde, now out of action. FA	
	19		ADOS gave instns to move store to Morlancourt. Informed 3rd Div DADOS that my store at Grovetown would be vacant. Visited M'court. FA	
	20		Found store at Morlancourt. Recd 2 German Field Guns. FA	
	21		Stopped receipts from Base. FA	
	22		Moved to Morlancourt. FA	
Morlancourt	23		Sent some stores to rest area at Pont Remy. No issues made troops moving. FA	
Pont Remy	24		Pont Remy. Distance about 34 miles from previous station. FA	
	25		Moved again. Pont Remy to Bruay, distance about 45 miles. Informed base to reconsign stores. FA	

1875 Wt. W593/826 1,000,000 4/15 J.B.C. & A. A.D.S.S./Forms/C. 2118.

Instructions regarding War Diaries and Intelligence Summaries are contained in F. S. Regs., Part II. and the Staff Manual respectively. Title pages will be prepared in manuscript.

WAR DIARY

or

INTELLIGENCE SUMMARY.

(Erase heading not required.)

Army Form C. 2118.

Place	Date	Hour	Summary of Events and Information	Remarks and references to Appendices
Bruay	July 26		Called on ADOS IX Corps. Arranged to hand over magazines for Lewis guns to 37 Divn. Visited base eng at Dieval station ref above. DAG moved in. Wired Base for machine guns deficient owing to recent action. [initials]	
	27		2070 magazines Lewis handed over to DADOS 37 Divn after examination by armourer. Many of these are US. [initials]	
	28		Visited Corbie with DAQMG ref packs left behind there, also ref handcarts left behind by SA at Méricourt. [initials]	
			Recd Vickers & Lewis guns from Base to complete.	
	29		Visited HQ of 1st 2nd & 4th SA Inf. Battns & 10th Argylls [initials]	
	30		Visited HQ 26th Inf: Bgde also units 8th Black Watch, 7th Seaforths, 5th Camerons & South Af: Fld. Amb: ref. equipment [illegible] [initials]	
	31		Issued all Lewis & Vickers guns to complete Div. 27th Bgde moved into Dieval area. [initials]	
			for Bgde Capt. DADOS 9th Div.	

1577 Wt. W10791/1773 500,000 1/15 D. D. & L. A.D.S.S./Forms/C. 2118.

9

Army Form C.-2118.

DADOS.

Instructions regarding War Diaries and Intelligence Summaries are contained in F. S. Regs., Part II. and the Staff Manual respectively. Title pages will be prepared in manuscript.

WAR DIARY
or
INTELLIGENCE SUMMARY.
(Erase heading not required.)

Place	Date	Hour	Summary of Events and Information	Remarks and references to Appendices
			Confidential	Vol 16
			War Diary of DADOS	
			9th Division	
			From 1. 8. 16	
			To 31. 8. 16	

1577 Wt. W10791/1773 500,000 1/15 D. D. & L. A.D.S.S./Forms/C. 2118.

Army Form C. 2118.

WAR DIARY

or

~~INTELLIGENCE~~ SUMMARY.

(Erase heading not required.)

Instructions regarding War Diaries and Intelligence Summaries are contained in F. S. Regs., Part II. and the Staff Manual respectively. Title pages will be prepared in manuscript.

Place	Date	Hour	Summary of Events and Information	Remarks and references to Appendices
Bruay	1/8/16		Visited HQ 27th I.B. & Q.M's stores of all units in Bgde. No shortages in items demanded from Ordnance complained of. [initials]	
	2nd		DDOS 1st Army visited. Suggested starting Ord Armourers shop, also a HQ shoemakers shop. The question of preventing waste of clothing & stores was discussed. [initials]	
	3rd		Visited HQ South African Bgde: at Fresnicourt, also stores of [illegible] SAR. [illegible] RA. spoke about difficulty in obtaining [illegible]. [initials]	
	4		Visited HQ RA. also D.50 Btty. & HQ 26th Bgde: at Bois de [illegible] [initials]	
	5		Spoke ADOS. 4th Corps ref: starting Divl Workshops, & decided that nothing could be done for the present until the Divn went into [illegible]. Visited QM stores 3rd S.A.I. & 8th B.W. Received cheque for purchase of unauthorized stores from Maj. King A.S.C. 1350 francs. [initials]	
	6			
	7		Visited HQ S.A. Bgde. also 1st 2nd & 4th Inf. Bttns; also HQ [illegible] at Estree Cauchie. Bethune heavily bombarded [illegible]. [initials]	
	8			
	9		Found suitable building at Estree Cauchie for store. Visited 2nd [illegible] this place. [initials]	

1577 Wt. W10791/1773 500,000 1/15 D. D. & L. A.D.S.S./Forms/C. 2118.

Army Form C. 2118.

Instructions regarding War Diaries and Intelligence Summaries are contained in F. S. Regs., Part II. and the Staff Manual respectively. Title pages will be prepared in manuscript.

WAR DIARY
or
~~INTELLIGENCE~~ SUMMARY.
(Erase heading not required.)

Place	Date	Hour	Summary of Events and Information	Remarks and references to Appendices
Bruay	10/8/16		Bought hammers for cookers at Lillers [initials]	
	11/8/16		Visited HQ 9th Scottish Rifles, 11th Royal Scots, 12th Rd. & inspected bootmakers & tailoring shops – these were working very satisfactorily in all cases – [initials]	
	12th		Transferred some reserve stores to Estrée Cauchie – [initials]	
	13th		Completed move to Estrée Cauchie – Discovered at 10.30 pm. that chief clerk (Sub Cr Pritchard) & WO. (Sub Cr McGafney) had not ~~returned~~ come ~~back~~ with the last lorry – Gave orders that their arrival should be immediately reported to me. [initials]	
Estrée Cauchie	14		Neither of the above WO's had arrived by 9 am when stores were opened for issue – Proceeded to Div HQ. to report the absence of these WO's & informed APM. Sub Crs Pritchard & McGafney arrived at 4 pm. & I placed both under open arrest.	
			Arranged with DADOS 37th Div: that he should hand over 1315 Lewis magazines to 27th Inf: Bgde. Recd 915 magazines from 103rd Bgde (37th D) [initials]	
	15		Visited DADOS 37th Div. ref. magazines – Recd 1 shield for Machine Gun – Court of Enquiry re: the above WO's Major Savage DSO DAAG of this Divn presiding – [initials]	
	16		Lt Evett AOD arrived ref. Armourers shop. Took him to inspect the armourers of Batns Court of Enquiry continued – both WO's deprived of acting rank for "absenting themselves without leave." [initials]	

1577 Wt. W10791/1773 500,000 1/15 D. D. & L. A.D.S.S./Forms/C. 2118.

Instructions regarding War Diaries and Intelligence Summaries are contained in F. S. Regs., Part II. and the Staff Manual respectively. Title pages will be prepared in manuscript.

WAR DIARY
or
~~INTELLIGENCE~~ SUMMARY.

(Erase heading not required.)

Army Form C. 2118.

Place	Date	Hour	Summary of Events and Information	Remarks and references to Appendices
Estrée Cauchie	17/8/16		Visited A.D.O.S. 4th Corps. Rec'd 1100 steel helmets.	
	18th		Visited D.D.O.S. 1st Army ref: the W.O.'s [illegible] referred to. Demanded magazines for Lewis guns to complete division, [illegible] hand over to 37th Div. for those borrowed. Rec'd 1500 more steel helmets.	
	19th		Spoke [illegible] Field Amb: ref: baths, [illegible] of [illegible] clothing issued to units. Ordered 2000 armbands at Merville for 26th Bgde. Rec'd 2 shields for machine guns.	
	20		Rec'd of 2 Lewis [illegible] back from 1st Army workshops Merville fitted with silencers — rec'd also 2 mountings.	
	21			
	22		Rec'd 2000 armbands from Merville, issued to 26th Bgde.	
	23		A/Sub Cdr Goodey arrived for duty as Chief Clerk — Sergt. Pritchard A.O.C. left 9th Div. for duty with 16th Div.	
	24		Request from R.E. H.Q. for purchase of [illegible] material. After discussion with Staff Capt: [illegible] matter [illegible] [illegible] supplied. Rec'd 5000 shirts & socks, issued to Divl Baths.	

1577 Wt. W10791/1773 500,000 1/15 D. D. & L. A.D.S.S./Forms/C. 2118.

Army Form C. 2118.

Instructions regarding War Diaries and Intelligence Summaries are contained in F. S. Regs., Part II. and the Staff Manual respectively. Title pages will be prepared in manuscript.

WAR DIARY
or
INTELLIGENCE SUMMARY.
(Erase heading not required.)

Place	Date	Hour	Summary of Events and Information	Remarks and references to Appendices
Estrée Cauchie	25/8/16		Sergt. Thomson reported for duty as A/Condr: in place of L/Cpl. McGeffney.	
			Removed reserve stores to another store in the village. [initials]	
			Removed store & office from shed to barns in another part of village. [initials]	
	26th		Lorry with A.O.D. stores & personnel caught fire. 3 wheeled stretchers burnt.	
	27th		Court of Inquiry arranged by Supply Col. [initials]	
	28th		Four armourers reported for duty. Col. Courtice A.D.O.S. 6th Corps visited making enquiries ref: missing 18 pr: Gave him all the information & correspondence recd from B.50 Bty concerned. [initials]	
	29		Took the Sergt. Maj: Lawson A.O.C. to visit 40th Div: armourers shop at Noeux les Mines for instn in running armourers shop. [initials]	
	30		Arm: Sergt. Maj: Lawson retd. from 40th Div. [initials]	
	31		Ordered further 2000 armbands from Abbeville for 26th Bde:	
			Wrote HQ proposing improved building for armourers shop.	
			Further enquiries ref: missing 18 pr. [initials]	
			31/8/16 [signature] Capt. DADOS 9th Div.	

1577 Wt. W10791/1773 500,000 1/15 D. D. & L. A.D.S.S./Forms/C. 2118.

Army Form C. 2118

Vol 17

Instructions regarding War Diaries and Intelligence Summaries are contained in F. S. Regs., Part II. and the Staff Manual respectively. Title Pages will be prepared in manuscript.

WAR DIARY
or
INTELLIGENCE SUMMARY
(Erase heading not required.)

Place	Date	Hour	Summary of Events and Information	Remarks and references to Appendices
			Confidential War Diary D.A.D.O.S. 9th Dn From 1st Sept. 1916 To 30th " "	

1875 Wt. W593/826 1,000,000 4/15 J.B.C. & A. A.D.S.S./Forms/C. 2118.

Instructions regarding War Diaries and Intelligence Summaries are contained in F. S. Regs., Part II. and the Staff Manual respectively. Title Pages will be prepared in manuscript.

WAR DIARY
or
~~INTELLIGENCE~~ SUMMARY
(Erase heading not required.)

Army Form C. 2118

Place	Date	Hour	Summary of Events and Information	Remarks and references to Appendices
Estrée Cauchie	Sep 1		Visited DADOS 37th Dn re missing gun. Visited Divl Laundry at Houdain & HQ 27th Inf Bgde re stores for Trench Mortars	GH
	2		Recd & issued 2000 white armbands for 26th Bgde. Purchased small electric torches for tactical purposes. GH	
	3		Visited A Corps HQ & OO 4th Corps Tpo: ref: medal ribbon	GH
	4		Nothing to report.	
	5		Do	
	6		ADOS 4th Corps called. Raised question with him re shortage of Blocks Brake. Spoke IOM. No 8 W'shop ref: possibility of supply. GH	
	7		Demand for purchase of 2 [illegible] for gas alarm recd from DHQ. Distributed telescopic rifles 5A 1 B.10 27th IB. 5.	GH

1875 Wt. W593/826 1,000,000 4/15 J.B.C. & A. A.D.S.S./Forms/C. 2118.

Instructions regarding War Diaries and Intelligence Summaries are contained in F. S. Regs., Part II. and the Staff Manual respectively. Title Pages will be prepared in manuscript.

WAR DIARY
or
~~INTELLIGENCE SUMMARY~~
(Erase heading not required.)

Army Form C. 2118

Place	Date	Hour	Summary of Events and Information	Remarks and references to Appendices
Estrée Cauchie	Sep- 8		Question of parts for Lewis Guns – asked 4th Corps to expedite supply if possible, & as to possibility of holding small reserve in Div: Armourers Shop – [initials]	
	9		Rec.d 2000 blankets from Base, being 1st consignment of 17000 demanded – Rec.d 4000 pr. gumboots thigh [initials]	
	10			
	11		Purchased 9 French horses for S.A. Bgde – issued also blankets –	
	12		Nothing to report – [initials]	
	13		Sent an armourer to H.M. workshops for instruction – Drew 4 handcarts from there – [initials]	
	14		Visited H.M. workshops Merville – [initials]	
	15		Ordered 4000 each 4 colours strips for shoulders – [initials]	
	16		Visited H.Q. 26th Bgde. ref: old clothing supplied for tactical purposes. [initials]	

1875 Wt. W593/826 1,000,000 4/15 J.B.C. & A. A.D.S.S./Forms/C. 2118.

Instructions regarding War Diaries and Intelligence Summaries are contained in F. S. Regs., Part II. and the Staff Manual respectively. Title Pages will be prepared in manuscript.

WAR DIARY
or
~~INTELLIGENCE SUMMARY~~
(Erase heading not required.)

Army Form C. 2118.

Place	Date	Hour	Summary of Events and Information	Remarks and references to Appendices
Estrée Cauchie	Sep. 16		Visited 4th Corps Tps. ref: tentage – Demanded howitzers for D 51. GA	
	17		Recd 100 prs: F.S. boots. being 25% of mounted men. GA	
	18		Purchased tin cutters for making discs for backs of men. GA	
	19		Indent for 390 prs: trousers for 12th R.S. Referred this to DHQ. as these are otherwise to repl: shorts. GA	
	20		Visited DADOS. 24th Dn. with ADOS 4th Corps. Arranged matter of taking over reserve of Smoke Helmets &c: GA	
	21		Visited new area with Camp: Commdt: found store + office – GA	
	22		Arranged to take over 17 box resp: from O.O. IV C.T. Visited HQ 26th I.B. also HQ S.A. Bgde GA	
	23		Nothing to report – GA	

Army Form C. 2118.

Instructions regarding War Diaries and Intelligence Summaries are contained in F. S. Regs., Part II. and the Staff Manual respectively. Title Pages will be prepared in manuscript.

WAR DIARY
or
~~INTELLIGENCE SUMMARY~~
(Erase heading not required.)

Place	Date	Hour	Summary of Events and Information	Remarks and references to Appendices
Estrée Cauchie	Sep. 24		Obtained 'straps' from Merville at 6d each – [initials]	
	25		DDOS & Col Scarborough called reference to procedure adopted during late battle by Ordnance – Spoke Staff Capt RA reference return of RA surplus stores – Cleared store preparatory to leaving – [initials]	
	26		Left for new area at Le Cauroy – [initials]	
	27		Visited SA. Bde. H.Q. with DDOS [initials]	
	28			
	29		Reopened store for issue – ADOS 17th Corps called. [initials]	
	30		Visited Railhead –	

[signature] Capt
DADOS 9th Div

1875 Wt. W593/826 1,000,000 4/15 J.B.C. & A. A.D.S.S./Forms/C. 2118.

Instructions regarding War Diaries and Intelligence Summaries are contained in F. S. Regs., Part II. and the Staff Manual respectively. Title pages will be prepared in manuscript.

WAR DIARY
or
INTELLIGENCE SUMMARY.
(Erase heading not required.)

Army Form C. 2118.

Vol 18

Place	Date	Hour	Summary of Events and Information	Remarks and references to Appendices
			Confidential War Diary D.A.D.O.S. 9th Division 1 - 10 - 16 31 - 10 - 16	

1577 Wt. W10791/1773 500,000 1/15 D. D. & L. A.D.S.S./Forms/C. 2118.

Army Form C. 2118.

Instructions regarding War Diaries and Intelligence Summaries are contained in F. S. Regs., Part II. and the Staff Manual respectively. Title pages will be prepared in manuscript.

WAR DIARY
or
~~INTELLIGENCE SUMMARY~~.
(Erase heading not required.)

Place	Date	Hour	Summary of Events and Information	Remarks and references to Appendices
Field	Sep. 28		Found new dump at Hauteville – many barns filled with straw which made finding suitable place very difficult. Meeting lorries with stores at railhead 5pm. reconducted them to new stores – [initials]	
	29		Visited A.D.O.S. XI Corps – [initials]	
	30		D.D.O.S. 3rd Army called, expressed himself dissatisfied with everything – [initials]	
	31		Arranged to work on "brigade" system from 1st of next month – [initials]	

[illegible] Capt
DADOS. 9th Dn
31/10/16

1577 Wt. W10791/1773 500,000 1/15 D. D. & L. A.D.S.S./Forms/C. 2118.

Army Form C. 2118.

Instructions regarding War Diaries and Intelligence Summaries are contained in F. S. Regs., Part II. and the Staff Manual respectively. Title pages will be prepared in manuscript.

WAR DIARY
or
INTELLIGENCE SUMMARY.
(Erase heading not required.)

Place	Date	Hour	Summary of Events and Information	Remarks and references to Appendices
Field	Sep: 1st		Visited HQ. S.A. Brigade, also 1st 2nd 3rd & 4th Batts: reference return of old Clothing. [initials]	
	2		Visited ADOS. 17th Corps. & DADOS 24th D. ref transfer of 9th Div: RA. to them for Ordnance Services. [initials]	
	3		Visited ADOS. 17th Corps: ref: tentage. 105 tents lent to division. Went to 26th Bgde: regarding receipt of tents. [initials]	
	4		Stopped stores from Base. Visited HQ S.A Bgde. also 26th & 27th Bgde. Arranged collection of all tents lent by Corps. [initials]	
	5.		Visited new area, & fixed dump. [initials]	
	6		Moved to new area, for one night. DAAG moved to Dernancourt [initials]	
	7		Moved again. to near Albert. tents. Stores being rec'd again. Numerous troops moving. [initials]	
	8		Ordered to move to Mametz Wood. [initials]	
	9		Visited area of Mametz. Roads impracticable for purpose. Div: Train removed after one "refill". Pitched tents near Albert-Fricourt Rd.	

1577 Wt. W10791/1773 500,000 1/15 D. D. & L. A.D.S.S./Forms/C. 2118.

Instructions regarding War Diaries and Intelligence Summaries are contained in F. S. Regs., Part II. and the Staff Manual respectively. Title pages will be prepared in manuscript.

WAR DIARY
or
~~INTELLIGENCE SUMMARY~~.
(Erase heading not required.)

Army Form C. 2118.

Place	Date	Hour	Summary of Events and Information	Remarks and references to Appendices
Field	10		Moved stores to E.S. [illegible] at Albert. 2 store tents. Issues made to troops – [initials]	
	11		Went to Amiens to order signalling [illegible] – [initials]	
	12		Of DAC called. Went through indents with him. Called on	
	13		Col. [illegible] ref. arrangement for new railhead at [illegible] – [initials]	
	14		Visited ADOS 3rd Corps. R.A. units reported & called for stores awaiting – [initials]	
	15		Conference at A.D.O.S. III Corps [initials]	
	16		Visited new proposed railhead with DAQMG. Also advanced dump, Salvage Coy. Recommended that additional labour be provided to assist in sorting equipment & cleaning rifles – Visited railhead – [initials]	
	17		Visited ADOS. Ordered more socks in view of failure of laundry contract – [initials]	
	18		Borrowed 1000 prs: socks from 50th Dn. Visited railhead. [initials]	
	19		Borrowed further 1000 prs: socks from 50th Dn. Drew Trench mortar from [illegible] workshops – for dispatch to 2nd Dn [initials]	

1577 Wt. W10791/1773 500,000 1/15 D. D. & L. A.D.S.S./Forms/C. 2118.

Instructions regarding War Diaries and Intelligence Summaries are contained in F. S. Regs., Part II. and the Staff Manual respectively. Title pages will be prepared in manuscript.

WAR DIARY

or

~~INTELLIGENCE SUMMARY.~~

(*Erase heading not required.*)

Army Form C. 2118.

Place	Date	Hour	Summary of Events and Information	Remarks and references to Appendices
Field	Sep. 20th		Dispatched T.M. to 24th Div. to replace one borrowed.	
	21st		Visited railhead Edgehill, arranged to collect steel helmets & equipment. Recd. 8600 leather jerkins.	
	22nd			
	23		Finished issue of leather jerkins as above. More winter clothing received.	
	24		Arranged to move again to 50th Div. dump.	
	25		Removed office, & remainder of stores to Millencourt. [illegible] Handed over 3800 gum boots thigh, & exchanged smoke helmets.	
	26			
	27		9th Div. R.A. handed over to 50th Div. for Ordnance services. Also 107 Coy A.S.C. [illegible]	
	28		~~Visited~~ Visited Hqrs. to find new dump owing to move. Found on arriving back that dump would have to be elsewhere owing to change of railhead.	

1577 Wt. W10791/1773 500,000 1/15 D. D. & L. A.D.S.S./Forms/C. 2118.

Instructions regarding War Diaries and Intelligence Summaries are contained in F. S. Regs., Part II. and the Staff Manual respectively. Title pages will be prepared in manuscript.

WAR DIARY
or
INTELLIGENCE SUMMARY.
(*Erase heading not required.*)

Army Form C. 2118.

Vol 19

Place	Date	Hour	Summary of Events and Information	Remarks and references to Appendices
			Confidential War Diary D.A.D.O.S. 9th Div 1.11.16 to 30-11-16 [illegible] Capt D.A.D.O.S.	

A5834 Wt. W4973/M687 750,000 8/16 D. D. & L. Ltd. Forms/C.2118/13.

Army Form C. 2118.

Instructions regarding War Diaries and Intelligence Summaries are contained in F. S. Regs., Part II. and the Staff Manual respectively. Title pages will be prepared in manuscript.

WAR DIARY
or
~~INTELLIGENCE~~ SUMMARY.
(Erase heading not required.)

Place	Date	Hour	Summary of Events and Information	Remarks and references to Appendices
Field	Nov. 1st		Moved from Hautville to Juvy in Artois – Store satisfactory but far removed from DHQ. Two Bgdes: in vicinity a third 15 miles away – Artillery away South – GH	
	2		DADOS & ADVS visited store – Heavy consignment of stores which are satisfactorily coped with – GH	
	3		Visited 12 Divl Ordnance to see system adopted there – Accomodation better than customary in more advanced villages – GH	
	4		Message from RO Doullens at 9 pm that stores had arrived there for me – 20 miles away – Finished 1.30 am. GH	
	5		Visited DHQ: XI Corps and Railhead – GH	
	6			
	7		Inspected QM stores [illegible] Bgde: The units of this Bgde: are doing better than formerly and making efforts to economise GH	
	8		Arranged with Camp Commdt to have barns cleared of straw at Boclecourt. Accomodation bad in that district for store – Asked for hut to be erected – GH	
	9		Visited DHQ. 4 trucks stores chiefly boots & clothing arrived – GH	

A5834 Wt. W4973/M687 750,000 8/16 D. D. & L. Ltd. Forms/C.2118/13.

Army Form C. 2118.

WAR DIARY
or
INTELLIGENCE SUMMARY.
(Erase heading not required.)

Instructions regarding War Diaries and Intelligence Summaries are contained in F. S. Regs., Part II. and the Staff Manual respectively. Title pages will be prepared in manuscript.

Place	Date	Hour	Summary of Events and Information	Remarks and references to Appendices
Field	Nov 10		Had to obtain more lorries for distribn of stores to units – These lorries now under Corps orders – GH	
	11		Supervised issues of stores to 27th Bgde: at [illegible] – Lunched with BG 27th Bgde (Gen: Maxwell) who discussed ordnance matters. GH	
	12		More accommodation suggested for stores – Erection of Armourers shop in progress – GH	
	13		Visited HQ 27th Bgde & units ref: muzzle protectors in possession – 9th Scottish Rifles in poss. of sufficient for whole Battn. Fitted one on to rifle to show that the particular kind in possession would do. GH	
	14		GOC asked for particulars regarding muzzle protectors – GH	
	15		Hastened supply of above – GH	
	16		Left for Etaples to consult [illegible] – GH	
	17			
	18		Medium box-respirators arrived 13545 in all – with repair outfit GH	
	19			
	20			
	21		Moved from [illegible] in Artois to Roellecourt –	
	22			
	23		Pte. Harrison for instruction to representative in repair of [illegible] – GH	

A5834 Wt. W4973/M687 750,000 8/16 D. D. & L. Ltd. Forms/C.2118/13.

Instructions regarding War Diaries and Intelligence Summaries are contained in F. S. Regs., Part II. and the Staff Manual respectively. Title pages will be prepared in manuscript.

WAR DIARY
or
INTELLIGENCE SUMMARY.
(Erase heading not required.)

Army Form C. 2118.

Place	Date	Hour	Summary of Events and Information	Remarks and references to Appendices
Field	Nov. 24th		Receipt of Box Respirators No 2 – 1794 – No 4 1634	
	25 –		Demanded 4000 Caps Macintosh – Arrived back for duty from Etaples – ADOS XI Corps called inspected store –	
	26		ADVS 9th Div – called ref. horse shoes – Hand made were much inferior to machine made – Samples of each produced – Use of frost nails preferable to cogs which necessitate the removal of shoe in case of inefficiency – GRO promulgated to this effect that frost nails were procurable –	
	27		Purchased 900 rifle covers from Bethune – 90 cms. each –	
	28		Dept. RA arrived from Somme – Visited 27th Bgde Laundry –	
	29			
	30 –		News of move – Taking over stores of 35th Div – Gen Furse for Div announced he was leaving – Gen Kitchin HQ 26th Bgde is given command of another Divn –	
			[illegible] Capt. DADOS 9th Div	

A5834 Wt. W4973/M687 750,000 8/16 D. D. & L. Ltd. Forms/C.2118/13.

Army Form C. 2118.

Instructions regarding War Diaries and Intelligence Summaries are contained in F. S. Regs., Part II. and the Staff Manual respectively. Title pages will be prepared in manuscript.

WAR DIARY
or
INTELLIGENCE SUMMARY.

(Erase heading not required.)

Vol 20

Place	Date	Hour	Summary of Events and Information	Remarks and references to Appendices
			War Diary D.A.D.O.S. 9th Div From 1-12-16 To 31-12-16	

A5834 Wt. W4973/M687 750,000 8/16 D. D. & L. Ltd. Forms/C.2118/13.

Instructions regarding War Diaries and Intelligence Summaries are contained in F. S. Regs., Part II. and the Staff Manual respectively. Title pages will be prepared in manuscript.

WAR DIARY
or
INTELLIGENCE SUMMARY.
(Erase heading not required.)

Army Form C. 2118.

Place	Date	Hour	Summary of Events and Information	Remarks and references to Appendices
Field	1/11/16		Visited Dursans to see capabilities of new store there - [initials]	
	2		DADOS 35th Dn called with reference to transfer of stores [initials]	
	3			
	4			
	5		Moved store & staff to Dursans - exchanging with 35th Dn [initials]	
	6		Divisional HQ removed to Dursans - [initials]	
	7		Applied for men to start Ordn Tailors & Bootmakers shops - but AA & QMG was not in agreement with idea, which for the moment is shelved - [initials]	
	8		Applied to DHQ for fatigue party to assist Salvage Coy. Considerable difficulty is experienced in obtaining men for the purpose of fatigues - [initials] Visited RA Headqrs: Bgde Laundry - Drying washed clothing is difficult owing to weather - this causes extra demands on Base for new - [initials]	
	9		Called on OC 9th DAC at Rebreuve - ref demands for technical stores - Issued notice for all QMs + 2 ms to attend conference at my office on 13th inst - [initials]	

A5834 Wt. W4973/M687 750,000 8/16 D. D. & L. Ltd. Forms/C.2118/13.

Army Form C. 2118.

Instructions regarding War Diaries and Intelligence Summaries are contained in F. S. Regs., Part II. and the Staff Manual respectively. Title pages will be prepared in manuscript.

WAR DIARY
or
INTELLIGENCE SUMMARY.

(Erase heading not required.)

Place	Date	Hour	Summary of Events and Information	Remarks and references to Appendices
Field	10/12/16		Visited HQ South African Bgde: + 26th Bgde: Arm. Again raised question of Tailors and Bootmakers Shops – with AA & QMG.	Ft
	11		Took Armr: Sergt Hemming to Divl Trench Warfare School to attend to rifles Ft	
	12		Took up question of reinforcements arriving without blankets with ADOS. Corps. Ft	
	13		Request from DADOS. 30th Dn for permission to see smoke Bombs made in my Armourers Shop – Referred him to TW School Ft	
	14		Referred matter raised by VI Corps letter regarding keeping stock of SD clothing for men coming out of trenches wet Ft	
	15		Conference of QMs & QMSs at my office, at which AA QMG and DA QMG were present – This is a useful institution and will be held monthly Ft	
	16		Asked CRE to attend to road leading to store. Obtained 10 tons red slag for purpose, & fatigue party – Ft	

A5834 Wt. W4973/M687 750,000 8/16 D. D. & L. Ltd. Forms/C.2118/13.

Army Form C. 2118.

Instructions regarding War Diaries and Intelligence Summaries are contained in F. S. Regs., Part II. and the Staff Manual respectively. Title pages will be prepared in manuscript.

WAR DIARY
or
~~INTELLIGENCE~~ SUMMARY.
(Erase heading not required.)

Place	Date	Hour	Summary of Events and Information	Remarks and references to Appendices
Field	17/12/16 18		Conference of DADOS at office of ADOS VI Corps – Subjects discussed included demands for technical stores thro' DAC. Temple Silencers required – ADOS suggested that 9th DRA. indents should be dealt with by 12th Dn who are near at hand – [initials]	
	19 20		Issued 3 Two inch Trench Hows to 9th Inf.B. Fitted with Temple Silencers received from IV Army – [initials]	
	22		27th Trench Mortar Bty issued one Barrel & BaseCap – Special Kettle recd from VI Corps for Trial issued to HQ 26th Bgde – [initials]	
	23		Issued 7 Chaff cutters drawn from VI C.T. to Town Majors of Duisans, Agnez, Louvres, Wanquetin, & Montenescourt – [initials]	
	24 25		Flat irons purchased and issued 16 per Battn – [initials]	
	26 27		Seven No 7 Dial Sights demanded – 6 were cancelled by order of ADOS VI Corps [initials]	

A5834 Wt. W4973/M687 750,000 8/16 D. D. & L. Ltd. Forms/C.2118/13.

Army Form C. 2118.

Instructions regarding War Diaries and Intelligence Summaries are contained in F. S. Regs., Part II. and the Staff Manual respectively. Title pages will be prepared in manuscript.

WAR DIARY
or
~~INTELLIGENCE~~ SUMMARY.

(Erase heading not required.)

Place	Date	Hour	Summary of Events and Information	Remarks and references to Appendices
Field	28/12/16		Issued to 2th Bde (Newton Patt) Authy: XI Corps Q 2/17/ 15/12/16	
			Tin boxes for Lewis mag: issued to each Battn: 48. ex: Pioneers	
	29		Two Cylinders for Strombus Horns issued to 26 Bgde. Hq.	
	30		Received consignment (4875) Green Identity Discs:	
	31		Issued 14 Rattles to Trench Warfare School - and one Lewis Gun for instructional purposes (recd from 14 Div) to TW School.	

J.S. Hyde Capt
DADOS. 9th Div

A5834 Wt. W4973/M687 750,000 8/16 D. D. & L. Ltd. Forms/C.2118/13.

Instructions regarding War Diaries and Intelligence Summaries are contained in F. S. Regs., Part II. and the Staff Manual respectively. Title pages will be prepared in manuscript.

WAR DIARY
or
INTELLIGENCE SUMMARY.
(Erase heading not required.)

Army Form C. 2118.

Place	Date	Hour	Summary of Events and Information	Remarks and references to Appendices
			Vol 21	
			War Diary D.A.D.O.S. 9th (Scottish) Divn From 1st Jany. 1917 To 31st " "	

A5834 Wt. W4973/M687 750,000 8/16 D. D. & L. Ltd. Forms/C.2118/13.

Army Form C. 2118.

Instructions regarding War Diaries and Intelligence Summaries are contained in F. S. Regs., Part II. and the Staff Manual respectively. Title pages will be prepared in manuscript.

WAR DIARY
or
~~INTELLIGENCE~~ SUMMARY.

(Erase heading not required.)

Place	Date	Hour	Summary of Events and Information	Remarks and references to Appendices
Duisans	1/1/17		Visited Railhead – Conference A.D.O.S. VI Corps – [illegible]	
	2		Made précis of correspondence regarding receipt of Trench Fittings [illegible]: for which there is difficulty in getting voucher cleared. Forwd to Corps [illegible]	
	3		Visited RA HQ ref: above –	
	4			
	5		D.D.O.S. 3rd Army called – Visited Div. Baths & HQ 27th Bgde – [illegible]	
	6		Trench Warfare School advised HQ that Lewis Gun supplied [illegible] not in good order – Drew 2 Stromber Horns & [illegible] Cylinders from VI Corps [illegible]	
	7		Visited O.C. Trench Warfare School ref. above Lewis Gun, and found that the gun in question was in perfect order and complaint not justified [illegible]	
	8		Ambala Pioneers arrived at Agny Duisans [illegible] for [illegible] Services – Visited HQ of these pioneers to see if they were properly provided with blankets – Interviewed Officer [illegible] ref unclosed voucher for receipt of Gun – Clear receipt obtained from him on looking through his records – [illegible]	

A5834 Wt. W4973/M687 750,000 8/16 D. D. & L. Ltd. Forms/C.2118/13.

Instructions regarding War Diaries and Intelligence Summaries are contained in F. S. Regs., Part II. and the Staff Manual respectively. Title pages will be prepared in manuscript.

WAR DIARY
or
INTELLIGENCE SUMMARY.
(*Erase heading not required.*)

Army Form C. 2118.

Place	Date	Hour	Summary of Events and Information	Remarks and references to Appendices
Duisans	9/1/17		Visited Railhead – Joined 17th Corps – Called on ADOS 17 Corps JH	
	10		Called on DADOS 3rd Canadian Divn ref taking over his store at Acq as move is projected – JH	
	11		Visited HQ 3rd Canadian Divn at Hermaville with DAQMG JH	
	12			
	13		Called on ADOS 6th Corps ref correspondence about the fittings for 18 pr. [illegible] vouchers	
	14		Wired Base ref. above to ask who signed waybill, & for number of waybill JH	
	15		Visited Rlhead ref withdrawal of Lewis Gun handcarts, & arranged with RTO & RAO to receive same from units JH	
	16		Visited HQ 8th Black Watch with DAQMG & also QM stores of unit – JH	
	17			

A5834 Wt. W4973/M687 750,000 8/16 D. D. & L. Ltd. Forms/C.2118/13.

Instructions regarding War Diaries and Intelligence Summaries are contained in F. S. Regs., Part II. and the Staff Manual respectively. Title pages will be prepared in manuscript.

WAR DIARY
or
INTELLIGENCE SUMMARY.
(Erase heading not required.)

Army Form C. 2118.

Place	Date	Hour	Summary of Events and Information	Remarks and references to Appendices
Duisans	18/1/17		Visited HQ 26th Inf. Bgde at Maroeuil	
	19		Recd III Army letter ref: return of Lewis Gun Handcarts – 20 await further orders reference these – sent to HQ workshops at present. JH	
	20		Heavy frost continues – Recd 60 white fabric suits for patrols working in snow. JH	
	21		Visited ÉTRUN where DAC is said to be going to see what accommodation there is for stores. JH	
	22		Examined outstanding indents of 27th Bgde. Gave instructions ref 2 mis of RA units clearing these with [illegible]. JH	
	23		Visited HQ 26th Bgde ref heavy tripods for Lewis Guns demanded. No description of these is known. JH	
	24		Received 5000 muzzle covers from Armies & arranged distribution. Supply inadequate. JH	
	25			

WAR DIARY

or

INTELLIGENCE SUMMARY.

(Erase heading not required.)

Army Form C. 2118.

Instructions regarding War Diaries and Intelligence Summaries are contained in F. S. Regs., Part II. and the Staff Manual respectively. Title pages will be prepared in manuscript.

Place	Date	Hour	Summary of Events and Information	Remarks and references to Appendices
DUISANS	26/1/17		DADOS 12th Div. called ref: system of checking disposal of surplus stores. Visited new area with DADC & 2m. JH	
	27th		Called at HQ 8th B.W. to instruct new 2m reference indents. Visited HQ 26th Inf Bde. JH	
	28		Received indents of S.A. Bde. JH	
	29		Warning received of removal of DHQ to Etrun for 31st inst. JH	
	30		Visited new baths at Marœuil with ADMS. Removed stores to ETRUN. Office remaining temporarily at Duisans.	
	31		Nissen hut arranged for for office at Etrun.	

[illegible] Capt.
DADOS 9th Div.

A5834 Wt. W4973/M687 750,000 8/16 D. D. & L. Ltd. Forms/C.2118/13.

Army Form C. 2118.

Instructions regarding War Diaries and Intelligence Summaries are contained in F. S. Regs., Part II. and the Staff Manual respectively. Title pages will be prepared in manuscript.

WAR DIARY
or
INTELLIGENCE SUMMARY.

(Erase heading not required.)

Place	Date	Hour	Summary of Events and Information	Remarks and references to Appendices
			Vol 22	
			War Diary of DADOS 9th Division From 1-2-17 To 28-2-17	

A5834 Wt. W4973/M687 750,000 8/16 D. D. & L. Ltd. Forms/C.2118/13.

Instructions regarding War Diaries and Intelligence Summaries are contained in F. S. Regs., Part II. and the Staff Manual respectively. Title pages will be prepared in manuscript.

WAR DIARY
or
INTELLIGENCE SUMMARY.
(Erase heading not required.)

Army Form C. 2118.

Place	Date	Hour	Summary of Events and Information	Remarks and references to Appendices
Field	1917 Feb 1		Visited railhead. Inspected Baths & Laundry at Maroeuil owing to reported difficulty in troops obtaining supplies of underclothing GH	
	2		Visited Baths & Laundry at St Michel with DAQMG Estimated output of 2000 per diem providing fuel is available for drying. GH	
	3		Move of DHQ cancelled. My office remains at DUISANS for time being GH	
	4			
	5		Issued 2 Bell sets Communication to each Light Trench Mortar Batty: Called at office ADOS 17th Corps. GH	
	6		Issued boxes for storing 4.5 how. ammunition GH	
	7		Received 959 steel helmets fitted with chain visor. Also pack saddlery for RFA for carrying rations & ammn. GH	

A5834 Wt. W4973/M687 750,000 8/16 D. D. & L. Ltd. Forms/C.2118/13.

Army Form C. 2118.

Instructions regarding War Diaries and Intelligence Summaries are contained in F. S. Regs., Part II. and the Staff Manual respectively. Title pages will be prepared in manuscript.

WAR DIARY
or
INTELLIGENCE SUMMARY.
(Erase heading not required.)

Place	Date	Hour	Summary of Events and Information	Remarks and references to Appendices
Field	1917 Feb 8		Issued 80 per Battn. steel helmets with visors G.H.	
	9		Purchased 3 wringers for laundry Maroeuil – Visited DAC ref. move of 2 sections & issue of stores – G.H.	
	10		Purchased flags for APM G.H.	
	11		Visited XVII Corps ref: Lewis Gun Handcart – G.H.	
	12			
	13		Recd. 30 carriers ammun. 4.5 How. G.H.	
	14		Issued 7 shutters signalling to each Inf Bde. G.H.	
	15		One periscope No. 25 issued to 9th Inf Bde. – G.H.	
	16		One carr. field 18 pr. issued to A 6x R.F.A. One Vickers .303" to 26th M.G.Co G.H.	
	17		Emergency pattern carriers Ammunn. 18 pr. 25 issued to each RA Bde. also 450 to each Battn. goggles anti-gas with sponge & spares G.H. — G.H.	

A5834 Wt. W4973/M687 750,000 8/16 D. D. & L. Ltd. Forms/C.2118/13.

Army Form C. 2118.

Instructions regarding War Diaries and Intelligence Summaries are contained in F. S. Regs., Part II. and the Staff Manual respectively. Title pages will be prepared in manuscript.

WAR DIARY
or
INTELLIGENCE SUMMARY.
(Erase heading not required.)

Place	Date	Hour	Summary of Events and Information	Remarks and references to Appendices
Field	1917 Feb 18		Further issues of goggles anti-gas with sponge eyepiece. [illegible]	
	19		Purchased forks for 9th Sanitary Sec. 6. One No 7 Dial Sight issued to C 52 RA. Issued Apparatus Sights Dial Illuminating to Batys - 9/6. [illegible]	
	20			
	21			
	22		One barrel Mk II 3" Stokes m. with stand breastplate and spare parts to 27th Inf. B. [illegible]	
	23		Issued one 4.5 how. to D 52 RA. also on 18 pr. 2F to 46 AFA without fittings. One Carr. Fld. [illegible] to A 64 (4.5 How) [illegible]	
	24		Visited HQ 27th Bgde: Railhead Aubigny. [illegible]	
	25		Placed order for coloured patches for distinguishing marks infantry. [illegible]	
	26		Visited 8 Black Watch, 7th Camerons, 9th Scottish Rifles & 9 Seaforths ref. [illegible] grenade carriers - 600 per batt. [illegible]	
	27		Visited HQ 26 Bgde.	
	28		Visited HQ 27th Bgde. ref. flags for tactical purposes - also reference [illegible] of tape for marking.	

[illegible] Capt
D.A.D.O.S. 9th Div.

A5834 Wt. W4973/M687 750,000 8/16 D. D. & L. Ltd. Forms/C.2118/13.

Army Form C. 2118.

Instructions regarding War Diaries and Intelligence Summaries are contained in F. S. Regs., Part II. and the Staff Manual respectively. Title pages will be prepared in manuscript.

WAR DIARY
or
INTELLIGENCE SUMMARY.
(Erase heading not required.)

Vol 23

Place	Date	Hour	Summary of Events and Information	Remarks and references to Appendices
			Confidential	
			War Diary	
			D.A.D.V.S. 9th Div	
			From 1st March 1917	
			To 31st " "	

A5834 Wt. W4973/M687 750,000 8/16 D. D. & L. Ltd. Forms/C.2118/13.

Instructions regarding War Diaries and Intelligence Summaries are contained in F. S. Regs., Part II. and the Staff Manual respectively. Title pages will be prepared in manuscript.

WAR DIARY
or
INTELLIGENCE SUMMARY.
(Erase heading not required.)

Army Form C. 2118.

Place	Date	Hour	Summary of Events and Information	Remarks and references to Appendices
Field	March 1917 1		Inspected Qm. stores 9th Black Watch, 7th Seaforths, 5th Camerons & 10th A.&S.H. Hastened Qm's in making grenade carriers – Visited HQ 27th Brigade – JH	
	2			
	3		Issued 327 flags for training area 27th Bgde:	
	4		Issued 1 German machine gun for practice to 27th Bgde. and Collected trophies from 9th Scottish Rifles gained during raid, which consisted of machine gun, dart thrower, Hotchkiss, stand. JH	
	5		Visited Qm stores 26th Brigade – JH	
	6		Purchased 12000 patches disting! for Inf. JH	
	7		Visited 26th & 27th Bgde. HQ ref supplies. JH	
	8		Railhead – Visited Q.M's S.A. Brigade. JH	
	9		Inspected all outstanding indents – JH	
	10			
	11			

A5834 Wt. W4973/M687 750,000 8/16 D. D. & L. Ltd. Forms/C.2118/13.

Instructions regarding War Diaries and Intelligence Summaries are contained in F. S. Regs., Part II. and the Staff Manual respectively. Title pages will be prepared in manuscript.

WAR DIARY
or
INTELLIGENCE SUMMARY.
(*Erase heading not required.*)

Army Form C. 2118.

Place	Date	Hour	Summary of Events and Information	Remarks and references to Appendices
	March 1917			
Field	12		Visited DOM 17th Corps ref: breech mechanisms – Arranged that all U/S should be returned to him – Saw Staff Capt 2nd ref: above [initials]	
	13		Conference at ADOS 17th Corps. [initials]	
	14		Visited 9th DAC with ADVS ref clipping machines – Blades to be returned to Base – Issued emergency pat: amm: carriers to 34th Div: [initials]	
	15		Collected extractors new type from DADOS 51st Div these for Light Trench Mortar Bttys [initials]	
	16		Further supplies of Carr Amm: Emergency pat: from 17th Corps – also 16 Carr Amm: 4.5 How, 8 each issued to D50 D51 [initials]	
	17		Completed Division to establishment with Cups for firing rifle grenades – Issued 3 panniers signalling to M G Coys. [initials]	
	18		Visited ADOS 17th Corps, & 51st Divn DADOS ref new sling for Lewis gun – Battns completed to 88 each Lewis carr magazine. [initials]	
	19		Two 18 pr: QF fitted with air recuperators issued to A 51 Bty. [initials]	

A5834 Wt. W4973/M687 750,000 8/16 D. D. & L. Ltd. Forms/C.2118/13.

Army Form C. 2118.

WAR DIARY
or
~~INTELLIGENCE SUMMARY.~~
(*Erase heading not required.*)

Instructions regarding War Diaries and Intelligence Summaries are contained in F. S. Regs., Part II. and the Staff Manual respectively. Title pages will be prepared in manuscript.

Place	Date	Hour	Summary of Events and Information	Remarks and references to Appendices
	Mch. 1917			
Field	20th		Purchased flatirons 2s. GH	
	21		Visited Salvage Coy: & R'head GH	
	22		Visited 57th Dn DADOS. Issued 8 Scales Range Correction to Btys GH	
	23		Purchased badges for runners &c at Bethune. Issued 100 rods & adapters to Divl Bomb Store GH	
	24		Special sling for Lewis Gun handed over to O.C. 9th Train for experiment & comparison with another pattern GH	
	25		Sent 8 Armourers to inspect arms of 11th Royal Scots. The whole battn completed in 6 hours. GH	
	26		Purchased 10,000 yds tape & material for flags for 27th Bde. Recd remainder of distg patches 12000 GH	
	27		Visited Salvage Dump at Marœuil. Lost of Lewis Gun handcarts recalled from units issued to 30th Bn GH	
	28		Arranged for Conference of 4 QMs for estimating the winter clothing, according to Army letter GH	

A5834 Wt. W4973/M687 750,000 8/16 D. D. & L. Ltd. Forms/C.2118/13.

Instructions regarding War Diaries and Intelligence Summaries are contained in F. S. Regs., Part II. and the Staff Manual respectively. Title pages will be prepared in manuscript.

WAR DIARY
or
INTELLIGENCE SUMMARY.
(Erase heading not required.)

Army Form C. 2118.

Place	Date	Hour	Summary of Events and Information	Remarks and references to Appendices
	Mch:	1917		
Field	29th		Visited ADOS 17th Corps. Spoke 21st MVS ref: clippers. JH	
	30		Visited Maroeuil to find Corps Salvage Officer & locate dump for Salvage. JH	
	31st		Visited QM stores 6th KOSB 10th Argylls, 8th Black Watch. Maroeuil bombarded. Inspected wagons of 14th Army F.A. Bgde: which are in a different order. JH	
			[illegible] Capt DADOS. 9th Div 1/4/17	

A5834 Wt. W4973/M687 750,000 8/16 D. D. & L. Ltd. Forms/C.2118/13.

Instructions regarding War Diaries and Intelligence Summaries are contained in F. S. Regs., Part II. and the Staff Manual respectively. Title pages will be prepared in manuscript.

WAR DIARY
or
INTELLIGENCE SUMMARY.
(Erase heading not required.)

Army Form C. 2118.

Vol 24

Place	Date	Hour	Summary of Events and Information	Remarks and references to Appendices
			Confidential	
			War Diary D.A.D.O.S. 9th Div From 1. 4. 17 To 30. 4. 17	

1577 Wt. W10791/1773 500,000 1/15 D. D. & L. A.D.S.S./Forms/C. 2118.

Instructions regarding War Diaries and Intelligence Summaries are contained in F. S. Regs., Part II. and the Staff Manual respectively. Title pages will be prepared in manuscript.

WAR DIARY
or
INTELLIGENCE SUMMARY.
(Erase heading not required.)

Army Form C. 2118.

Place	Date	Hour	Summary of Events and Information	Remarks and references to Appendices
	1917			
Field	April 1st		Inspected G.S. wagons of newly attached 23rd Army F.A. Bgde. and find 5 of obsolete pattern, and others in bad condition. Arranged with A.S.C. Coy to whom attached to indent forthwith. Visited H.Q. Train ref. stores. [initials]	
	2nd		Visited A.D.O.S. 17th Corps with Staff Capt 9th R.A. [initials]	
	3rd		Called on A.D.O.S. 17th Corps with D.A.Q.M.G. ref supply of machine gun parts, very pistols &c. [initials]	
	4th		Visited Corps workshops. also Divl Train ref. moves during action. Drew Depression Stops (16) from Corps workshops. [initials]	
	5th		Visited Battn. ledgers of units 26th Bgde: & Quartermasters stores in view of coming Events. Stores coming well from Base. [initials]	
	6th			
	7th		Visited Inf. Battns. 27th Bgde: & Divns stores. [initials]	
	8th		Carr. 18 pr. for 108/23rd Bgde. R.F.A. recd from Frevent. Visited Army Gun Park Frevent. [initials]	
	9th		Battle begun. Demanded gun for B/57. Lewis Guns for 8th Black Watch (5) Armourers can supply 2 of these. [initials]	

1577 Wt. W10791/1773 500,000 1/15 D. D. & L. A.D.S.S./Forms/C. 2118.

Instructions regarding War Diaries and Intelligence Summaries are contained in F. S. Regs., Part II. and the Staff Manual respectively. Title pages will be prepared in manuscript.

WAR DIARY
or
~~INTELLIGENCE SUMMARY.~~

(Erase heading not required.)

Army Form C. 2118.

Place	Date	Hour	Summary of Events and Information	Remarks and references to Appendices
Field	1917 Dec. 10th		Demanded Lewis guns for 3rd + 4th S.A. Regt (7). Drew Lewis guns for 9th B.W. from Gun Park, + spare parts for 17th Corps from w'shops. Visited A.D.O.S. 17th Corps. [initials]	
	11th		Demanded 1 Lewis gun for 1st S.A. Regt + one 18pr. for A/52. Gun Park indent for supplies not being met. Visited I.O.M. Corps ref. supplies of parts. [initials]	
	12th		Demanded 9 Lewis guns for various units [initials]	
	13th		Recd. army letter ref. return of Winter Clothing, thro: D.H.Q. Conferred with D.A.Q.M.G. reference above. [initials]	
	14th		Receiving the 2nd blanket. Engaged factory at Marœuil for reception [initials]	
	15th		Division comes out of line [initials]	
	16th		D.H.Q. removed to Hermaville. My store + I remain at Etrun. Visited 17th Corps. Advised Gun Park of deficiencies of issues of gun parts. [initials]	

Instructions regarding War Diaries and Intelligence Summaries are contained in F. S. Regs., Part II. and the Staff Manual respectively. Title pages will be prepared in manuscript.

WAR DIARY

or

~~INTELLIGENCE SUMMARY.~~

(Erase heading not required.)

Army Form C. 2118.

Place	Date 1917	Hour	Summary of Events and Information	Remarks and references to Appendices
Field	Apl. 17th		Visited Bgde. H.Q. 27th 26th + S.A. with DADVS. ref: refitting – Also railhead.	
	18th		Advised of belated truck containing 700 horserugs. Spoke A.D.V.S. ref: these. The long winter suggests the necessity of retaining these for sometime –	
	19th			
	20th			
	21st		Visited railhead, and A.D.V.S. 17th Corps.	
	22nd		Moved store from Etrun to Chelers. taking over from 34th D. Cleared all winter clothing from Maroeuil.	
	23rd		Visited H.Q. South African Bgde and ADOS. 17th Corps	
	24th			
	25th		H.Q. moved back to Hermaville from Chelers. I remain at Chelers. Two Bgdes. 26th & 27th move up – S.A. remain in present area	
	26th		Horse rugs 700 arrive – Arranged with A.D.V.S. to reconsign to Base	

1577 Wt. W10791/1773 500,000 1/15 D. D. & L. A.D.S.S./Forms/C. 2118.

Army Form C. 2118.

Instructions regarding War Diaries and Intelligence Summaries are contained in F. S. Regs., Part II. and the Staff Manual respectively. Title pages will be prepared in manuscript.

WAR DIARY
or
~~INTELLIGENCE SUMMARY.~~
(Erase heading not required.)

Place	Date	Hour	Summary of Events and Information	Remarks and references to Appendices
	1917 Apr			
Field	27th		Visited Arras to see store for proposed depot and 26th Anglo[?] ref: care of stores – Arranged to stop all bulk stores. [initials]	
	28		Railhead moved to Arras – for one day thence to Agnez les Duisans – [initials]	
	29		Cleared all salvage from Chelers & Hermaville – [initials]	
	30		ADMS. 9th Div: killed E of Arras – moved from Chelers [initials]	

[signature] Capt
DADOS. 9th Div.
May 1st 1917

Army Form C. 2118.

Vol 25

Instructions regarding War Diaries and Intelligence Summaries are contained in F. S. Regs., Part II. and the Staff Manual respectively. Title pages will be prepared in manuscript.

WAR DIARY
or
INTELLIGENCE SUMMARY.
(Erase heading not required.)

Place	Date	Hour	Summary of Events and Information	Remarks and references to Appendices
			War Diary DADOS 9th (Scottish) Divn From 1st May 1917 To 31st Confidential	

A5834 Wt. W4973/M687 750,000 8/16 D. D. & L. Ltd. Forms/C.2118/13.

Instructions regarding War Diaries and Intelligence Summaries are contained in F. S. Regs., Part II. and the Staff Manual respectively. Title pages will be prepared in manuscript.

WAR DIARY
or
INTELLIGENCE SUMMARY.
(Erase heading not required.)

Army Form C. 2118.

Place	Date	Hour	Summary of Events and Information	Remarks and references to Appendices
Field	1/5/17		Returned Machine Gun belts for Vickers .303 borrowed from 57th Div. Two Carriages 18pr. issued to A/50 and one do to B/50. JA	
	2nd		293rd AFA Bde. attached for Ordnance. Issued 2 Lewis Guns to 9th Scottish Rifles. Issued 1 18pr. Carr to B/51 & one to C/50. JA	
	3rd		Arras heavily shelled. ADOS 17th Corps called. Issued 1 Vickers .303 to 197th Machine Gun Co. & 1 Carr 18pr. to B/51. JA	
	4th		Visited railhead. FA Bde [illegible] and battalions. JA	
	5th		Arras shelled again. Issued 1 Vickers to 28th [illegible] Co & 9 Lewis guns to 27th Bgde. & 3 Lewis guns to 6th [illegible]. JA	
	6th		Correspondence with Base ref. delays in reply to memos. Asked Staff Capt RA to urge his unit to reply promptly. Issued 5 Vickers guns to 27th [illegible] Co. & 9 Lewis to 5th Camerons. JA	
	7th		Issued one 4.5 How. to D/50. 1 18pr. Carr to ~~[illegible]~~ A/57 23 AFA Bde. JA	
	8th		Ammn. Dump blown up in Arras. Issued 1 18pr. to B/50 & 1 18pr Carr to 23/108 AFA. JA	

A5834 Wt. W4973/M687 750,000 8/16 D. D. & L. Ltd. Forms/C.2118/13.

Instructions regarding War Diaries and Intelligence Summaries are contained in F. S. Regs., Part II. and the Staff Manual respectively. Title pages will be prepared in manuscript.

WAR DIARY
or
INTELLIGENCE SUMMARY.
(*Erase heading not required.*)

Army Form C. 2118.

Place	Date	Hour	Summary of Events and Information	Remarks and references to Appendices
Field	9th May 1917		Visited Chelers to arrange transfer of Dump. Asked Supply Column for add[l] Lorry. Issued 2 Lewis Guns 5/7th Seaforths and One 18pr. to C/23 AFA, One Carr 18pr. to C/23 AFA [initials]	
	10th		Visited Corps HQ re: Transfer of AFA Bgdes. [initials]	
	11th		Moved to Chelers. Left 1 NCO clerk & storeman behind at St Nicholas to attend to all our [illegible] RA units. Issued 1 Carr 4.5 to D/51. One Carr. 18pr to 108/23 AFA. 2 18pr. [illegible] to A/52. One 4.5 How. to D/51. Two Carr 18pr. to A/52. One Carr 18pr. to T/42 AFA. [initials]	
	12th		Transferred AFA Bgdes to 17 & 51st Div. Issued 1 18pr. to A/298 [initials]	
	13th		Moved to Roellecourt. DDOS called. [initials]	
	14th		Called on HQ SA Bgde. HQ 27th Bgde. Indented for canvas to make water carriers. [initials]	
	15		Visited advanced store at St Nicholas. Issued one 18pr. to B/51 [initials]	

A5834 Wt. W4973/M687 750,000 8/16 D. D. & L. Ltd. Forms/C.2118/13.

Instructions regarding War Diaries and Intelligence Summaries are contained in F. S. Regs., Part II. and the Staff Manual respectively. Title pages will be prepared in manuscript.

WAR DIARY
or
INTELLIGENCE SUMMARY.
(Erase heading not required.)

Army Form C. 2118.

Place	Date	Hour	Summary of Events and Information	Remarks and references to Appendices
Field	16/5/17		Issued 4 Lewis Guns to 8th Black Watch. Withdrew NCO and men from advanced dump St Nicholas. JA	
	17		Visited HQ. 26th Inf Bgde and stores of 10th Argyll & Suth., 9th Seaforth, 7 Seaforths. JA	
	18		Visited HQ 27th Bgde & Qm stores 11th & 12th Ryl. Scots & 9th Scott. Rifles. Asked specially about condition of boots, & inspected repair shops. JA	
	19 20		Visited HQ. SA Bgde: units: & found much improvement with regard to the Qm stores. JA	
	21		Arranged with AD Signals XVII Corps for return of gum boots on loan to them since January. JA	
	22		3rd Army AA4 ref: Keeping stocks in Divl Canteens of badges, titles & necessaries. Gave DAQMG average issues for month of April. JA	
	23			
	24		Visited HQ of 27th Bgde with DAQMG also HQ 26th Bgde and SA. JA	
	25		Demanded 1 Carr. 18 pr. for C.S.R. Visited DADOS 7th Div ref move, & exchange of reserves. JA	

A5834 Wt. W4973/M687 750,000 8/16 D. D. & L. Ltd. Forms/C.2118/13.

Army Form C. 2118.

Instructions regarding War Diaries and Intelligence Summaries are contained in F. S. Regs., Part II. and the Staff Manual respectively. Title pages will be prepared in manuscript.

WAR DIARY
or
INTELLIGENCE SUMMARY.
(Erase heading not required.)

Place	Date	Hour	Summary of Events and Information	Remarks and references to Appendices
Field	26/5/17		Nothing of particular [illegible]	
	27th		Presentation of rewards [illegible] [illegible]	
28			[illegible]	
29			Visited A.D.O.S. [illegible] Arranged with [illegible]	
30			[illegible]	
31			Dismounted [illegible]	
			[illegible] Capt. D.A.D.O.S. [illegible] 31/5/17	

A5834 Wt. W4973/M687 750,000 8/16 D. D. & L. Ltd. Forms/C.2118/13.

9

Instructions regarding War Diaries and Intelligence Summaries are contained in F. S. Regs., Part II. and the Staff Manual respectively. Title pages will be prepared in manuscript.

WAR DIARY
or
INTELLIGENCE SUMMARY.
(Erase heading not required.)

Army Form C. 2118. 9

Vol 26

Place	Date	Hour	Summary of Events and Information	Remarks and references to Appendices
			Confidential	
			War Diary D.A.D.O.S 9th Divn	
			From 1st June 1917	
			To 30th June 1917	

1577 Wt. W10791/1773 500,000 1/15 D. D. & L. A.D.S.S./Forms/C. 2118.

Army Form C. 2118.

Instructions regarding War Diaries and Intelligence Summaries are contained in F. S. Regs., Part II. and the Staff Manual respectively. Title pages will be prepared in manuscript.

WAR DIARY
or
~~INTELLIGENCE SUMMARY.~~

(Erase heading not required.)

Place	Date	Hour	Summary of Events and Information	Remarks and references to Appendices
Field	June 1st 1917		Moved office + store to G.13.d. central. on Arras–St Pol Rd. – taking over from 51st Divn 3 Armstrong huts + store tents –	
	2nd		Divisional Headquarters moved to Candle Factory at St. Nicolas –	
	3rd		A.D.O.S. called and inspected store &c:	
	4th		Underaged men from S.A. regiments temporarily attached to A.O.D. for duty rejoined their units – Took stock of pack saddles handed over by 51st Divn. Demanded 18 pr carriage for 255 Btty R.F.A.	
	5th		Called on A.D.O.S. 17th Corps. Inspected transport of Divisional Train Companies. Wheels coming up better from Base. German automatic rifle received from 12th Royal Scots	
	6th		Visited HQ 26th Inf. Bde. with D.A.Q.M.G. Hostile aeroplanes show considerable activity at night, dropping bombs and using machine guns.	
	7th		3 new battalions attached to the Division – 2/4 Queens 3/4 R. W Kents – 3/10 Middlesex.	

Instructions regarding War Diaries and Intelligence Summaries are contained in F. S. Regs., Part II. and the Staff Manual respectively. Title pages will be prepared in manuscript.

WAR DIARY
or
~~INTELLIGENCE SUMMARY.~~
(*Erase heading not required.*)

Army Form C. 2118.

Place	Date 1917	Hour	Summary of Events and Information	Remarks and references to Appendices
Field June	8th		Visited Quartermasters of newly joined battalions, and gave each written instructions on various points on formalities new to them – DAAG, & DAQMG also went – Arranged for each of 2 i/c's to visit my store – [initials]	
	9th		Received visit from above 2 i/c. who saw exactly how stores were received and issued – and how the office work was carried on – [initials]	
	10th			
	11th		Received sanction from Corps to go on leave on 15th [initials]	
	12th		Left store on Arras Road and moved to TINCQUES – Tents again – no buildings available – Took over the Artillery of 51st Divn for Ordnance – [initials]	
	13th		Visited all Inf: Brigades with DAQMG [initials]	
	14th		Took telescopic rifles to 3rd Army Sniping School, for adjustment & issue to 3/4 Queen's Regt [initials]	

1577 Wt. W10791/1773 500,000 1/15 D. D. & L. A.D.S.S./Forms/C. 2118.

Instructions regarding War Diaries and Intelligence Summaries are contained in F. S. Regs., Part II. and the Staff Manual respectively. Title pages will be prepared in manuscript.

WAR DIARY
or
~~INTELLIGENCE SUMMARY.~~
(Erase heading not required.)

Army Form C. 2118.

Place	Date	Hour	Summary of Events and Information	Remarks and references to Appendices
Field June	15 ↓ 25th	}	On leave –	
	26th 27th		Visited 17th Corps with DADOS also 27th Inf. Bgde. The Division well equipped again excepting for a few technical items, & Webley pistols in which the shortage is well known. JFH	
	28th		DADOS asked me to arrange purchase in England of material for making distinguishing patches for men's shoulders. The units finding the allowance of 20 francs a month insufficient – JFH	
	29th		9th Seaforth (Pioneers) left for north – attached to 32nd Divn. Transferred indents – 57th Divl R.A. indents transferred also. JFH	
	30th		Nothing to report. JFH	

[illegible] Capt
DADOS 9th Div

1577 Wt. W10791/1773 500,000 1/15 D. D. & L. A.D.S.S./Forms/C. 2118.

Instructions regarding War Diaries and Intelligence Summaries are contained in F. S. Regs., Part II. and the Staff Manual respectively. Title pages will be prepared in manuscript.

WAR DIARY
or
INTELLIGENCE SUMMARY.
(Erase heading not required.)

Army Form C. 2118.

Vol 27

Confidential

Place	Date	Hour	Summary of Events and Information	Remarks and references to Appendices
			War Diary DADOS 9th Div From 1st July 1917 To 31st " "	

1577 Wt. W10791/1773 500,000 1/15 D. D. & L. A.D.S.S./Forms/C. 2118.

Army Form C. 2118.

Instructions regarding War Diaries and Intelligence Summaries are contained in F. S. Regs., Part II. and the Staff Manual respectively. Title pages will be prepared in manuscript.

WAR DIARY
or
~~INTELLIGENCE SUMMARY.~~
(Erase heading not required.)

Place	Date	Hour	Summary of Events and Information	Remarks and references to Appendices
TINCQUES	July 1st		Divl. H.Q. removed from Rocllecourt to Chelers - Visited XVII Corps Salvage Dump for stores. Recd. 3 chaff cutters from XVII Corps. GH	
	2nd		26th + 27th Inf. Bgdes. moved to new area. - GH	
	3rd		Moved from Tincques to Avesnes le Comte - Taking over buildings vacated by 12th Dl. Laundry. GH	
	4		Issued 3 chaff cutters 1 to DAC + one each to 105 + 107 Coy A.S.C. GH	
	5		Moved from Avesnes to Warlus - Accommodation good - 26th Bgde. H.Q. removed to same place - S.A. to Berneville - 27th Manin. GH	
	6		Railhead changed from Tincques to Agnez les Duisans - visited railhead - Sent lorry to Gun Park, Albert for 'considerable' stores distance 60 miles run. GH	
	7		Arranged for Salvage Coy. to come to Warlus. GH	
	8		Visited XVII Corps. GH	
	9		A.D.O.S. called + inspected store GH	

Instructions regarding War Diaries and Intelligence Summaries are contained in F. S. Regs., Part II. and the Staff Manual respectively. Title pages will be prepared in manuscript.

WAR DIARY
or
~~INTELLIGENCE SUMMARY.~~
(*Erase heading not required.*)

Army Form C. 2118.

Place	Date	Hour	Summary of Events and Information	Remarks and references to Appendices
Warlus	July 10th		Visited HQ Divl: RA and HQ Coy Train at Boisleux au Mont ref: disposal of coloured cloth for shoulders &c. [initials]	
	11th		Held conference of QMs + QMS. of 26th + S.A. Bgde: 30 present. including AA&QMG + DAQMG. Discussion ref: supply of necessaries. [initials]	
	12th		Transferred 9th D.R.A. with HQ Coy: Train to 50th Divn. [initials]	
	13th		Visited railhead - Arranged with Corps Lorry Pk to collect How: carriage for ~~D~~ 51 + take to Logny - [initials]	
	14		Held conference of QMs + QMS. of 27th Bgde: at HQ 27th Bgde. [initials]	
	15			
	16		Inspected QM stores of SA Bgde: + visited HQ Bgde. [initials]	
	17		Inspected general condition of kit + clothing of 5th Cameron Hrs: Visited 26th Bgde HQ. [initials]	
	18		Inspected transport lines of 9th Train - Rains scarce - wheels generally good - [initials]	

Army Form C. 2118.

Instructions regarding War Diaries and Intelligence Summaries are contained in F. S. Regs., Part II. and the Staff Manual respectively. Title pages will be prepared in manuscript.

WAR DIARY
or
~~INTELLIGENCE SUMMARY.~~
(Erase heading not required.)

Place	Date	Hour	Summary of Events and Information	Remarks and references to Appendices
Warlus	July 19 20th		Visited new area to arrange transfer. ADOS called in my absence.	
	21		DADOS 58th Div called to inspect accomodation.	
	22		Inspected 2nd stores of 27th Bde: visited HQ 27th Bgde.	
	23		Visited ADOS 17th Corps, railhead, & Corps Salvage Coy.	
	24		Issued muslin for shoulder patches to HQ Coy: [illegible] for issue to battns on repayment. Visited r'head, & SA Bgde.	
	25		26th Bgde. moved to new area.	
	26		Arranged numbers of reserve stores to be transferred to 58th Division.	
Bus	27 28		Moved to new area in allotted four lorries. Distance 25 miles. [illegible] to store, 2 marquees, 6 bell tents.	
	29		Visited 26th Bgde. Hq. in advanced area.	
	30		Visited new railhead, & Salvage Coy at Rocquigny. Heavy rain.	
	31		Railhead, & Corps Troops.	

[illegible] Capt
DADOS. 9th Div.

1577 Wt. W10791/1773 500,000 1/15 D. D. & L. A.D.S.S./Forms/C 2118.

Army Form C. 2118.

Instructions regarding War Diaries and Intelligence Summaries are contained in F. S. Regs., Part II. and the Staff Manual respectively. Title pages will be prepared in manuscript.

WAR DIARY
or
INTELLIGENCE SUMMARY.
(Erase heading not required.)

Vol 28

Place	Date	Hour	Summary of Events and Information	Remarks and references to Appendices
			Confidential War Diary D.A.D.O.S. 9th Dn. From 1st August 1917 To 31st " " [illegible] Capt D.A.D.O.S. 9th Dn	

1577 Wt. W10791/1773 500,000 1/15 D. D. & L. A.D.S.S./Forms/C. 2118.

Instructions regarding War Diaries and Intelligence Summaries are contained in F. S. Regs., Part II. and the Staff Manual respectively. Title pages will be prepared in manuscript.

Army Form C. 2118.

WAR DIARY

or

~~INTELLIGENCE SUMMARY.~~

(Erase heading not required.)

Place	Date	Hour	Summary of Events and Information	Remarks and references to Appendices
Field	1/8/17		Visited units stores 26th Bgde: and 27th Field Ambce: [initials]	
	2		Spoke railway constn: officer at railhead reference light railway – Track incomplete – [initials]	
	3		Visited Office of No 6 Ry. Construction Coy: inspected plans and arranged for siding to be put into my yard – [initials]	
	4		Transferred my 4 lorries to 9th Supply Col. and arranged to draw from railhead by horse transport pro tem – Arranged with No 9 Ry Operating Co: ref. no. of trucks to be available for Ordnance Sx – [initials]	
	5		Track at railhead still incomplete – Visited R.A. Bgdes: HQ – Interviewed 2nd in presence of Staff Capt. and OC – & spoke particularly re extravagance – [initials]	
	6		Visited proposed refilling points on Lt Ry System Interviewed Ry foreman at r'head & made arrangement with OC Divl Train to fit in with loading [initials]	

1577 Wt. W10791/1773 500,000 1/15 D. D. & L. A.D.S.S./Forms/C. 2118.

Army Form C. 2118.

WAR DIARY
or
~~INTELLIGENCE SUMMARY.~~
(Erase heading not required.)

Instructions regarding War Diaries and Intelligence Summaries are contained in F. S. Regs., Part II. and the Staff Manual respectively. Title pages will be prepared in manuscript.

Place	Date	Hour	Summary of Events and Information	Remarks and references to Appendices
Field Bns.	7/8/17		Siding into my depôt constructed - 100 yds long - GH	
	8		First run of Lt. railway with Ordce. Stores. Visited r'head at 6 a.m. Arrangements satisfactory - GH	
	9		Visited all refilling points - tall issues made to 2 [illegible], they having huts there - GH	
	10		Visited refilling points again - all satisfactory - GH	
	11			
	12		Went & settled with 58th Dn. H.Q. ref. transfer of Stokes guns & parts by S.A. Bgde. - Took various parts due to 58th Dn and brought back those due to S.A. Bgde. GH	
	13		Visited A.D.O.S. IX Corps - GH	
	14		Went round refilling points. Drew 35 Strombos horns 79 cylinders & 400 rattles from Corps. GH	

1577 Wt. W10791/1773 500,000 1/15 D. D. & L. A.D.S.S./Forms/C. 2118.

Army Form C. 2118.

WAR DIARY
or
~~INTELLIGENCE~~ SUMMARY.
(Erase heading not required.)

Instructions regarding War Diaries and Intelligence Summaries are contained in F. S. Regs., Part II. and the Staff Manual respectively. Title pages will be prepared in manuscript.

Place	Date	Hour	Summary of Events and Information	Remarks and references to Appendices
Field Bus	15/8/17 16		Drew stores from 3rd Army Gun Pk: Bed & base plates for 27th Bgde. GH	
	17		Called on ADOS. 4th Corps. Asked DADVS ref: blow lamps. 4. GH	
	18		Purchased blow lamps for DADVS. 3. GH	
	19		Visited QM. stores 27th Bgde. railhead, & refilling pts. GH	
	20 21		Hot food containers req^d in this area. Those in possn mostly perished, & require retinning. GH	
	22		Visited QM. stores 26th Bgde at Neuville & Rozelcourt. Demanded 30 hot food containers. GH	
	23		Visited ADOS. 6th Corps. & Achiet le Grand ref: forthcoming move - limits necessary. GH	

WAR DIARY
or
~~INTELLIGENCE SUMMARY.~~
(Erase heading not required.)

Army Form C. 2118.

Instructions regarding War Diaries and Intelligence Summaries are contained in F. S. Regs., Part II. and the Staff Manual respectively. Title pages will be prepared in manuscript.

Place	Date	Hour	Summary of Events and Information	Remarks and references to Appendices
Field Bns.	24/8/17		Purchased 50 prs. slippers for tactical purposes at Amiens – [illegible]	
	25		Arranged with D.A.D.O.S. 36th Div. ref taking over. A.D.O.S. called [illegible]	
	26		Transferred 9th R.A. to 36th Div. Drew 11 carriers emerg? from 4th Corps Tps. [illegible]	
	27		Sent reserves to Achiet le Grand. High wind at night which blew down tents all over area. [illegible]	
	28		Move to new area postponed until tomorrow, owing to gale. [illegible]	
	29		Moved to new area. [illegible]	
Achiet	30			
	31		HQ Divn moved to Achiet le Petit. [illegible]	

[illegible] Capt
DADOS. 9th Div.

1/9/17

1577 Wt. W10791/1773 500,000 1/15 D. D. & L. A.D.S.S./Forms/C. 2118.

Army Form C. 2118.

Instructions regarding War Diaries and Intelligence Summaries are contained in F. S. Regs., Part II. and the Staff Manual respectively. Title pages will be prepared in manuscript.

WAR DIARY
or
INTELLIGENCE SUMMARY.
(Erase heading not required.)

Vol 29

Confidential

Place	Date	Hour	Summary of Events and Information	Remarks and references to Appendices
			War Diary DADOS 9th Div From 1st Sept 1917 To 30th " 1917	

1577 Wt. W10791/1773 500,000 1/15 D. D. & L. A.D.S.S./Forms/C. 2118.

Instructions regarding War Diaries and Intelligence Summaries are contained in F. S. Regs., Part II. and the Staff Manual respectively. Title pages will be prepared in manuscript.

WAR DIARY
or
~~INTELLIGENCE SUMMARY.~~
(Erase heading not required.)

Army Form C. 2118.

Place	Date	Hour	Summary of Events and Information	Remarks and references to Appendices
ACHIET le GRAND	Sep 1		Received stores from Base again chiefly clothing + wheels GH	
	2		Visited A.D.O.S. 6th Corps – Fetched 9th RA indents from 36th Dn + arranged for of stores to be drawn by them from 5th A. Gun Park GH	
	3		Visited various units stores of 26th Inf: Bgde:	
	4		Arranged with Gas Officer to inspect all anti-gas appliances of staff, and give instruction + allow all to go through gas chamber. GH	
	5		Went through gas chamber myself – watched experiments with various gas bombs GH	
	6		Nothing to report GH	
	7		Inspected 4th SA Regt reference excessive demands for ground sheets and boots. GH	
	8		Went to new area near Vlamertinghe – inspected site for dump – Saw the ADOS 5th Corps GH	
	9		Arranged to send certain stores by train – + to move ~~[illegible]~~ Received lorry load of stores for RA from 36th Dn GH	
	10		Arranged with 9th Supply Col: for another lorry, + decided not to send any stores by train as system unsatisfactory – GH	
	11		Stores + office move to Brandhoek nr. Vlamertinghe – trek of about 60 miles GH	

1577 Wt. W10791/1773 500,000 1/15 D. D. & L. A.D.S.S./Forms/C. 2118.

Army Form C. 2118.

Instructions regarding War Diaries and Intelligence Summaries are contained in F. S. Regs., Part II. and the Staff Manual respectively. Title pages will be prepared in manuscript.

WAR DIARY
or
~~INTELLIGENCE SUMMARY.~~
(Erase heading not required.)

Place	Date	Hour	Summary of Events and Information	Remarks and references to Appendices
	Sep			
BRANDHOEK	12		Divl HQ moved to Poperinghe	
	13		Notified Base that stores could be received on 16th inst. Ordered all huts to be sandbagged round in view of hostile shelling & bombing	
	14		Units not yet in area.	
	15			
	16		~~Brandhoek~~ Camp shelled at 8 pm. one dropping in the middle doing no damage worth considering. Apparently a 5.9. About 18 in all fell around the camp	
	17		Moved to Poperinghe, good accommodation. DHQ moved to Brandhoek taking over from 42nd Dn.	
	18		Issued to Transport lines of 197 M.G. Co. Vickers gun & 2 2" T.Ms to [illegible] T.M.B.	
	19		Issued 200 Nation fans to 58th & 27th Bydes at advd HQ	
	20		9th Dn attacked successfully taking all objectives.	
	21			
	22		Visited new area, & DADOS 59th Dn reg. taking over	

Instructions regarding War Diaries and Intelligence Summaries are contained in F. S. Regs., Part II. and the Staff Manual respectively. Title pages will be prepared in manuscript.

WAR DIARY
or
~~INTELLIGENCE SUMMARY.~~
(Erase heading not required.)

Army Form C. 2118.

Place	Date	Hour	Summary of Events and Information	Remarks and references to Appendices
	Sep^t			
WINNIZEELE	23		Moved office + stores to Winnezeele – [illegible] GH.	
	24		DHQ moved to above area, with Bdes: less RA + Fld Coys + Pioneers GH	
	25		Visited HQ RA Bde: 26th Bde: return to late area as reserve. GH	
	26		Move again indicated. Visited Arneke to find accommod^n. Very full of troops. GH	
ARNEKE	27		Moved to Arneke with DHQ. GH	
	28		26th Bde: + 3 Fld Coys return. GH	
	29		Visited all units of 27th Bde: + BHQ. Refitting going on well. Gun Park system very satisfactory for all. GH	
	30		Visited BHQ of RA also 4th + 3rd Regts + QM Stores also 27th MG Coy. Heavy bombing at night. bright moonlight. GH	

1/10/17

[signature] Capt
DADOS 9th Div

Army Form C. 2118.

Vol 30

Instructions regarding War Diaries and Intelligence Summaries are contained in F. S. Regs., Part II. and the Staff Manual respectively. Title pages will be prepared in manuscript.

WAR DIARY
or
INTELLIGENCE SUMMARY.

(*Erase heading not required.*)

Place	Date	Hour	Summary of Events and Information	Remarks and references to Appendices
			Confidential War Diary [illegible] From 1st October 1917 To 31st " " [illegible]	

WAR DIARY
or
~~INTELLIGENCE SUMMARY.~~
(Erase heading not required.)

Army Form C. 2118.

Instructions regarding War Diaries and Intelligence Summaries are contained in F. S. Regs., Part II. and the Staff Manual respectively. Title pages will be prepared in manuscript.

Place	Date	Hour	Summary of Events and Information	Remarks and references to Appendices
	Oct			
Arneke	1		Held Court of Enquiry on instruments of Divl: Band - 197 M.G. Coy. lent to 48th Divn for operations - GH	
	2		Visited HQ of 26th Inf: Bde: and inspected Qm. Stores of 10th Argyll & Sutherland Hrs, 5th Camerons, & 7th Seaforths - GH	
	3		Visited HQ 27th Brigade, & Qm. Stores of 6th K.O.S.B. 12th Royal Scots 11th Royal Scots & 9th Scottish Rifles. GH	
	4			
	5		Advised of dispatch of 1st Blanket - GH	
	6		Received 150 Yukon packs from Base - Visited new area and fixed site for dump. GH	
	7			
	8		Moved from Arneke to Border Camp near Vlamertinghe, in tents - GH	
	9		58th Bde RA attached for ordnance stores - GH	
	10		Units arrive to draw stores in new area -	
	11			

1577 Wt. W10791/1773 500,000 1/15 D. D. & L. A.D.S.S./Forms/C. 2118.

Instructions regarding War Diaries and Intelligence Summaries are contained in F. S. Regs., Part II. and the Staff Manual respectively. Title pages will be prepared in manuscript.

WAR DIARY
or
~~INTELLIGENCE SUMMARY.~~

(Erase heading not required.)

Army Form C. 2118.

Place	Date Oct	Hour	Summary of Events and Information	Remarks and references to Appendices
Border Camp	12		Blankets arrive at new railhead. Saw SMTO. 18 Corps and arranged to employ additional six lorries. Arranged fatigue parties from South African Bgde: Visited Reigersburg railhead. GH	
	13		Visited advanced HQ at Canal Bank, railhead GH	
	14		Visited ADOS. 18 Corps.	
	15		Purchased torches electric for advanced HQ. Refills not being available from Base GH	
	16		Received stores from Base again. Enemy aircraft active in bombing neighbourhood, particularly horse lines. GH	
	17		Sent lorry to Calais for 6000 pairs socks, and more blankets GH	
	18		Sent another lorry for blankets. GH	
	19		Issued blankets & socks to units coming out of line at Irish Farm north of Ypres. GH	
	20		Issued by lorry to Essex Farm further stores of blankets & socks. GH	
	21			
	22		DDOS. 5th Army called & inspected store GH	
	23		Owing to move reconsigned leather jerkins. GH	

1577 Wt. W10791/1773 500,000 1/15 D. D. & L. A.D.S.S./Forms/C. 2118.

Army Form C. 2118.

Instructions regarding War Diaries and Intelligence Summaries are contained in F. S. Regs., Part II. and the Staff Manual respectively. Title pages will be prepared in manuscript.

WAR DIARY
or
INTELLIGENCE SUMMARY.
(*Erase heading not required.*)

Place	Date Oct.	Hour	Summary of Events and Information	Remarks and references to Appendices
Border Camp	24		Visited ADOS. 18 Corps - + SMTO reference lorries for move, managed to obtain 5.	
	25		Moved to Coudekerke Branche near DUNKIRK.	
	26		Took Cinema at above place for additional accomodation	
	27		Orders to move again - Issued horse rugs to RA units.	
	28		Moved to St Idesbald 12 m. north of Dunkirk	
	29		Line trucks at r'head, chiefly winter clothing. Arranged with SMTO for 4 lorries - + two to be att^d permanently -	
	30		Handed over various stores to 41st Div RA. Visited ADOS. XV Corps	
	31		Winter clothing, + 2nd blanket being issued. Vests not yet to hand	

[signature] Capt
DADOS 9 Div

2/11/17

A5834 Wt. W4973/M687 750,000 8/16 D. D. & L. Ltd. Forms/C.2118/13.

Instructions regarding War Diaries and Intelligence Summaries are contained in F. S. Regs., Part II. and the Staff Manual respectively. Title pages will be prepared in manuscript.

WAR DIARY
or
INTELLIGENCE SUMMARY.
(Erase heading not required.)

Army Form C. 2118.

Vol 31

Place	Date	Hour	Summary of Events and Information	Remarks and references to Appendices
			Confidential –	
			War Diary	
			DADOS 9th Division	
			From 1st Nov 1917	
			To 30th " "	
			[illegible] Capt	

A5834 Wt. W4973/M687 750,000 8/16 D. D. & L. Ltd. Forms/C.2118/13.

Instructions regarding War Diaries and Intelligence Summaries are contained in F. S. Regs., Part II. and the Staff Manual respectively. Title pages will be prepared in manuscript.

WAR DIARY
or
~~INTELLIGENCE SUMMARY.~~

(*Erase heading not required.*)

Army Form C. 2118.

Place	Date Nov	Hour	Summary of Events and Information	Remarks and references to Appendices
Field	1		Received indents from 9th RA Brigade to make up deficiencies for stores handed over to 41st DRA. who are mobilizing for Italy GH	
	2		DADOS 42nd Div. called – Recd list of stores reqd from 51st Bgd: RA Dispatched indents to Base – Gave list to ADOS 15 Corps GH	
	3		Recd list of stores handed over, from 50th Bgde: RA. Dispatched indents to Base, & list to Corps – GH	
	4		Recd bulk of winter clothing with exception of vests, issued to troops – GH	
	5		Nothing to report. GH	
	6			
	7		Four H.V. shells dropped near DHQ. about 8.10 pm. no damage Returned surplus blankets to Base GH	
	8		Recd instructions ref: return of Area Stores owing to French taking over. Conference with AA. 2nd Corps & Divn	
	9		Drew 5 mountings Vickers from XV Corps Tps: Visited ADOS. Corps – 14 Gothas came over in broad daylight – bombed at night – Returned 2100 gum boots to Base GH	

A5834 Wt. W4973/M687 750,000 8/16 D. D. & L. Ltd. Forms/C.2118/13.

Instructions regarding War Diaries and Intelligence Summaries are contained in F. S. Regs., Part II. and the Staff Manual respectively. Title pages will be prepared in manuscript.

WAR DIARY
or
~~INTELLIGENCE SUMMARY.~~
(Erase heading not required.)

Army Form C. 2118.

Place	Date Nov	Hour	Summary of Events and Information	Remarks and references to Appendices
Field	10		Further discussion ref. return of Area Stores – I am to leave a W.O. & clerk behind to take tally [initials]	
	11		Issued instns: to all units concerned to return Area stores to existing Salvage Dumps – only those not immediately reqd [initials]	
	12 / 13		Visited XV Corps HQ. was bombed on the way at 11 am near the Canal at Adinkerke – 12 bombs dropped doing considerable damage [initials]	
	14		Visited new area at Houquelières near Frugès, & found site for store [initials]	
	15		moved stores & office to Houquelières – Trek of 10 hours for lorries – [initials]	
	16		Visited 10 Corps HQ [initials]	
	17		DHQ arrived excepting DAQMG [initials]	
	18		DAQMG arrived from northern area – [initials]	
	19 / 20		Nothing in particular to report – [initials]	
	21 / 22		Visited 27th Bgde: HQ. just arrived after march from north – All in good order [initials]	

A5834 Wt. W4973/M687 750,000 8/16 D. D. & L. Ltd. Forms/C.2118/13.

Instructions regarding War Diaries and Intelligence Summaries are contained in F. S. Regs., Part II. and the Staff Manual respectively. Title pages will be prepared in manuscript.

Army Form C. 2118.

WAR DIARY
or
INTELLIGENCE SUMMARY.
(Erase heading not required.)

Place	Date Nov.	Hour	Summary of Events and Information	Remarks and references to Appendices
Field	23rd		Visited 26th Bgde: on trek at Renescure – Number of men fell out, & horses too – Had been in line probable reason. GA	
	24		Visited HQ 2nd Army – & SA. Bgde on trek. GA	
	25		Applied for leave. Went to railhead at Hesdin. – Tried to find place for stores without success. GA	
	26		Recd army letter ref: census of guns – Went to R.A. HQ & Conferred with Staff Capt. & Bgde: Major – ref this GA	
	27		Again visited RA HQ ref: above – GA	
	28		Recd & dispatched pro: forma giving actual position as regards guns in pos: &c: GA	
	29		Visited RA HQ again reference one how: & carr: alleged deficient – Understood all complete excepting one on indent – No satisfactory information forthcoming – GA	
	30		Handed over to Lt Ingesfield who acts for me when on leave – GA	

[signature] Capt
DADOS 9th Dn

A5834 Wt. W4973/M687 750,000 8/16 D. D. & L. Ltd. Forms/C.2118/13.

Instructions regarding War Diaries and Intelligence Summaries are contained in F. S. Regs., Part II. and the Staff Manual respectively. Title pages will be prepared in manuscript.

WAR DIARY
or
INTELLIGENCE SUMMARY.
(*Erase heading not required.*)

Army Form C. 2118.

VR 32

Place	Date	Hour	Summary of Events and Information	Remarks and references to Appendices
			Confidential	
			War Diary DADOS 9 Div	
			From 1st December 1917	
			to 31st " "	
			[illegible] Capt	
			DADOS 9 Div	

A5834 Wt. W4973/M687 750,000 8/16 D. D. & L. Ltd. Forms/C.2118/13.

Instructions regarding War Diaries and Intelligence Summaries are contained in F. S. Regs., Part II. and the Staff Manual respectively. Title pages will be prepared in manuscript.

Army Form C. 2118.

WAR DIARY
or
~~INTELLIGENCE SUMMARY.~~
(Erase heading not required.)

Place	Date	Hour	Summary of Events and Information	Remarks and references to Appendices
Field	Dec 1		Left Frances area for Peronne – had all night wait for arrival of stores – weather bitterly cold and frosty – [initials]	
	2		Visited OO 7th Corps Troops & selected site with him for dump – no buildings – tents at side of Bapaume Peronne Rd – Issued all available boots to infantry battns – [initials]	
	3		Issued various stores to units from bulk [initials]	
	4		Lorries arrived from other area with office & remainder of stores and tents erected – weather fortunately fine – [initials]	
	5		Received wire from Calais Base stating that all bulk wires were cancelled – Informed ADOS 3rd Corps of this – which means that all bulk items urgently reqd will be delayed – [initials]	
	6		Units moving to forward area – DAQ to Haut Allaines [initials]	
	7		Visited DAQ & dump of area stores left by 12th D. Had 12th Div RA attached – wired Base for bulk. [initials]	
	8		Urgent demands for Boots being recd. Started advanced store at Leramont – [initials]	
	9		Visited advanced store & DAQ at Leramont [initials]	
	10		Called on various Batty Commanders of attached RA units now composing 12th 20th & Guards Divnl [initials]	

A5834 Wt. W4973/M687 750,000 8/16 D. D. & L. Ltd. Forms/C.2118/13.

Instructions regarding War Diaries and Intelligence Summaries are contained in F. S. Regs., Part II. and the Staff Manual respectively. Title pages will be prepared in manuscript.

WAR DIARY
or
INTELLIGENCE SUMMARY.
(Erase heading not required.)

Army Form C. 2118.

Place	Date Dec	Hour 1917	Summary of Events and Information	Remarks and references to Appendices
Field	11		Visited ADOS 7th Corps + discussed various subjects with him. GA	
	12		Bulk items recd from Base + sent up to advanced dump and issued GA	
	13		Heavy demands being recd. from all units – especially attached RA owing to recent events in field GA	
	14		Paid visits to attached units stores. GA	
	15 16 17		Severe frost. Demanded extra lorries from Corps to cope with incoming stores. Transferred Guards Div RA to their own Divn GA	
	18		Frost continues. 31 tons stores arrived – demanded extra lorries + despatched to advd dump – GA	
	19		Moved from Peronne to YTRES [?] – taking over premises vacated by 36th Div DHQ now at Sorel le Grand –	
	20 21		Visited DHQ Salvage Coy and HQ 27th Bgde. Closed store at Lieramont and collected staff at Ytres – GA	
	22		Visited Salvage Coy + 27th Field Amb. [?] of Salvage left by 36th Div chiefly rifles and clothing GA	

A5834 Wt. W4973/M687 750,000 8/16 D. D. & L. Ltd. Forms/C.2118/13.

Instructions regarding War Diaries and Intelligence Summaries are contained in F. S. Regs., Part II. and the Staff Manual respectively. Title pages will be prepared in manuscript.

WAR DIARY
or
INTELLIGENCE SUMMARY.
(Erase heading not required.)

Army Form C. 2118.

Place	Date	Hour	Summary of Events and Information	Remarks and references to Appendices
[illegible]	Dec 23		Thaw sets in at night rendering roads in dangerous condition for	
	24		Visited Corps HQ. asked for passes for lorries which were not allowed [illegible]	
	25		24 tons Clothing arrived. Thaw precautions being off these were	
	26		drawn by lorry. Frost continues. [illegible]	
			Visited Corps. ref: light railway system — also Corps Troops [illegible]	
	27			
	28		Billets cold wind. Snow again. Visited workshops [illegible]	
	29		Suggested new system of submitting Bulk demands by units — One day a week for submitting Bulk demands for the week, thereby saving paper and journeys of D.R's. [illegible]	
	30		Made arrangements with Light Railway Coy: for disposition of trucks when the thaw precautions come into operation.	
	31			

[illegible] Capt.
DADOS 9th Div. [illegible]/17

A5834 Wt. W4973/M687 750,000 8/16 D. D. & L. Ltd. Forms/C.2118/13.

Instructions regarding War Diaries and Intelligence Summaries are contained in F. S. Regs., Part II. and the Staff Manual respectively. Title pages will be prepared in manuscript.

9

WAR DIARY
or
INTELLIGENCE SUMMARY.
(Erase heading not required.)

Army Form C. 2118.

V/133

Place	Date	Hour	Summary of Events and Information	Remarks and references to Appendices
			War Diary D.A.D.O.S. 9th Division From 1st Jany: 1918 To 31st Jany: 1918	

1577 Wt. W10791/1773 500,000 1/15 D. D. & L. A.D.S.S./Forms/C. 2118.

Army Form C. 2118.

Instructions regarding War Diaries and Intelligence Summaries are contained in F. S. Regs., Part II. and the Staff Manual respectively. Title pages will be prepared in manuscript.

WAR DIARY
or
INTELLIGENCE SUMMARY.
(Erase heading not required.)

Place	Date	Hour	Summary of Events and Information	Remarks and references to Appendices
Field	Jany/18 1st to 10th		No officer functioning during this period but following Special issues made:- Palliasses & mattresses Boots Gum Thigh Fans Ayrton Flapper Rules Howitzer Correction Gloves Hedging Buckets Latrine completed issues of Jerkins Leather to all units In addition to above the detachment erected two huts for Stores	

A5834 Wt. W4973/M687 750,000 8/16 D. D. & L. Ltd. Forms/C.2118/13.

Instructions regarding War Diaries and Intelligence Summaries are contained in F. S. Regs., Part II. and the Staff Manual respectively. Title pages will be prepared in manuscript.

WAR DIARY
or
INTELLIGENCE SUMMARY.
(*Erase heading not required.*)

Army Form C. 2118.

Place	Date 1918 Jany	Hour	Summary of Events and Information	Remarks and references to Appendices
Field	11th		Lt W. Howard 9th London Regt att A.O.D. reported for duty in absence of Capt Hyde on leave. Arrival reported to Corps Army D.O.S. & O/c 400 Section 3rd Echelon by D.R.L.S. Personally to Divisl HQ	W.H.
	12th		Shops & stores inspected. Corps Salvage dump visited & clinometer collected from Corps HQ	W.H.
	13th		Drew 400 frs from Field Cashier Corps. Collected 2 Strombos horns & 6 full cylinders from 7th Corps Troops. M.G. spares collected from 3rd Army Gun Park sent to 16th Divsn	W.H.
	14th		Large dump of stores left by 63rd & 36 Divsns. Under instructions A.D.O.S. VII commenced to evacuate this dump to base & Corps troops. Drew paliasses from 21 Ind Labour Coy.	W.H.
	15th		Conference at VII Corps. Work on new camp proceeded. Thaw precautions on at 6 pm arranged with "Anlimbro" Ry for stores to be sent up by them.	W.H.
	16th		All men who could be spared employed on new camp. Visited by A.D.O.S.	W.H.
	17th		Moved Armourers and Tailors shops and office	W.H.
	18th		Moved remainder of stores & men's kits & cookhouses.	W.H.

A5834 Wt. W4973/M687 750,000 8/16 D. D. & L. Ltd. Forms/C.2118/13.

Army Form C. 2118.

Instructions regarding War Diaries and Intelligence Summaries are contained in F. S. Regs., Part II. and the Staff Manual respectively. Title pages will be prepared in manuscript.

WAR DIARY
or
INTELLIGENCE SUMMARY.
(Erase heading not required.)

Place	Date	Hour	Summary of Events and Information	Remarks and references to Appendices
	Jan 1/18			
Field	19		Salvage dumps + 27 F.A visited.	WMH
	20"		Collected rifles from Salvage dump. Corps troops + railhead visited Conference at Corps HQ 5.30pm	WMH
	21		To Amiens for local purchases Lamp glasses + blackboard for Signal School	WMH
	22		Corps + SA Bgde visited	WMH
	23		3 Salvage men arrived as per arrangement with Divn HQ for the receipt of u/s clothing.	WMH
	26		New area visited to arrange details of move with 39th Divn	WMH
	27		ADOS called to check outstanding indents	WMH
	28		To Corps to discuss special issue of SD trousers to Highland Brigade as these no longer required arranged to return to Base	WMH
	30		Armourers + shop moved to Mericourt sur Somme (new area)	WMH
	31		Moved to Mericourt Attached units 48 San Sec + 7 M.M G Coy transferred to 39th Divn	WMH

Wm Upward Lt
for Capt. DADOS
9 Divn

A5834 Wt. W4973/M687 750,000 8/16 D. D. & L. Ltd. Forms/C.2118/13.

Instructions regarding War Diaries and Intelligence Summaries are contained in F. S. Regs., Part II. and the Staff Manual respectively. Title pages will be prepared in manuscript.

WAR DIARY
or
INTELLIGENCE SUMMARY.
(Erase heading not required.)

Army Form C. 2118.

Vol 34

Place	Date	Hour	Summary of Events and Information	Remarks and references to Appendices
			War Diary S.R.W.B. 9th Bn From 1st Feb. 1918 to 28th "	

A5834 Wt. W4973/M687 750,000 8/16 D. D. & L. Ltd. Forms/C.2118/13.

Instructions regarding War Diaries and Intelligence Summaries are contained in F. S. Regs., Part II. and the Staff Manual respectively. Title pages will be prepared in manuscript.

WAR DIARY
or
INTELLIGENCE SUMMARY.
(Erase heading not required.)

Army Form C. 2118.

Place	Date	Hour	Summary of Events and Information	Remarks and references to Appendices
Field	1/2/18		Arrived back from leave – one month – FH	
	2		Visited 27th 28th S.A. Bgde. HQ and 3rd Regt S.A. ref demobilization FH	
	3		Visited 3rd S.A. regt. again – FH	
	4		9th Scottish Regt. transferred to 14th Divn. complete – Inspection of Vickers guns of 27th M.G. Coy begun – FH	
	5		Fitting of butt catches to Lewis guns, also [illegible] process begun	FH
	6		Collected 500 bayonet fighting sticks FH	
	7		Visited 2nd stores of 2nd & 4th S.A. regts: also [illegible] FH	
	8		Assistant Insp. of Armourers in [illegible] Armourers Shop. [illegible] refs details – FH Inspection of guns 27th M.G. Coy finished	
	9		12 6" Newtons recd for Artillery – FH	
	10		Lt Upward who acted in my absence, returned to go to 7th Corps HQ	FH
	11		Inspection of guns of 28th M.G. Coy begun – FH	
	12		Inspection of arms for 2nd S.A. Inf: sent 5 armourers – FH	
	13		Getting to report – FH	

A5834 Wt. W4973/M687 750,000 8/16 D. D. & L. Ltd. Forms/C.2118/13.

Army Form C. 2118.

Instructions regarding War Diaries and Intelligence Summaries are contained in F. S. Regs., Part II. and the Staff Manual respectively. Title pages will be prepared in manuscript.

WAR DIARY
or
INTELLIGENCE SUMMARY.
(Erase heading not required.)

Place	Date	Hour	Summary of Events and Information	Remarks and references to Appendices
Field	14.12.18		10th Argyll & Suth'd Hrs left for 32nd [illegible] JH	
	15		Inspection of 25th Inf. Bde [illegible] . Reported on [illegible] for Asst. Insp. Armr. JH	
	16		Visited HQ [illegible] 2nd Army. [illegible] of 26th Inf Bde [illegible] JH	
			Inspection [illegible] 26th Inf Bde [illegible]	
	17		stores on demobilization. JH	
	18		Took 5 Rifle [illegible] Army [illegible] School JH	
	19		Arranged with [illegible] to [illegible] from [illegible] JH	
	20		Visited HQ 50th & 51st Bdes RA [illegible] JH	
	21		Asked for meeting of [illegible] reduction of mob: tech. equipment JH	
	22		Raised question of supply of [illegible] to batteries RA. [illegible] [illegible] JH	
	23		Sent armourers to 12th Royal Scots for [illegible] of arms JH	

A5834 Wt. W4973/M687 750,000 8/16 D. D. & L. Ltd. Forms/C.2118/13.

Instructions regarding War Diaries and Intelligence Summaries are contained in F. S. Regs., Part II. and the Staff Manual respectively. Title pages will be prepared in manuscript.

WAR DIARY
or
~~INTELLIGENCE~~ SUMMARY.

(*Erase heading not required.*)

Army Form C. 2118.

Place	Date	Hour	Summary of Events and Information	Remarks and references to Appendices
Field	24/2/18		Visited stores of 1st 2nd & 4th S A Batts [illegible]	
	25		Wrote D HQ re excellent return of surplus stores of 3rd SA Bn [illegible]	
	26		Visited Corps for conference - & 39th Div reference exchange of stores on move [illegible]	
	27		Visited HQ 27th Bgde & QM stores of 6th KOSB [illegible]	
	28		Recd orders for move arranged for 2nd march [illegible]	

1/3/18 [illegible] Capt
DADOS 9 Div

A5834 Wt. W4973/M687 750,000 8/16 D. D. & L. Ltd. Forms/C.2118/13.

Instructions regarding War Diaries and Intelligence Summaries are contained in F. S. Regs., Part II. and the Staff Manual respectively. Title pages will be prepared in manuscript.

WAR DIARY
or
INTELLIGENCE SUMMARY.
(Erase heading not required.)

Army Form C. 2118.

VA 35

Place	Date	Hour	Summary of Events and Information	Remarks and references to Appendices
			War Diary DADOS of 15th (Scottish) division From 1st March 1918 To 31st 1918	

A5834 Wt. W4973/M687 750,000 8/16 D. D. & L. Ltd. Forms/C.2118/13.

Instructions regarding War Diaries and Intelligence Summaries are contained in F. S. Regs., Part II. and the Staff Manual respectively. Title pages will be prepared in manuscript.

WAR DIARY
or
~~INTELLIGENCE SUMMARY.~~
(Erase heading not required.)

Army Form C. 2118.

Place	Date	Hour	Summary of Events and Information	Remarks and references to Appendices
Field	1/3/18		Divisional HQ took ordnance lorries for move. The first instance of this during my tenure as DADOS. Orders to move forward. Found store at Peronne. GH	
	2		Visited DDOS 7th Corps & informed him of my location. Fixed Armourers up in building opposite. Conference at Corps ref: igniters, alterations to. GH	
	3		DAQ fixed at Haut Allaines. Rec^d orders to proceed on Amm^n Course. GH	
	4		Left for Zeningham on Amm^n Course. Armourers employed on altering the igniters rec^d from Corps	
	5.		Lt. Upward took over my duties in my absence. GH	
	12		LP. of 11200 gramophone needles for purpose of alterations to igniters. These were for the whole of the VII Corps. GH	
	13		Office & store moved to [illegible], taking over from 39 Div. GH	
	14		Conference of QMs 27th Bde at my office. GH	
	20		Capt: Smail, Asst Staff Capt: [illegible], & [illegible] [illegible] [illegible] working of Ordnance. GH	
	21		Returned from Amm^n Course. [illegible] [illegible] [illegible] heavily. [illegible] to move back to [illegible] [illegible] began	

A5834 Wt. W4973/M687 750,000 8/16 D. D. & L. Ltd. Forms/C.2118/13.

Instructions regarding War Diaries and Intelligence Summaries are contained in F. S. Regs., Part II. and the Staff Manual respectively. Title pages will be prepared in manuscript.

WAR DIARY
or
INTELLIGENCE SUMMARY.
(Erase heading not required.)

Army Form C. 2118.

Place	Date	Hour	Summary of Events and Information	Remarks and references to Appendices
			(Continued)	
Field	21/3/18		at 3 a.m. Shell fell at X roads Nurlu [illegible] towards ammun: dump on Peronne Rd. Several casualties here – [illegible] being hit – Road badly damaged – [illegible] moving dump to Peronne to [illegible] buildings –	
	22/3/18		moved to Peronne – [illegible] to [illegible] from [illegible] Corps [illegible] stores [illegible] from Peronne – along with other [illegible] stores which had not to [illegible]	
	23.		Peronne became too hot, the enemy already advancing from Nurlu. I ordered the lorries, already packed ready, to proceed to Maricourt – at 3 a.m. D H Q moved to Maricourt – Issued 2 Lewis to M G Bn. I followed at 4 a.m. the enemy shelling both [illegible] – moved again under Corps orders to Bray Corbie Rd.	
	24		Issued 22 Lewis guns to 26th Bde – On Bray Corbie Rd – Division in 3 [illegible] [illegible] Ordered to move into Corbie [illegible] – [illegible] 200 belts [illegible] to M G Bn.	
	25		Corbie – stayed one night [illegible] Corps ordered me [illegible] to Beaucourt [illegible] – D H Q [illegible] [illegible] being shelled [illegible] in the day – Issued 28 L.G. to 27th Bde + 2 [illegible]	
	26		At Beaucourt. Division moved [illegible]	
	27		At Beaucourt –	
	28		moved to Villers Bocage	
	29		HQ moved to Bertangles –	
	30		Division moved north – Bdes come out to villages round about	
	31		R.A. of Div. relieved [illegible] on 2nd [illegible]	
			Summary [illegible]	

A5834 Wt. W4973/M687 750,000 8/16 D. D. & L. Ltd. Forms/C.2118/13.

WAR DIARY
or
INTELLIGENCE SUMMARY.
(*Erase heading not required.*)

Army Form C. 2118.

Instructions regarding War Diaries and Intelligence Summaries are contained in F. S. Regs., Part II. and the Staff Manual respectively. Title pages will be prepared in manuscript.

Place	Date	Hour	Summary of Events and Information	Remarks and references to Appendices
			Remarks on Operations since 21st March to end of battle –	
			The chief thing seemed to be to get rid of what might be called surplus impedimenta – Four lorries allotted to Ordnance will not suffice to move reserves, shops, & personnel under abnormal conditions where mobility is an urgent factor – I sent away service dress clothing (which had been demanded for inclement weather for relief battns, & for exchange of that impregnated by gas) gum boots, area stores (likely to be captured) part of my reserves of gas appliances – I sent the tailors back to the Employment Company – The supply of Lewis Guns & Vickers with various spares was well maintained by the V Army from OK, & no difficulties were encountered in obtaining those demanded – There was no great demand for gas appliances, some from "wandering" parties going to rejoin were issued irrespective of units or divisions – A small quantity of SD was left behind at Peronne in the Divl. Dump, as it was found impossible to clear, & railhead there was evacuated. Lewis Guns demanded during operations 55, Vickers 4 – The latter number owing to the Bn. not being in touch with their Coys – Numbers to refit 107 & 42 respectively.	
			[signature] Capt DADOS 9 Div	

A5834 Wt. W4973/M687 750,000 8/16 D. D. & L. Ltd. Forms/C.2118/13.

Instructions regarding War Diaries and Intelligence Summaries are contained in F. S. Regs., Part II. and the Staff Manual respectively. Title pages will be prepared in manuscript.

WAR DIARY
or
INTELLIGENCE SUMMARY.
(Erase heading not required.)

Army Form C. 2118.

Confidential

Vol 36

Place	Date	Hour	Summary of Events and Information	Remarks and references to Appendices
			War Diary D.A.D.O.S. 9th Div From 1st April 1918 To 30th " "	

A5834 Wt. W4973/M687 750,000 8/16 D. D. & L. Ltd. Forms/C.2118/13.

Instructions regarding War Diaries and Intelligence Summaries are contained in F. S. Regs., Part II. and the Staff Manual respectively. Title pages will be prepared in manuscript.

WAR DIARY
or
~~INTELLIGENCE SUMMARY.~~
(Erase heading not required.)

Army Form C. 2118.

Place	Date	Hour	Summary of Events and Information	Remarks and references to Appendices
Field –	1/4/18		Moved from Villers Bocage to Scherpenberg near Kemmel – Take over from 1st Australian Divn. GH	
	2		Issued 27 Vickers ·303 to 9th Machine Gun Bn. GH	
	3		Demanded 109 Lewis Guns to Complete – Visited DDOS. 2nd Army – Trucks for refitting arrive – GH	
	4		Issued 64 Lewis Guns – Great coats arrived reconsigned from South – Visited all 3 Bgdes: with DAQMG. GH	
	5		Patrol suits demanded by 27th Bgde: GH	
	6		Visited Gun Pk: and railhead – Issued 1 Lewis Gun. GH	
	7		Drew 20 prs. wiring gloves from Gun Park. for 26th Bgde.	
	8		Visited ADOS 9 Corps – GH	
	9 10		Moved dump & store to Steenvoorde under instns DHQ. Issued 23 Lewis Guns – GH	
	11		Sent 5 armourers back to rejoin units. French Divn passes through town GH	
	12		Issued 4 Vickers Guns to M.G. Bn GH	
	13		Suggested joining up with M.T. Coy: AA&QMG agrees GH	

Instructions regarding War Diaries and Intelligence Summaries are contained in F. S. Regs., Part II. and the Staff Manual respectively. Title pages will be prepared in manuscript.

WAR DIARY

or

~~INTELLIGENCE SUMMARY.~~

(Erase heading not required.)

Army Form C. 2118.

Place	Date	Hour	Summary of Events and Information	Remarks and references to Appendices
Field	4/5/18		Moved to South of Abeele with M.T. Coy: Some shelling of back areas. GA	
	15.		Obtain 4 more lorries from M.T. to cope with issues. GA	
	16		Issued 9 Vickers to M.G. Bn. GA	
	17 18		Again borrowed lorries to compete with issues. Staff working in many cases 18 hours per day GA	
	19 20		Moved to Ouderdom Poperinghe Road. Lorries continue to issue & are out until 1 am. GA	
	21		Shelled out, & move to Watou area with M.T. Coy. GA	
	22		9th Scottish Rifles, & 2nd R. Scots Fusiliers join Divn. Visited 2nd in C. of 9th Scot. Rifles.	
	23		Issued all available stores to 9th Scottish Rifles. GA	
	24		Went to Calais for No. 9 periscopes (50) and took to D.H.Q. & owing to change in operations were not wanted. GA	
	25 26		Issued 1 Lewis gun to A 51 Bty: R.F.A. GA	
	27 28		Issued 1 Lewis gun to 5th Cameron Hrs. GA	

1577 Wt. W10791/1773 500,000 1/15 D. D. & L. A.D.S.S./Forms/C. 2118.

Instructions regarding War Diaries and Intelligence Summaries are contained in F. S. Regs., Part II. and the Staff Manual respectively. Title pages will be prepared in manuscript.

WAR DIARY

or

~~INTELLIGENCE SUMMARY.~~

(Erase heading not required.)

Army Form C. 2118.

Place	Date	Hour	Summary of Events and Information	Remarks and references to Appendices
Field	Apl. 29		Moved to Wormhoudt - Cassel road - Considerable difficulty experienced in finding accommodation owing to the great number of French troops in area - FH	
	30		Delivery of stores to troops by MT continues - The difficulty of units finding transport sufficient to take stores is always in evidence - Issued 12 Lewis guns - FH	

[signature] Capt

DADOS 9th Dn

2/5/18

Instructions regarding War Diaries and Intelligence Summaries are contained in F. S. Regs., Part II. and the Staff Manual respectively. Title Pages will be prepared in manuscript.

WAR DIARY
or
INTELLIGENCE SUMMARY
(Erase heading not required.)

Army Form C. 2118

Vol 37

Place	Date	Hour	Summary of Events and Information	Remarks and references to Appendices
			Confidential War Diary DADOS 9th Div From 1st May 1918 To 31st " "	

1875 Wt. W593/826 1,000,000 4/15 J.B.C. & A. A.D.S.S./Forms/C. 2118.

Instructions regarding War Diaries and Intelligence Summaries are contained in F. S. Regs., Part II. and the Staff Manual respectively. Title Pages will be prepared in manuscript.

May 1918

WAR DIARY
or
INTELLIGENCE SUMMARY
(Erase heading not required.)

Army Form C. 2118

Place	Date	Hour	Summary of Events and Information	Remarks and references to Appendices
FIELD	1/5/18		Recd. instns from DHQ. to arrange to take Dump to Staple – visited Area Commandant Staple – GH	
	2		Issued 35 Vickers complete to Machine Gun Bn. GH	
	3		Visited Zeggers Cappel, suggested Imom there, order since countermanded GH	
	4		Visited railhead Bergues, & ordered trucks to be re-consigned to new railhead – GH	
	5		Moved to Staple – tents and small building – Visited Bergues to confer with RTO re: trucks GH	
	6		Division moving to Blaringhem – decide to remove there – R'head at Ebblinghem – GH	
	7		Moved to Blaringhem – barn & good office – GH	
	8		Visited Hq. 28th Bgde; & S.A. Bn. 9th Scottish Rifles and 2nd R. Scots Fus. also 5th Camerons – inspecting 2m. stores in each Bn. GH	
	9		Visited ADOS. 15th Corps. & RA Hq. at Ledrzeele with DAQMG. GH	
	10		Visited Hq. 27th Bgde: at Lynde & all 2m. of units, also South African Bn. GH	

1875 Wt. W593/826 1,000,000 4/15 J.B.C. & A. A.D.S.S./Forms/C. 2118.

Instructions regarding War Diaries and Intelligence Summaries are contained in F. S. Regs., Part II. and the Staff Manual respectively. Title Pages will be prepared in manuscript.

May

WAR DIARY
or
INTELLIGENCE SUMMARY
(Erase heading not required.)

Army Form C. 2118

Place	Date	Hour	Summary of Events and Information	Remarks and references to Appendices
FIELD	11/5/18		Purchased 10 flat irons for SA Bn. Visited Qm stores of 2nd Royal Scots Fusiliers, + SA. Bn.	
	12		Considerable difficulty experienced with amalgamation of SA Bn owing to the staffs of the merged units having been sent away. Urged particularly that particulars of [illegible] be rendered without delay.	
	13			
	14		Visited Brigades and Batterys of the Div RA in the Watou area with DAQMG.	
	15		Inspected Qm stores of 27th Bgde + called on Bgde HQ.	
	16		Visited with AA+QMG 28th Bgde. South African Bgde HQ and SA Batn ref return of [illegible] from surplus on reorganisation.	
	17		Called on 9th Seaforth H (Pioneers) near Watou Cappel	
	18		Again urged return of surplus [illegible] from SA Bn. 2nd Royal Scots Fus: in need of shoemakers tools. These purchased	
	19		51st Bgde RFA arrive from Watou – inspected the horses &c	
	20		HQ RA at Racquinghem – enquired position re guns from Staff Capt. Inspected [illegible] wagons surplus with DADOS, 1st Australian [illegible] 3 for [illegible]	

1875 Wt. W593/826 1,000,000 4/15 J.B.C. & A. A.D.S.S./Forms/C. 2118.

Army Form C. 2118

Instructions regarding War Diaries and Intelligence Summaries are contained in F. S. Regs., Part II. and the Staff Manual respectively. Title Pages will be prepared in manuscript.

WAR DIARY
or
~~INTELLIGENCE SUMMARY~~
(Erase heading not required.)

Place	Date	Hour	Summary of Events and Information	Remarks and references to Appendices
FIELD	21/5/18		Orders to move again – Store at Hondeghem where the 31st Dn DADOS taken over by DHQ. GH	
	22		Arranged for barn at Staple with Camp Commdt. GH	
	23		Called on DADOS 31st Dn and ADOS XV Corps. GH	
	24		Opened store at Longue Croix nr Staple – barn + tents – GH	
	25		With DAQMG inspected 2nd Army Laundry. + ADOS Corps visited. Demanded 1000 long + 2500 short drawers – GH	
	26		21 MVS complain of damaged water troughs issued – Inspected and returned to unit for local repair – GH	
	27		Inspected harness of Train Coys: with view to Economy in demands. Consider more repairs could be effected locally – Tendency to demand new for appearance sake – GH	
	28		Pressed SA Bn again for statement ref. Ldy. GH	
	29		Blankets of 26th Bgde: recalled 5470 received + dispatched. Relief for Armr Sht. Lawson arrived from Base. GH	

1875 Wt. W593/826 1,000,000 4/15 J.B.C. & A. A.D.S.S./Forms/C. 2118.

Instructions regarding War Diaries and Intelligence Summaries are contained in F. S. Regs., Part II. and the Staff Manual respectively. Title Pages will be prepared in manuscript.

WAR DIARY
or
~~INTELLIGENCE~~ SUMMARY
(Erase heading not required.)

Army Form C. 2118

Place	Date	Hour	Summary of Events and Information	Remarks and references to Appendices
FIELD	30/5/18		A.D.O.S. called – Pressed for return from South African Bn ref. L.G. R.A. blankets recalled – Made searching enquiries regarding 18 L.G. said to have been retd to Salvage Coy: by S.A. Bn &c	
	31		Recd statement from S.A. Bn ref. L.G. retd to Salvage Coy. &c	

1/6/18 G. Hyde Capt
DADOS. 9 Dn

1875 Wt. W593/826 1,000,000 4/15 J.B.C. & A. A.D.S.S./Forms/C. 2118.

Instructions regarding War Diaries and Intelligence Summaries are contained in F. S. Regs., Part II. and the Staff Manual respectively. Title Pages will be prepared in manuscript.

WAR DIARY
or
INTELLIGENCE SUMMARY
(Erase heading not required.)

Army Form C. 2118

Confidential

Vol 38

Place	Date	Hour	Summary of Events and Information	Remarks and references to Appendices
			War Diary DADOS 9th Div From 1st June 1918 To 30th " "	

1875 Wt. W593/826 1,000,000 4/15 J.B.C. & A. A.D.S.S./Forms/C. 2118.

Instructions regarding War Diaries and Intelligence Summaries are contained in F. S. Regs., Part II. and the Staff Manual respectively. Title Pages will be prepared in manuscript.

WAR DIARY
or
INTELLIGENCE SUMMARY
(Erase heading not required.)

Army Form C. 2118

Place	Date	Hour	Summary of Events and Information	Remarks and references to Appendices
Field	June 1		Submitted statement of [illegible] to Corps of the South African Bde. – Drew 4 6" Newton mortars from 1st Australian Divn DADOS. [initials]	
	2		Submitted special indents to Base for bicycles urgently required. – Wrote South African Brigade reference return of Mob: Stores on reorganization – for instruction of 8th [illegible] [illegible] of GOC. [initials]	
	3			
	4		Received 2 additional 6" Newton mortars from 1st Aust. Div. [initials]	
	5		Inspected vehicles of 9th Divl Train – Paint generally condemned as of inferior quality. [initials]	
	6		Purchased 50 prs. rope soled shoes for patrol work. [initials]	
	7		Inspected chaff-cutter issued to DAC. who complain that it is too bulky to carry about – weighs about 7 cwt. – I concur & suggest to Corps that this particular one is kept in area as area store. [initials]	
	8		Additional purchase of shoes for patrol. [initials]	
	9			
	10		DHQ [illegible] for chevrons – Last indents already submitted – [initials]	
	11			
	12		Visited Div. RA ref. springs running out. [initials]	

1875 Wt. W593/826 1,000,000 4/15 J.B.C. & A. A.D.S.S./Forms/C. 2118.

Army Form C. 2118.

Instructions regarding War Diaries and Intelligence Summaries are contained in F. S. Regs., Part II. and the Staff Manual respectively. Title Pages will be prepared in manuscript.

WAR DIARY
or
INTELLIGENCE SUMMARY
(Erase heading not required.)

Place	Date	Hour	Summary of Events and Information	Remarks and references to Appendices
Field	July 13		Drew seven snipers rifles from 2nd Army School, Lumbres. 4 for 5th Cameron Hrs: 3 for 2nd Royal Scots Fus: Chevron indents returned from Base. GH	
	14		Visited Corps ref: springs running out. Bicycle question becoming acute. GH	
	15		Divl. Hq moved to U6 a 3.4. vice Hondeghem which is being shelled. GH	
	16		Visited ADOS. XV Corps taking 7 Very pistols required. Visited Army Hq. who state extra Lewis guns may be drawn making 32 per battn. GH	
	17 18		ADOS. called with Inspector of Armourers. Purchased featherom for Baths. GH	
	19		Received 300 rattles from Base for Gas Officer. GH	
	20		Recd authority from 2nd Army for the issue of 8 addl. Lewis guns per battn. GH	
	21		Recd special sample Horse Clippers for Mobile Vet. Sec. GH	
	22		Inspected limbers fitted with new patt: racks for carriage of Lewis Guns. most satisfactory. GH	
	23		The carriage of the additional magazines discussed. It is generally conceded with this Divn that the scale of 44 per gun is too big. GH	

1875 Wt. W593/826 1,000,000 4/15 J.B.C. & A. A.D.S.S./Forms/C. 2118.

Army Form C. 2118

WAR DIARY
or
INTELLIGENCE SUMMARY
(Erase heading not required.)

Instructions regarding War Diaries and Intelligence Summaries are contained in F. S. Regs., Part II. and the Staff Manual respectively. Title Pages will be prepared in manuscript.

Place	Date	Hour	Summary of Events and Information	Remarks and references to Appendices
Field	July 24		Visited 2nd stores 2nd Royal Scots Fusiliers, 9th Scottish Rifles, 12th Royal Scots	
	25		Collected 704 rifles from Labour Group for reissue after cleaning overhaul	
	26		Lent armourers to 40th Div DADOS for one day for inspection of arms	
	27–30		Acting as ADOS 15th Corps.	

War Diary [signature] Major
2/7/18 DADOS 9th Div

1875 Wt. W593/826 1,000,000 4/15 J.B.C. & A. A.D.S.S./Forms/C. 2118.

9

Instructions regarding War Diaries and Intelligence Summaries are contained in F. S. Regs., Part II. and the Staff Manual respectively. Title Pages will be prepared in manuscript.

WAR DIARY
or
INTELLIGENCE SUMMARY
(Erase heading not required.)

Army Form C. 2118

Confidential

Vol 39

Place	Date	Hour	Summary of Events and Information	Remarks and references to Appendices
			War Diary – DADOS 9th Div. From July 1st 1918 To " 31st 1918	

1875 Wt. W593/826 1,000,000 4/15 J.B.C. & A. A.D.S.S./Forms/C. 2118.

Instructions regarding War Diaries and Intelligence Summaries are contained in F. S. Regs., Part II. and the Staff Manual respectively. Title Pages will be prepared in manuscript.

WAR DIARY
or
~~INTELLIGENCE SUMMARY~~
(Erase heading not required.)

Army Form C. 2118

Place	Date	Hour	Summary of Events and Information	Remarks and references to Appendices
Field	July 1	1918	Acting ADOS XV Corps –	
	13		Visited wagon lines SA Brigade – Inspected QM stores of 9th Scottish Rifles and 2nd Royal Scots Fusiliers – GA.	
	14		Capt McDowell USA attached for instruction on British ordnance methods. GA	
	15		Showed above officer the office work as carried on in DADOS office – Visited various QM stores, showing how the QM disposes of his stores recd from Ordnance – & arranged that the American off. should proceed with ration wagons forward – GA	
	16		Proceeded to railhead with Mr Dowell – Saw taking over of stores from truck to my lorries by my representative, & subsequent splitting up of stores at the dump previous to issuing to units. GA	
	17		Visited ADOS XV Corps – also Salvage Coy: & QM stores of 7th Seaforths – GA	
	18		Returned 120 Vigilant periscopes to SA Bgde: these were borrowed for a special purpose GA	
	19		Visited railhead. Inspected harness of 104, 105 & 106 Coys ASC GA	
	20		Visited No 14 workshops (light) ref. gun carriage for 51st Bgde RFA. Saw Staff Capt. RA. GA	

1875 Wt. W593/826 1,000,000 4/15 J.B.C. & A. A.D.S.S./Forms/C. 2118.

Army Form C. 2118

Instructions regarding War Diaries and Intelligence Summaries are contained in F. S. Regs., Part II. and the Staff Manual respectively. Title Pages will be prepared in manuscript.

WAR DIARY
or
~~INTELLIGENCE SUMMARY~~
(Erase heading not required.)

Place	Date	Hour	Summary of Events and Information	Remarks and references to Appendices
Field	July 21		Visited railhead - various Ordn. stores - Spoke of train reference economy in harness - JH	
	22		Visited advanced rear Hq. 26th Bgde. with A.A. + QMG. JH	
	23		Question of supply of hammers for cookers raised - Suggested DHQ. should put the question up to Army - JH	
	24		Purchased 17 Claw hammers through Divl. Canteen for above purpose JH	
	25		Inspected certain harness at Salvage Coy: + brought to notice of DHQ. the condition of certain pieces - This matter taken up by me with unit concerned, also by DHQ + Train Hq. JH	
	26		Inspected hot food containers sent in to Salvage - These showed rough usage by unit - This brought before notice of DHQ JH	
	27		Suggested employment of Saddler from Train Coy: for attachment to DADOS. + to receive all returned harness at my place - JH	
	28		Demanded 3" Stokes to replace one burst. 27th Bde. JH	
	29		Rect. 20 new hot food containers - also catch enough to meet all indents. JH	
	30		Conference at ADOS office. JH	
	31		Visited Salvage Dump, + railhead - Discrepancies more frequent JH	

1/7/18 [signature] Major DADOS 9 Div

1875 Wt. W593/826 1,000,000 4/15 J.B.C. & A. A.D.S.S./Forms/C. 2118.

Instructions regarding War Diaries and Intelligence Summaries are contained in F. S. Regs., Part II. and the Staff Manual respectively. Title Pages will be prepared in manuscript.

WAR DIARY
or
INTELLIGENCE SUMMARY
(Erase heading not required.)

Army Form C. 2118

VR 40

Place	Date	Hour	Summary of Events and Information	Remarks and references to Appendices
			Confidential	
			War Diary	
			D.A.D.O.S. 9th Divn	
			From 1 - 8 - 1918	
			To 31 - 8 - 1918	

1875 Wt. W593/826 1,000,000 4/15 J.B.C. & A. A.D.S.S./Forms/C. 2118.

Instructions regarding War Diaries and Intelligence Summaries are contained in F. S. Regs., Part II. and the Staff Manual respectively. Title Pages will be prepared in manuscript.

WAR DIARY
or
~~INTELLIGENCE SUMMARY~~
(Erase heading not required.)

Army Form C. 2118

Place	Date	Hour	Summary of Events and Information	Remarks and references to Appendices
Field	Aug 1st		Visited ADOS XV Corps ref: modified Bar Indicators required by RA. Took burst 3" Stokes Mortar to ADOS. GH	
	2		Received first batch of chevrons 12000. GH	
	3		Arranged with HQ Div Train for assistance of Saddlers to condition horses & saddlery returned by units. GH	
	4		Inspected Salvage Dump & visited railhead, also visited ADOS. ref: modified Bar Indicators. GH	
	5		Visited & inspected QM stores of 6th KOSB 11th & 12th Royal Scots. GH	
	6		Visited stores of 7th Seaforths, & SA Battn. Question of new clothing for latter discussed. Tendency to exceed limit of economy. GH	
	7		Visited all ASC Coys: ref. repair to wagons, & asked them to send numbers repaired during past two months. GH	
	8		Vehicle question again gone into - inspected books of Coys: GH	
	9		QM stores of 9th Scot. Rifles, & 2nd R.S. Fusiliers visited. Inspected transport. GH	
	10		Visited 8th Black Watch, interviewed new Quartermaster GH	

1875 Wt. W593/826 1,000,000 4/15 J.B.C. & A. A.D.S.S./Forms/C. 2118.

Instructions regarding War Diaries and Intelligence Summaries are contained in F. S. Regs., Part II. and the Staff Manual respectively. Title Pages will be prepared in manuscript.

WAR DIARY
or
INTELLIGENCE SUMMARY
(Erase heading not required.)

Army Form C. 2118

Place	Date	Hour	Summary of Events and Information	Remarks and references to Appendices
Field	Aug 11		Demand rec'd from M.G.Bn for 40 barrels Vickers - referred back for the proper authority - Question taken up with Corps - GH	
	12		Visited S.A.A. Section of DAC. ref paint & varnish reqd. for the making	
	13		of Vasley Smoke Bombs. GH	
	14		Received 5000 more chevrons - GH	
	15		Arranged with Corps: reference 40 barrels Vickers GH	
			Went to Calais for 200 Vigilant periscopes, & to G.P. for 40 barrels Vickers GH	
	16		Issued the periscopes above to Brigades for special tactics GH	
	17			
	18		Received 12 L.G. handcarts from Base - issued 2 to Salvage Coy	
	19		2 to Employment Coy & G.H.Q. 26th Bgde. GH	
	20		Visited Army HQ to see DDOS. GH	
	21		Discussed returned ordnance stores with DAQ - no Ordnance stores returned by units as such come in the Salvage returns. GH	
	22		Visited HQ 9th Seaforth (Pioneers) GH	

1875 Wt. W593/826 1,000,000 4/15 J.B.C. & A. A.D.S.S./Forms/C. 2118.

Army Form C. 2118

Instructions regarding War Diaries and Intelligence Summaries are contained in F. S. Regs., Part II. and the Staff Manual respectively. Title Pages will be prepared in manuscript.

WAR DIARY
or
~~INTELLIGENCE SUMMARY~~
(Erase heading not required.)

Place	Date	Hour	Summary of Events and Information	Remarks and references to Appendices
Field	Aug 23		Moved office & store to Wardrecques – Barn & outbuildings. JH	
	24		Visited R.A. H.Q: Artillery still staying in the line – DHQ moved to Wardrecques. JH	
	25		Conference of DADOS. at 15th Corps – JH	
	26		Visited S.A. Bgde: HQ. & S.A. Bns. JH	
	27		ADOS called at Dump. & inspected the place. JH	
	28		Visited 26th Brigade HQ. & 7th Seaforths, 8th Black Watch & 5th Camerons JH	
	29		Called on S.A. Brigade, now moved to Lumbres ref: Ordnance personnel to	
	30		serve the Brigade on leaving the Divn. JH	
	31		Called with DADMS. on 26th Bgde: HQ. also 27th Bgde: HQ. JH	

1/9/18

J H Byde Major
DADOS 9th Divn

1875 Wt. W593/826 1,000,000 4/15 J.B.C. & A. A.D.S.S./Forms/C. 2118.

Army Form C. 2118

Instructions regarding War Diaries and Intelligence Summaries are contained in F. S. Regs., Part II. and the Staff Manual respectively. Title Pages will be prepared in manuscript.

WAR DIARY
or
INTELLIGENCE SUMMARY
(Erase heading not required.)

VR 41

Place	Date	Hour	Summary of Events and Information	Remarks and references to Appendices
			War Diary DADOS 9th Divn From 1-9-18 To 30-9-18	

1875 Wt. W593/826 1,000,000 4/15 J.B.C. & A. A.D.S.S./Forms/C. 2118.

Instructions regarding War Diaries and Intelligence Summaries are contained in F. S. Regs., Part II. and the Staff Manual respectively. Title Pages will be prepared in manuscript.

WAR DIARY
or
~~INTELLIGENCE SUMMARY~~
(Erase heading not required.)

Army Form C. 2118

Place	Date	Hour	Summary of Events and Information	Remarks and references to Appendices
Field	Sep 1		Issued 5000 rounds S.A.A. blank to S.A. Brigade – Conference of D.A.D.O.S. at Corps. F.H.	
	2		Visited A.D.O.S. Corps –	
	3		Issued 11000 rds. S.A.A. blank to 27th Bgde: + 10,000 to S.A. Bgde. F.H.	
	4		Went on leave – Major Wright acting for me. Visits made to 27th Fld Ambce: reference heavy issues of clothing – F.H.	
	~~5~~ 5		South African Composite Bn: visited – also 2nd S.A. Regt. No. 4 Coy Train ref heavy issues of clothing – Transfer arranged of S.Sergt. Edwards & Pte. Hopgood of 1st S.A.R. for Ordnance Services. F.H.	
	6		9th Bde Inf. Coy visited also 26th Bgde H.Q. F.H.	
	7		Conference of D.A.D.O.S. postponed. F.H.	
	8		Recd orders to remove north – F.H.	
	9			
	10		Esquelbec visited for store F.H.	
	12		Moved to Esquelbec: Railhead at Watten. F.H.	
	13		Chief Clerk visited A.D.O.S. 2nd Corps F.H.	
	14		Nothing to report. F.H.	
	15		Delivered 8 Stokes 3" mortars to 28th I.A.B. 2nd Corps School also stores to 26th Bgde units. F.H.	

1875 Wt. W593/826 1,000,000 4/15 J.B.C. & A. A.D.S.S./Forms/C. 2118.

Instructions regarding War Diaries and Intelligence Summaries are contained in F. S. Regs., Part II. and the Staff Manual respectively. Title Pages will be prepared in manuscript.

WAR DIARY
or
INTELLIGENCE SUMMARY
(Erase heading not required.)

Army Form C. 2118

Place	Date	Hour	Summary of Events and Information	Remarks and references to Appendices
Field	Sep 17		Cleared 1st blanket per man from Roesbrugge Rhead & issued to units from Couthove Aerodrome. GH	
	18		Visited DADOS 14th Div ref. taking over GH	
			Fixed purchase of 1200 [illegible] for packsaddlery GH	
	19		Called on ADOS. Moved to Couthove Aerodrome. Drew 250	
	20		sets packsaddlery from Corps Troops. also emergency ammunition carriers – GH	
	21		Issued packsaddlery to Bdes also ammn carriers to [illegible] of DAC GH	
	22		Recd 2000 water bottles from Base for Bdes. asked for further 1000 – GH	
	23		Moved ordered again GH	
	24		Found site on main Poperinghe – Elverdinghe road, and arranged office accommodation at A 30 central GH	
	25		Collected 10 Stadia range finders from 50.2nd CT. GH	
	26		Nothing to report GH	

Instructions regarding War Diaries and Intelligence Summaries are contained in F. S. Regs., Part II. and the Staff Manual respectively. Title Pages will be prepared in manuscript.

Army Form C. 2118

WAR DIARY
or
INTELLIGENCE SUMMARY
(Erase heading not required.)

Place	Date	Hour	Summary of Events and Information	Remarks and references to Appendices
Field	Sep. 27		Moved store coys to A22 d. & A30 central respectively – fit.	
	28		Ypres offensive begun. Camp bombed at night – fit.	
	29		No demands rec^d for machine guns – unusual after battle.	
	30		Pte. Phillips attached from 61st Lab. Coy. for instruction in rifle repairs returned to unit.	
			[illegible] Major D.A.D.O.S. 9 D. 2/10/18	

1875 Wt. W593/826 1,000,000 4/15 J.B.C. & A. A.D.S.S./Forms/C. 2118.

Instructions regarding War Diaries and Intelligence Summaries are contained in F. S. Regs., Part II. and the Staff Manual respectively. Title Pages will be prepared in manuscript.

WAR DIARY
or
INTELLIGENCE SUMMARY
(Erase heading not required.)

Army Form C. 2118

Confidential

Vol 42

Place	Date	Hour	Summary of Events and Information	Remarks and references to Appendices
			War Diary – D.A.D.O.S. 9th Division From 1 - 10 - 18 To 31 - 10 - 18.	

1875 Wt. W593/826 1,000,000 4/15 J.B.C. & A. A.D.S.S./Forms/C. 2118.

Instructions regarding War Diaries and Intelligence Summaries are contained in F. S. Regs., Part II. and the Staff Manual respectively. Title Pages will be prepared in manuscript.

WAR DIARY
or
INTELLIGENCE SUMMARY
(Erase heading not required.)

Army Form C. 2118

Place	Date	Hour	Summary of Events and Information	Remarks and references to Appendices
Field	1/10/18		Arranged to remove office + store to further forward area - Looked for a forward site N.E. Ypres. JH	
	2		moved to near new railhead at St Jean. Sent lorry to Calais for harness &c: JH	
	3		ADOS called - Walked to new DHQ at Broodseinde east of Zonnebeke - Roads bad - Recd demand for 9 Lewis Guns for 2nd Royal Scot Fus. JH	
	4		Had to issue stores by ration wagons owing to state of roads JH	
	5		Walked again DHQ. ASC continue to issue battle stores in lieu of sundry by lorries. JH	
	6		Issued 100 prs. socks to each Battalion. JH	
	7		Nothing in particular to report JH	
	8		Visited DHQ and 9th Machine Gun Co. Also transport lines of 26th + 27th Bgdes: JH	
	9		26th Bgde. come out to rest for 2 days. Inspected all Qm. stores of Bgde, + arranged for requirements to be met. JH	
	10		Issued drawers woollen vests: to all units. JH	
	11		27th Bgde: come out to rest. Inspected all QM stores and arranged for immediate needs to be met JH	

1875 Wt. W593/826 1,000,000 4/15 J.B.C. & A. A.D.S.S./Forms/C. 2118.

Instructions regarding War Diaries and Intelligence Summaries are contained in F. S. Regs., Part II. and the Staff Manual respectively. Title Pages will be prepared in manuscript.

Army Form C. 2118

WAR DIARY
or
INTELLIGENCE SUMMARY
(Erase heading not required.)

Place	Date	Hour	Summary of Events and Information	Remarks and references to Appendices
Field	12th	–	Nothing to report. [initials]	
	13		Issued leather jerkins to 27th & 28th Bgdes: [initials]	
	14		Moved office to Broodseinde east of Zonnebeke. [initials]	
	15		Prospected new area, Menin–Roulers Road for site for office & camp – [initials]	
	16		Moved store from St Jean, & office to Lord Farm on Menin–Roulers Road. [initials]	
	17		Owing to operations units decline all stores – [initials]	
	18		DHQ moved to near Wakkel St Eloi. [initials]	
	19		Issued leather jerkins to 26th Bgde: [initials]	
	20		Nothing to report. [initials]	
	21		Units leave various dumps behind – inspected as many as possible – Issued two guns Lewis to 8th B.W. by 105 Coy. ASC. [initials]	
	22		Was able to issue stores to 27th & 28th Bgdes: 26th could take nothing – My lorries hindered by shelling of road near Ravebeke. [initials]	
	23		Moved Office & Store to Stokerij. Inspected stores dumped by units in huts nr. Wakkel St Eloi – Discussed transport difficulties with DAQMG. [initials]	

1875 Wt. W593/826 1,000,000 4/15 J.B.C. & A. A.D.S.S./Forms/C. 2118.

Army Form C. 2118

Instructions regarding War Diaries and Intelligence Summaries are contained in F. S. Regs., Part II. and the Staff Manual respectively. Title Pages will be prepared in manuscript.

WAR DIARY
or
INTELLIGENCE SUMMARY
(Erase heading not required.)

Place	Date	Hour	Summary of Events and Information	Remarks and references to Appendices
Field	24th		Visited SAA Section, and 9th M.Gun Bn ref: question of limbers &c. demanded by the latter. — J.A.	
	25		D.H.Q. moved to Harlebeke. — J.A.	
	26		Asked D.H.Q. for return to Division of Salvage personnel taken by Corps. Staff unable to cope with salvaged stores. — J.A.	
	27		Dispatched about 15 tons of salvaged stores to railhead. — J.A.	
	28		Went with D.A.Q.M.G. to Wounded St. Eloi, to again inspect & decide what surplus stores that could be returned to Base. — J.A.	
	29		Visited railhead – ref pontoons for Field Coy. & arranged trucks for Salvage. — J.A.	
	30		Section of Salvage Coy: joined me for duty. — J.A.	
	31		Visited M.Gun. Battn ref: limbers &c. — J.A.	

2/11/18 [signature] Major
D.A.D.O.S. 9th Div.

1875 Wt. W593/826 1,000,000 4/15 J.B.C. & A. A.D.S.S./Forms/C. 2118.

Instructions regarding War Diaries and Intelligence Summaries are contained in F. S. Regs., Part II. and the Staff Manual respectively. Title Pages will be prepared in manuscript.

WAR DIARY
or
INTELLIGENCE SUMMARY
(Erase heading not required.)

Army Form C. 2118

VII 42

Place	Date	Hour	Summary of Events and Information	Remarks and references to Appendices
			Confidential War Diary DADOS 9th Div From 1. 11 16 To 30. 11 17	

1875 Wt. W593/826 1,000,000 4/15 J.B.C. & A. A.D.S.S./Forms/C. 2118.

Instructions regarding War Diaries and Intelligence Summaries are contained in F. S. Regs., Part II. and the Staff Manual respectively. Title Pages will be prepared in manuscript.

WAR DIARY
or
INTELLIGENCE SUMMARY
(Erase heading not required.)

Army Form C. 2118

Place	Date	Hour	Summary of Events and Information	Remarks and references to Appendices
Field	Nov 1		Visited units of 26th Bgde: at Lendelede - GH	
	2		Visited railhead at Heule and SAA Sect. ref L.G.S. wagon - GH	
	3		Further supplies of winter clothing arrived - GH	
	4 5		9th Divn inspected by King of Belgians who presented decorations. Visited railhead ref: returned salvage - GH	
	6		Section of Salvage Coy: joined - Heavy receipts of salvage - Lorries and staff fully engaged at unloading. GH	
	7		Estimate 30 tons of salvage returned during past few days to the railhead sorted and labelled. GH	
	8		Question of abandoned water-cart taken up with RA. GH	
	9		Visited ADOS. 2nd Corps. GH	
	10			
	11		Armistice signed - GH	
	12		Visited M.G. Coy ref limbers, also SAA Sectn on same business GH	
	13		Visited QM stores of units of 27th Bgde. GH	

1875 Wt. W593/826 1,000,000 4/15 J.B.C. & A. A.D.S.S./Forms/C. 2118.

Instructions regarding War Diaries and Intelligence Summaries are contained in F. S. Regs., Part II. and the Staff Manual respectively. Title Pages will be prepared in manuscript.

WAR DIARY
or
INTELLIGENCE SUMMARY
(Erase heading not required.)

Army Form C. 2118

Place	Date	Hour	Summary of Events and Information	Remarks and references to Appendices
Field	Nov. 14		Visited railhead – Heule – [illegible]	
	15		Collected Lewis guns and trench mortars dumped by units prior to advance at various points in area and placed in central dumps. [illegible]	
	16		Moved to Renaix – Collected 1000 blankets from Corps Dump Harlebeke. Issued picketing gear etc [illegible]	
	17		Visited 26th Bgde and ASC units. [illegible]	
	18		Visited 27th + 28th Brigades and ASC Coys. [illegible]	
	19		Moved to Nederbrakel – Sent lorries to railhead, about 50 kilometres away – Went to Menin to see Reception Camp, arranged for 1000 blankets to be issued by 19th Corps – [illegible]	
	20		Moved to Grammont – Arranged for trucks at railhead [illegible]	
	21		Moved to Hal [illegible]	
	22		Entry of King of Belgians into Brussels. One composite Batt. took part in procession. Lorries arrived from r'head with various stores – [illegible]	
	23		Moved to Mont St Jean, nr Waterloo. [illegible]	

1875 Wt. W593/826 1,000,000 4/15 J.B.C. & A. A.D.S.S./Forms/C. 2118.

WAR DIARY
or
INTELLIGENCE SUMMARY
(Erase heading not required.)

Army Form C. 2118

Instructions regarding War Diaries and Intelligence Summaries are contained in F. S. Regs., Part II. and the Staff Manual respectively. Title Pages will be prepared in manuscript.

Place	Date	Hour	Summary of Events and Information	Remarks and references to Appendices
Field	Nov 24		Made issues of horseshoes boots and clothing to all troops – 8H	
	25		moved to Wavre area – Trouble with tyres for lorry 8H	
	26		moved to Bourdinne area 8H	
	27		Went to Namur to take over clothing &c: for Repat.d P of W. No trucks arrived – left 1 WO. & Staff Sergt. 8H	
	28		moved to Ampsin – went Namur again – Still no truck 8H	
	29		moved to Flemalle Grande –	
	30		R Head moved to Ayen – moved to Verviers.	

[illegible] Major
DADOS 9 Div
3/12/18

Army Form C. 2118

Instructions regarding War Diaries and Intelligence Summaries are contained in F. S. Regs., Part II. and the Staff Manual respectively. Title Pages will be prepared in manuscript.

WAR DIARY
or
INTELLIGENCE SUMMARY
(Erase heading not required.)

VOL 4

Place	Date	Hour	Summary of Events and Information	Remarks and references to Appendices
			Confidential War Diary – D.A.D.O.S. 9th Div. from 1st Decr 1918 to 31st " "	

1875 Wt. W593/826 1,000,000 4/15 J.B.C. & A. A.D.S.S./Forms/C. 2118.

Instructions regarding War Diaries and Intelligence Summaries are contained in F. S. Regs., Part II. and the Staff Manual respectively. Title Pages will be prepared in manuscript.

WAR DIARY
or
INTELLIGENCE SUMMARY
(Erase heading not required.)

Army Form C. 2118

Place	Date	Hour	Summary of Events and Information	Remarks and references to Appendices
Field	1/12/18		Remain at Verviers [initials]	
	2		Visited railhead (Pepinster), also HQ 26th + 27th Brigades to whom I issued maps – [initials]	
	3 4	}	Still at Verviers, entrucked to the Rhine – made issues of horse shoes & frost cogs – [initials]	
	5		Moved to Duren, distance of 35 Kilometres, & crossed frontier – [initials]	
	6 7		Vehicles arrived Duren & head for M.G. Coy, 7th Seaforths and 9th Scottish Rifles – [initials]	
	8		Visited 28th Bgde: at Cologne – [initials]	
	9		Arrived at Cologne & arranged for store & office, & 7 addit'l lorries to bring stores from Duren	
	10		Informed units issues will be made tomorrow & split up all stores in anticipation – [initials]	
	11		About 50 tons of stores issued to units, chiefly boots [initials]	
	12		Further truck of boots arrived – 1st pairs fitted from truck – [initials]	

1875 Wt. W593/826 1,000,000 4/15 J.B.C. & A. A.D.S.S./Forms/C. 2118.

Army Form C. 2118

Instructions regarding War Diaries and Intelligence Summaries are contained in F. S. Regs., Part II. and the Staff Manual respectively. Title Pages will be prepared in manuscript.

WAR DIARY
or
~~INTELLIGENCE SUMMARY~~
(Erase heading not required.)

Place	Date	Hour	Summary of Events and Information	Remarks and references to Appendices
Field	Dec. 13/18		The Division, inspected by Corps Commander crossed the Rhine. JH	
	14		Proceeded to Ohligs to arrange office & stores near railhead – Visited railhead & nos 105 & 107 Coys ASC. JH	
	15		Moved stores & office to Ohligs – Visited 26th Bgde: HQ at SOLINGEN & train Coy with OC Train. 7 tons stores advised & vehicles – JH	
	16		Railhead at Opladen – visited there JH	
	17			
	18		Truck horseshoes dispatched from Base 12th not yet arrived JH	
	19		Visited batteries of 28th A.F.A. Bgde: Soap needed. Also visited B.H.Q. of R.F.A. Bgde & 107 Coy ASC JH	
	20		Proceeded railhead Opladen – Drawers woollen & vests recd. JH	
	21		Shortage of nosebags for ASC Coys reported. The large size seems to be the difficulty in supply from Base. JH	
	22		Wired Base respecting truck of horseshoes dispatched 12th JH	
	23		ADOS called – 1 truck in – JH	
	24		Visited SAA Sec: DAC ref: limbered GS wagons drawn from railhead at Poperinghe JH	

1875 Wt. W593/826 1,000,000 4/15 J.B.C. & A. A.D.S.S./Forms/C. 2118.

Instructions regarding War Diaries and Intelligence Summaries are contained in F. S. Regs., Part II. and the Staff Manual respectively. Title Pages will be prepared in manuscript.

WAR DIARY

or

~~INTELLIGENCE SUMMARY~~

(Erase heading not required.)

Army Form C. 2118

Place	Date	Hour	Summary of Events and Information	Remarks and references to Appendices
Ohligs	Dec 25–26		Three trucks arrived, one of which was considerably overdue and should have arrived on 18th inst – [initials]	
	27			
	28		Visited units of 27th Bgde: also 9th Scottish Rifles – [initials]	
	29		Provided medal ribbons for presentation by Corps Commander – [initials]	
	30		Visited Army + Corps HQ. [initials]	
	31		Two W.O's mentioned in dispatches – Sub.C. Rolfe + S.Cr. Thornton [initials]	

[signature] Major
DADOS 9th Dn
3/1/19

1875 Wt. W593/826 1,000,000 4/15 J.B.C. & A. A.D.S.S./Forms/C. 2118.

9

Instructions regarding War Diaries and Intelligence Summaries are contained in F. S. Regs., Part II. and the Staff Manual respectively. Title Pages will be prepared in manuscript.

WAR DIARY
or
INTELLIGENCE SUMMARY
(Erase heading not required.)

Army Form C. 2118

VR 45

1448

Confidential

Place	Date	Hour	Summary of Events and Information	Remarks and references to Appendices
			War Diary — DADOS 9th Divn From 1st Jany 1919 To 31st " "	

1875 Wt. W593/826 1,000,000 4/15 J.B.C. & A. A.D.S.S./Forms/C. 2118.

Army Form C. 2118

Instructions regarding War Diaries and Intelligence Summaries are contained in F. S. Regs., Part II. and the Staff Manual respectively. Title Pages will be prepared in manuscript.

WAR DIARY
or
INTELLIGENCE SUMMARY
(Erase heading not required.)

Place	Date	Hour	Summary of Events and Information	Remarks and references to Appendices
Ohligs Germany	January 1st		New Years Day. Visited railhead. – JH	
	2		Inspected 2nd stores of units of 27th Brigade. – JH	
	3		Visited with O.C. 9th Train, 7th Seaforths, + 105 Coy. A.S.C. JH	
	4		Visited H.Q. 8th Black Watch ref boots – Some sizes chiefly 7's + 8's are not coming up well from Base. – JH	
	5		Part of 27th Field Ambulance moved to another part of Germany for duty. – JH	
	6		Visited 8th Black Watch – issued boots to them also kilts which were wanted badly. – JH	
	7		Issued more boots to 8th Black Watch – Inspected clothing of battalion. – JH	
	8		Visited all three Companies of A.S.C. ref shortage of nosebags – Large size of which very short from Base matter put up to Corps. – JH	
	9		Nothing to report. – JH	

1875 Wt. W593/826 1,000,000 4/15 J.B.C. & A. A.D.S.S./Forms/C. 2118.

Instructions regarding War Diaries and Intelligence Summaries are contained in F. S. Regs., Part II. and the Staff Manual respectively. Title Pages will be prepared in manuscript.

WAR DIARY
or
INTELLIGENCE SUMMARY
(Erase heading not required.)

Army Form C. 2118

Place	Date	Hour	Summary of Events and Information	Remarks and references to Appendices
Ohligs-Germany	Jany 10		Shortages frequent at railhead from Base - Boots in particular - Bales tampered with in some cases. [initials]	
	11		Royal Newfoundland Regt which joined the Divn last autumn is reported leaving the Divn. [initials]	
	12		Visited HQ. RAA. Sec DAC and 9th Scottish Rifls. Inspected Harness at small arm Sect. [initials]	
	13		Nothing to report. [initials]	
	14		Visited ADOS. 2nd Corps. [initials]	
	15		Away on leave.	
	16			
	31			
			3/2/19 [illegible] Major DADOS 9th Divn	

1875 Wt. W593/826 1,000,000 4/15 J.B.C. & A. A.D.S.S./Forms/C. 2118.

Instructions regarding War Diaries and Intelligence Summaries are contained in F. S. Regs., Part II. and the Staff Manual respectively. Title Pages will be prepared in manuscript.

WAR DIARY
or
INTELLIGENCE SUMMARY
(Erase heading not required.)

Army Form C. 2118

Vol 46

Confidential

Place	Date	Hour	Summary of Events and Information	Remarks and references to Appendices
			War Diary – D.A.D.O.S. 9th Divn From 1 – 2 – 19 To 28th – 2 – 19	

1875 Wt. W593/826 1,000,000 4/15 J.B.C. & A. A.D.S.S./Forms/C. 2118.

Army Form C. 2118

WAR DIARY
or
INTELLIGENCE SUMMARY
(Erase heading not required.)

Instructions regarding War Diaries and Intelligence Summaries are contained in F. S. Regs., Part II. and the Staff Manual respectively. Title Pages will be prepared in manuscript.

Place	Date	Hour	Summary of Events and Information	Remarks and references to Appendices
	Feb 1919			
Ohligs Germany	1		Arrived back from leave. Went through papers.	
	2		ADOS called ref supplies of clothing & boots to the Divn generally	
	3		Asked to prepare statement of all bulk stores outstanding from Base.	
	4		Interviewed GOC Divn ref recent shortages.	
	5		Submitted above statement to DHQ.	
	6		Visited ADOS 2nd Corps with DAQMG ref requisitioning of stores for Div'l Hostel at Cologne – ADOS asked me to requisition locally	
			Visited 2nd Army HQ ref: questions of demobilization	
	7		Visited 26th Bde HQ Requisitioned brooms for 7th Seaforths	
	8		Lecture for inspection of horses duty of ADVS.	
	9		Visited HQ 8th Black Watch ref: clothing & boots	
	10		Inspected 106th Bde harness – nosebags required –	
	11		Went to Army HQ on questions of demobn. ADOS called whilst I was out.	
	12		Recd most of stores requisitioned for Cologne Hostel. Visited 9 MT Coy ref clothing question.	

1875 Wt. W593/826 1,000,000 4/15 J.B.C. & A. A.D.S.S./Forms/C. 2118.

Instructions regarding War Diaries and Intelligence Summaries are contained in F. S. Regs., Part II. and the Staff Manual respectively. Title Pages will be prepared in manuscript.

WAR DIARY
or
INTELLIGENCE SUMMARY
(Erase heading not required.)

Army Form C. 2118

Place	Date	Hour	Summary of Events and Information	Remarks and references to Appendices
Ohligs Germany	Feb 13		Replied at length to D.A.D.O.S. ref. shortages in stores – to questions raised by DADMG [illegible] Corps –	
	14		Sent to Cologne [illegible] 6 bicycles from the Yorks. Hussars – [illegible]	
	15		Went to H.Q. 28th A.F.A. Bgde: with DAQMG.	
	16		Recommended Gunner [illegible] 17th Bgde. RFA. for gallantry in stopping pair of runaway horses in town – Lt [illegible] called. [illegible]	
	17		ADOS called ref 28th A.F.A. Bgde: Went through figures to: Looked at site for S.Cs. [illegible]	
	18			
	19		Visited 1st Bty 28th AFA. Bgde. with C.O. Compared of indents Up to date with bulk – Some detail still o/s. [illegible] [illegible] – [illegible]	
	20		Visited [illegible] 9th Seaforths. ref. return of [illegible] also 8th Black Watch at Solingen – [illegible]	
	21		Arranged place for S.Cs. opposite to [illegible]	[illegible]

1875 Wt. W593/826 1,000,000 4/15 J.B.C. & A. A.D.S.S./Forms/C. 2118.

Instructions regarding War Diaries and Intelligence Summaries are contained in F. S. Regs., Part II. and the Staff Manual respectively. Title Pages will be prepared in manuscript.

WAR DIARY
or
INTELLIGENCE SUMMARY
(Erase heading not required.)

Army Form C. 2118

Place	Date Feb	Hour	Summary of Events and Information	Remarks and references to Appendices
[illegible] Germany	22		Called on Armourers of 9th Scottish Rifles, 11th Royal Scots, 12th Royal Scots, ref: [illegible] [illegible]. Only one [illegible] (11th R.S.) willing to volunteer. [illegible]	
	23 24		Staff Capt. R.A. called with list of "outstanding" [illegible]. List quite inaccurate. Consider that the [illegible] not being provided with Quartermaster is a source of trouble to the Btty. & to the A.O.D. Records are badly kept in almost every case in the battys. [illegible]	
	25		A.D.O.S. called & interviewed Pte Bilton ref. [illegible] [illegible] for demobilization. [illegible]	
	26		Visited A.D.O.S. [illegible] Corps. New Base at Cologne. Also [illegible] N.Z. divn. for special store. [illegible] Drew further stores from N.Z. Divn.	
	27 28		Visited HQ 26th Bde: Seaforths & [illegible] Camerons. [illegible]	

[illegible] Major
D.A.D.O.S. 9th Dn.

1875 Wt. W593/826 1,000,000 4/15 J.B.C. & A. A.D.S.S./Forms/C. 2118.

Army Form C. 2118.

Instructions regarding War Diaries and Intelligence Summaries are contained in F. S. Regs., Part II. and the Staff Manual respectively. Title pages will be prepared in manuscript.

WAR DIARY
or
INTELLIGENCE SUMMARY.
(Erase heading not required.)

Place	Date	Hour	Summary of Events and Information	Remarks and references to Appendices
			Confidential Vol 47 War Diary – DADOS Lowland Divn – From 1 March 1919 To 31 "	

A5834 Wt. W4973/M687 750,000 8/16 D. D. & L. Ltd. Forms/C.2118/13.

Instructions regarding War Diaries and Intelligence Summaries are contained in F. S. Regs., Part II. and the Staff Manual respectively. Title pages will be prepared in manuscript.

WAR DIARY
or
INTELLIGENCE SUMMARY.
(Erase heading not required.)

Army Form C. 2118.

Place	Date	Hour	Summary of Events and Information	Remarks and references to Appendices
[illegible] Germany	Mar. 1		Went with Staff Capt. RA. to HQ 2nd A.F.A. Bde: ref [illegible]. Visited COs and QMs of incoming units 1/4 R.S.F. 15th & 16th H.L.I. The latter badly off for clothing – [illegible]	
	2		6 pairs Binoculars reported missing from truck vouchered for [illegible] Div Signals – being the 2nd consignment for this unit which has been pilfered – Taking matter up with Corps – [illegible]	
	3		Visited 1/5 K.O.S.B. newly joined Division – Complete in Mob. [illegible] [illegible] needed – otherwise well off for clothing [illegible] generally [illegible]	
	4		Scrutiny of indents of 1/5 KOSB. The [illegible] and [illegible] came in for information – [illegible]	
	5		Visited 90th Field Co. R.E. also 1/4 Adjutant [illegible] – [illegible] clothing needed for the [illegible] [illegible]	
	6		Complaint from C.R.E. ref [illegible] said to be unserviceable [illegible] when issued – [illegible]	
	7		M.G. Bn said to be moving from [illegible] to [illegible] [illegible]	
	8		A.D.O.S. lectured to RA on Ordnance matters – large attendance [illegible]	

A5834 Wt. W4973/M687 750,000 8/16 D. D. & L. Ltd. Forms/C.2118/13.

Instructions regarding War Diaries and Intelligence Summaries are contained in F. S. Regs., Part II. and the Staff Manual respectively. Title pages will be prepared in manuscript.

WAR DIARY
or
INTELLIGENCE SUMMARY.
(*Erase heading not required.*)

Army Form C. 2118.

Place	Date	Hour	Summary of Events and Information	Remarks and references to Appendices
Ohligs	Mar 9		Nothing to report. [initials]	
	10		Dispatched ambulance vehicles from [illegible] – Reported on defect in harness to 2nd Corps. [initials]	
	11		Again visited 1/4 RSF ref. clothing – also 28th AFA Bde HQ.	
			Recd indents from all RA battys. for 50 jackets SD. [initials]	
	12		Visited CRA ref: 28th AFA Bde. [initials]	
	13		Nothing to report. [initials]	
			Issued 50 SD jackets to each batty. RFA. [initials]	
	14		Visited HQ. 5/6 RS joined the Div: newly – also 1/5 KOSB. [initials]	
	15			
	16		Attended lecture by AA & QMG on duties of Courts martial officers. [initials]	
	17			
	18		GOC left Division. Visited ADOS 2nd Corps. [initials]	
	19		Requisitioned 1 ton steel bars for making of mule shoes. [initials]	
	20		Visited 1/5 KOSB at Solingen: also 1/4 RSF Div. Stores.	
	21			
	22		Steel bars for making mule shoes received – issue to be made tomorrow. [initials]	
	23		Inspected equipment & [illegible] of 7th Seaforths & 28th AFA Bde leaving as Cadre unit for UK. [initials]	

A5834 Wt. W4973/M687 750,000 8/16 D. D. & L. Ltd. Forms/C.2118/13.

Instructions regarding War Diaries and Intelligence Summaries are contained in F. S. Regs., Part II. and the Staff Manual respectively. Title pages will be prepared in manuscript.

WAR DIARY
or
INTELLIGENCE SUMMARY.
(Erase heading not required.)

Army Form C. 2118.

Place	Date	Hour	Summary of Events and Information	Remarks and references to Appendices
Ohligs	Mar 23		[illegible] W.O. To visit Div. inspect list of 57 [illegible] newly arrived from England – gave complete instructions re [illegible] etc. [illegible]	
	24 25 26		Visited 5/6 Royal Scots: and all Armourers in the Division referring to [illegible] on [illegible] of [illegible] – [illegible]	
	27		Visited ADOS 2nd Corps: ref. various questions – [illegible]	
	28		Held conference at HQ 28th Arty. Bde. ref. 1/3 reduction of existing Mob Tables on being reduced to Cadre & going home as 4 gun batty. [illegible]	
	29		Inspected Mob. Tables of all Battys: & B.H.Q. of 128 [illegible] Bgde. [illegible]	
	30 31		ADOS called: & inspected stores &	

[illegible] Major
DADOS Lowland Div.

2/4/19

A5834 Wt. W4973/M687 750,000 8/16 D. D. & L. Ltd. Forms/C.2118/13.

DADOS Lowland Div

Army Form C. 2118.

Instructions regarding War Diaries and Intelligence Summaries are contained in F. S. Regs., Part II. and the Staff Manual respectively. Title pages will be prepared in manuscript.

WAR DIARY
or
~~INTELLIGENCE SUMMARY.~~

(Erase heading not required.)

Vol 48

Place	Date	Hour	Summary of Events and Information	Remarks and references to Appendices
OHLIGS Germany	April 1		Visited BAC 28th AFA Brigade – 2nd Royal Scots Fus: and 1/14 London Scottish. Inspected 2nd Stores – Visited 51st HLI with DAQMG. FH	
	2		Arranged to take over various stores left by London Scottish for re-issue FH	
	3		2nd Royal Scots Fus: and 12th Royal Scots ~~[illegible]~~ left for UK. FH	
	4		Made issues of Grindery, bicycles & parts from Armourers Shop to 51st HLI. FH	
	5		Visited HQ 126 AFA Brigade attached for Ordnance services to this Division from ~~[illegible]~~ London Divn temporarily – FH	
	6		Sunday	
	7		Received 27 Tons of stores from Base – 1/14 London Scottish left Dn for UK. FH	
	8		Visited 51st HLI. and interviewed CO. also visited 1/5 KOSB. FH	
	9		Inspected Companies of 1/8 Scottish Rifles & found newly arrived drafts badly clothed – Instructed QM. to put in indents for requirements without delay – FH	
	10		Sent stores to 16th HLI. at Mülheim – Submitted list of training stores required to Corps – FH	
	11		ADOS & DADOS NZ Dn called – Went round Brigades ref: stores – Clothing required by 3 Brigade – Supplied 300 jackets trousers & puttees to 1/8 Scot Rif. FH	
	12		Interviewed GOC. with ADOS, & DADOS NZ Divn – Spoke GOC RA ref Soap for cleaning harness FH	
	13		Sunday –	

A5834 Wt. W4973/M687 750,000 8/16 D. D. & L. Ltd. Forms/C.2118/13.

Army Form C. 2118.

*Instructions regarding War Diaries and Intelligence Summaries are contained in F. S. Regs., Part II. and the Staff Manual respectively. Title pages will be prepared in manuscript.

WAR DIARY
or
~~INTELLIGENCE SUMMARY.~~

(Erase heading not required.)

Place	Date	Hour	Summary of Events and Information	Remarks and references to Appendices
OHLIGS Germany	April 14		Visited 51st H.L.I. ref: harness - also 105 A.S.C. who were repairing same - 1/8 Scottish Rifles inspected vehicles & harness. JH	
	15		Nothing to report JH	
	16		Dados No 2 Divn came to take over - JH	
	17		Visited OC 51st HLI with reference to condition of transport in his unit and arranged to have it attended to. Took over Imprest a/c G 127.	
	18		Ordinary Routine.	
	19		Visited 1/8 Scottish Rifles and inspected vehicles of this unit made arrangements to exchange some of these. Saw OC 1/5 K.O.S.B. re equipment, also 1/4 Royal Scots Fusiliers.	
	20		Nothing to report.	
	21		" " "	
	22		Visited OC 11th Royal Scots inspected harness & vehicles and arranged for material for repair	

A5834 Wt. W4973/M687 750,000 8/16 D. D. & L. Ltd. Forms/C.2118/13.

Army Form C. 2118.

Instructions regarding War Diaries and Intelligence Summaries are contained in F. S. Regs., Part II. and the Staff Manual respectively. Title pages will be prepared in manuscript.

WAR DIARY
or
INTELLIGENCE SUMMARY.
(Erase heading not required.)

Place	Date	Hour	Summary of Events and Information	Remarks and references to Appendices
Ohligs Germany	23		Inspected equipment of 28th A.F.A ~~No~~ Signal Sub Section signed M.S.T. of this unit which is going Home as Cadre	
	24		Ordinary Routine	
	25		" "	
	26		" "	
	27		Visited O/C 6 K.O.S.B. in regard to his equipment everything in good order	
	28		Visited O/C 1/8 Scottish Rifles who has just exchanged his vehicles and harness at NZ D.C.S. everything satisfactory	
	29		Ordinary Routine	
	30		" "	

A5834 Wt. W4973/M687 750,000 8/16 D. D. & L. Ltd. Forms/C.2118/13.

9TH DIVISION

ASST DIR. VETY SERVICES

MAY 1915 - ~~DEC 1918~~ 1919 OCT

WAR
DIARY

A. D. V. S.

9th DIVISION

MAY 1915

Nil
M.T.
23.8.15

121/5573

A.D.V.S. 9th Division

Vol I, ~~II~~ 9 — 27.5.15 — ~~28.6.15~~

Army Form C. 2118.

Instructions regarding War Diaries and Intelligence Summaries are contained in F. S. Regs., Part II. and the Staff Manual respectively. Title pages will be prepared in manuscript.

WAR DIARY
or
INTELLIGENCE SUMMARY.
(Erase heading not required.)

Hour, Date, Place	Summary of Events and Information	Remarks and references to Appendices
1915		
10-30 A.M. 9th May Borden	Entrained for Southampton	
1 P.M. " Southampton	Embarked for Overseas	
7 A.M. 10th Le Havre	Disembarked + Halted for the day	
9-30 P.M. " "	Entrained	
10 P.M. 11th Arques	Disentrained + billetted in Arques Area	
2-30 P.M. 16th "	Marched to Le Neippe + billetted for the night	
5-30 A.M. 17th Le Neippe	Marched to Neippe + billetted in that area	
2 P.M. " Neippe		
23rd "	Cameron Highlanders 26th Infy Bde. shoeing unsatisfactory, action taken	
27th	Divisional Ammunition Col. a large number of Mules unshod + shoeing on the whole unsatisfactory, due to Shortage of Shoeing Smiths and men shown on paper as Farrier Sergts + shoeing smiths who are practically untrained. Action taken	
	A.D.V.S. experiences difficulty in the execution of his various Duties for want of Small 2 Seated Motor Car authorised for A.D.V.S., division being extended over a large Area.	

H d G
9th (Scottish) Divn
3/5/15

[illegible] Capt A.V.C.
A.D.V.S.
9th (Scottish) Divn

(73989) W4141—463. 400,000. 9/14. H.&J.Ltd. Forms/C. 2118/10.

WAR
DIARY

A. D. V. S.

9th DIVISION

JUNE 1915

A.D.M.S. 9th Div.
Vol: 2

121
7761

June 15.

AUD

Instructions regarding War Diaries and Intelligence Summaries are contained in F. S. Regs., Part II. and the Staff Manual respectively. Title pages will be prepared in manuscript.

WAR DIARY
or
INTELLIGENCE SUMMARY.
(Erase heading not required.)

Army Form C. 2118.

Hour, Date, Place	Summary of Events and Information	Remarks and references to Appendices
June. 4th 1915.	Weekly conference of Vety Officers	[illegible]
" 5.	Left Nieppe about 4 p.m. for Busnes arrived midnight.	[illegible]
" 7	D.D.V.S. called inspected Office and 21st Mobile Vety Section of this Divn.	[illegible]
" 11.	Weekly conference of Vety Officers	[illegible]
" 16	Standing to. for quick move.	[illegible]
" 18.	Weekly conference of Vety Officers	[illegible]
" 20.	D.D.V.S. at this Office again paid visit to Mobile Vety Section	[illegible]
" 25.	Weekly conference of Vety Officers Left Busnes about 2 p.m. for Lillers arrived about 3 p.m. to opened new Office.	[illegible]
" 27	again standing to for move.	[illegible]
" 28.	Left Lillers for Locon about 10 a.m. arrived Midday	[illegible]

[illegible] Capt
A.D.V.S. [illegible]
1/7/15

(73989) W4141—463. 400,000. 9/14. H.&J.Ltd. Forms/C. 2118/10.

Army Form C. 2118.

Instructions regarding War Diaries and Intelligence Summaries are contained in F. S. Regs., Part II. and the Staff Manual respectively. Title pages will be prepared in manuscript.

WAR DIARY
or
INTELLIGENCE SUMMARY.
(Erase heading not required.)

Hour, Date, Place	Summary of Events and Information	Remarks and references to Appendices
4 P.M. 5/6/15 Nieppe	left for new area	
12 P.M. " Busnes	arrived	
Mid-day 8/6/15 "	Inspected by D.D.V.S. 1st Army who also inspected No 21 Mobile Veterinary Section of the Division	
2-30 P.M. 10/6/15 "	Conference of Veterinary Officers in A.D.V.S. Office. Decided to have weekly Conference of Veterinary Officers of the Division every Friday morning at eleven o'clock.	
15/6/15 until 18/6/15 "	Standing to, ready to move with short notice " " "	
19/6/15 "	Resumed usual Routine	
2 P.M. 25/6/15 "	left for new area	
3 P.M. 25/6/15 Lilliers	arrived	
10 A.M. 28/6/15 "	Inspected Horses at Mobile Veterinary Section for despatch to Base Veterinary Hospital, including 2 Suspicious Cases of Mange	
2 P.M. "	left for new area.	
4 P.M. " Locon	arrived	

1/7/15

[illegible] Capt AVC
A.D.V.S. 9th (Scottish) Divn

(73989) W4141—463. 400,000. 9/14. H.&J.Ltd. Forms/C. 2118/10.

WAR DIARY

A. D. V. S.

9th DIVISION

JULY 1915

9th Division

181/6250

Headquarters 9th Division
A.D.V.S.

Vol III

1 - 26 - 4 - 15

Incl

Instructions regarding War Diaries and Intelligence Summaries are contained in F. S. Regs., Part II. and the Staff Manual respectively. Title pages will be prepared in manuscript.

WAR DIARY
or
INTELLIGENCE SUMMARY.
(Erase heading not required.)

Army Form C. 2118.

Hour, Date, Place	Summary of Events and Information	Remarks and references to Appendices
1st July Locon to 21st July "	Usual Routine	
22nd July "	One suspicious Case of Mange belonging to D/Bty 50th Bde. R.F.A. evacuated to L.S.[illegible] C. Microscopic examination of skin scrapings were made with negative Results. Usual precautionary measures taken.	
25th July Locon	Practical demonstration of the intra dermal palpebral mallenisation of horses by Lt Hobday A.V.C.	
26th July Locon	Horses of 53rd Bde R.F.A. falling off in condition due to want of supervision + bad stable management. Action taken.	

1/8/15

[illegible] Major AVC
A.D.V.S. 9th (Scottish) Divn

(73989) W4141—463. 400,000. 9/14. H.&J.Ltd. Forms/C. 2118/10.

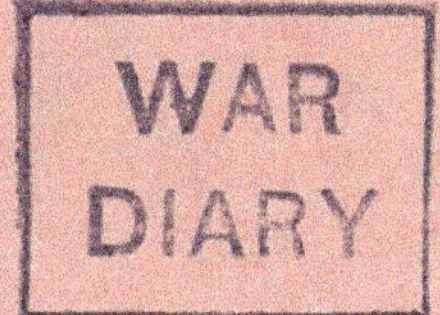

A. D. V. S.

9th DIVISION

AUGUST SEPTEMBER OCTOBER

1915

9th Division

121/7598

H.Q. 9th Division A.D.V.S.

Vols 4, 5, 6

Aug Sept & Oct. 15

a.v.d.

Army Form C. 2118.

Instructions regarding War Diaries and Intelligence Summaries are contained in F. S. Regs., Part II. and the Staff Manual respectively. Title pages will be prepared in manuscript.

WAR DIARY
or
INTELLIGENCE SUMMARY.
(Erase heading not required.)

Hour, Date, Place	Summary of Events and Information	Remarks and references to Appendices
August 6th 1915.	Weekly conference of Veterinary Officers.	[illegible]
8.	1 Suspected Case of Mange in 50th B'de R.F.A. 53rd B'de R.F.A. & Dw. Train respectively evacuated to C of C. by 21st Mobile Vety Section (In contacts) isolated and all necessary steps taken to prevent possible spread of disease. These units personally inspected by A.D.V.S. Microscopical Test of Skin Scrapings negative.	[illegible]
13.	Weekly conference of Vety Officers	[illegible]
18.	Dw. left Cocon. for Busnes arrived Busnes noon same day.	[illegible]
19	1 Suspected case of Mange from each of the following Units evacuated to C of C by 21st Mobile Vety Section. 52nd B'de R.F.A. 53rd B'de R.F.A. 9th Signal Co. & (7th Siege B'de R.G.A. attached) 2 of these Horses were Remounts, one from advanced Remount Section Gonnehem & one from Thienne. Microscopical Test of Skin Scrapings negative. Units personally inspected by A.D.V.S. and all necessary action taken to prevent spread of disease.	[illegible]
20.	Weekly conference of Veterinary Officers.	[illegible]
21.	D.D.V.S. 1st Army (Lt Col. Newsom) called at this Office and interviewed A.V.C. N.C.O's attached to Infty Brigades.	[illegible]
27.	Weekly conference of Vety Officers.	[illegible]
31.	Dw. left Busnes for Busnettes arrived Busnettes same day.	[illegible]

[illegible] Major [illegible]
31/8/15.

(73989) W4141—463. 400,000. 9/14. H.&J.Ltd. Forms/C. 2118/10.

Instructions regarding War Diaries and Intelligence Summaries are contained in F. S. Regs., Part II and the Staff Manual respectively. Title pages will be prepared in manuscript.

WAR DIARY
or
INTELLIGENCE SUMMARY.
(Erase heading not required.)

Army Form C. 2118.

Hour, Date, Place	Summary of Events and Information	Remarks and references to Appendices
September 1st 1915.	With approval of D.D.V.S. 1st Army Lt. H. Torrance A.V.C. S.R. appointed O.C. 21st Mobile Veterinary Section to relieve Lt. H. McCullough A.V.C. placed in Vety charge of 53rd B'de R.F.A. & other details	[illegible]
" 2.	D.W. left Busnettes for Bethune arrived same day	[illegible]
3.	Weekly conference of Veterinary Officers	[illegible]
" 5.	A.D.V.S. attended conference at Rostaires of A.D.s V.S. 1st Army under supervision of D.D.V.S. 1st Army re working of Mobile Vety Sections during active operations	[illegible]
6.	A.D.V.S. met D.D.R. 1st Army to inspect Horses for Casting	[illegible]
10	Weekly conference of Vety Officers. Duties detailed to O.C. Mobile Vety Section and Vety Officers in charge of Units re active operations	[illegible] No I attached [illegible] No II attached
	arrival of A.V.C. Sergeants from L of C for R.F.A. Units	
17	Weekly conference of Vety Officers	[illegible]
21	All arrangements completed for Advanced Collecting Station. Lt. F.F. Steward A.V.C. to take command H.Q. Mobile Vety Section during absence of O.C. Mobile Vety Section at Advanced Collecting Station	[illegible] No III + IV attached
22.	Advanced Veterinary Collecting Station opened at E 23 a. 7 8.	[illegible]
24.	Weekly conference of Vety Officers	[illegible]
25	Lt. J. Simpson A.V.C. from 1st Div. replaced Lt. H. McCullough A.V.C. sent to L of C.	[illegible]
27	Active operations cease. Total casualties during active operations animals killed in action 8. Wounded 7 (Shrapnel)	[illegible]
29	Advanced Collecting Station withdrawn & rejoined H.Q. Mobile Vety Section. Lt. H. Torrance A.V.C. resuming Command.	[illegible]
30.	Lt. J. Simpson A.V.C. went sick to Hospital in Bethune (Influenza)	[illegible]

[illegible] Major [illegible] 30/9/15

(73989) W4141—463. 400,000. 9/14. H.&J.Ltd. Forms/C. 2118/10.

Army Form C. 2118.

Instructions regarding War Diaries and Intelligence Summaries are contained in F. S. Regs., Part II. and the Staff Manual respectively. Title pages will be prepared in manuscript.

WAR DIARY
or
INTELLIGENCE SUMMARY.
(Erase heading not required.)

Hour, Date, Place	Summary of Events and Information	Remarks and references to Appendices
October 1. 1915	Weekly conference of Veterinary Officers	HH
3	Left Bethune for 5th Corps, 2nd army area. arrived [illegible]	HH
4	D D V S 2nd army visited this office	HH
8	Weekly conference of Vety Officers	HH
15	Weekly conference of Vety Officers	HH
16	A D V S and D D R 2nd army inspecting animals of the Divl Train and Divl Amm Column	HH
18	A D V S and D D R inspecting animals of the Glasgow Yeomanry	HH
22	Weekly conference of Vety Officers	HH
24	H M the King inspecting troops of the 9th Divn 1 N.C.O & 5 men of the 21st Mobile Vety Section on parade	HH
28	1 Case of Suspected mange in C Battery 53rd Bde RFA microscopic examination of skin scrapings negative. In contacts isolated and all necessary steps taken to prevent spread of disease. Case evacuated to C of C and Unit personally inspected by A D V S	HH
29	Weekly conference of Vety Officers	HH

HH [illegible] Major
ADVS
9th Divn
31/10/15

(73989) W4141—463. 400,000. 9/14. H.&J.Ltd. Forms/C. 2118/10.

Y. Sent. Copy

D A & Q M G

9th Scottish Division

Hereunder please find copy of Orders (Veterinary) for favour of consideration and mention in operating orders.

Veterinary. The O.C. Mobile Section A.V.C at E 3. a.g.b will post an advanced collecting Station at E 23a7.8.

N.C.O's and men on arrival with sick & wounded horses at a Veterinary collecting station will hand the animals over to the Veterinary Pers-onnel and return forthwith to their Units.

I propose in the case of an advance at any moment taking place and necessitating the forward movement of any considerable number of horses to open an advanced collecting station within touch of the main body of horses.

Wounded horses will not be evacuated until after dark unless large numbers are received and congestion is feared.

Orders have been prepared for issue to V.O's and O.C. No 2nd Mobile Vety Section A.V.C and will be issued on receipt of instructions from H.Q.

H.Q.
9th Divn
4/9/15

W.H. Hurst Major
ADVS
9th Divn

Secret

Copy

O.C. 21st Mobile Vety Section

On 22nd inst you will proceed with 10 N.C.O's + men (marching order) one Wagon, rations for 20 horses and the Party for one day. Unit Chest Wallet. Cattle Killer, Picketing Gear, hemp halters, nose bags, canvas water buckets &c arriving at E 23.a.7.8 at on. Travelling by roads indicated

On arrival there, you will open a Veterinary Collecting Station, indicating its presence by the Signboard, a white triangle on a red ground in a prominent position.

All sick & wounded animals received during the day will be retained here and sent to the M.V.S in the evening, unless you receive later orders from me.

Movements of animals to M.V.S will take place along roads already indicated

You should issue instructions to all concerned that:-

(1) at no time are roads blocked by sick & wounded animals

(2) No man leads more than 3 horses or mules

(3) at the few points where evacuation party crosses and follows main roads, they give way to all traffic if necessary by moving into fields.

(4) It is essential that all wounds be dressed prior to evacuation and if possible

[illegible] [illegible] foreign bodies removed therefrom.

Orders against washing wounds with water and regarding antiseptic to be used must be adhered to.

If a comparatively small number of animals are received, they will be retained at the M.V.S for evacuation in the usual course. If numbers are large and operations are expected to continue on the following day you will arrange to evacuate as soon as possible.

Your advance Collecting Post will be held in readiness to move immediately on receipt of orders from me.

The M.V.S will also be ready to move at short notice.

Total Casualties admitted and Total Evacuated daily during active Operations should be reported to me.

Instructions have been issued to V.O. [illegible] to take temporary command of the H.Q. of your section at E23. a. 7 8. during your absence with the advance Collecting Station.

<u>Note</u> The greatest value of a Veterinary <u>Service</u> in the field during active Operations lies in its ability to relieve units of the encumbrance of sick and wounded animals at the earliest possible moment and without

interfering with any military movement of troops.

To carry out this Service effectively it is essential that O.C.s of Collecting Centres take over sick and wounded animals immediately on arrival and send back the men in whose charge they arrived to their Unit.

When possible men should be sent back under one of their own N.C.O.s and not allowed to wander or straggle.

H.Q.
9th Divn
12/9/15

[illegible] Major
A.D.V.S. 9th Divn

Secret   Copy

V. Os

All Brigades

During active operations V. Os will arrange to be with –

A. In the case of R.A. Brigades: The Waggon Lines

B. In the case of Infy Brigades: The Brigade transport

If V. Os are called to attend horses of their units elsewhere they will return to these places <u>immediately</u> on completion of the duty.

They will arrange that all persons concerned know where they are to be found.

Position of Collecting Station will be E 23 a 7.8.

<u>NOTE</u> The greatest value of the Veterinary Service in the field during active operations lies in its ability to relieve units of the incubus of wounded and unworkable animals with the least possible delay.

Animals sufficiently seriously injured to be temporarily unworkable and yet not sufficiently serious to indicate destruction should be evacuated forthwith to the Veterinary Collecting Station.

Please report to me daily during continuance of active operations Number of Casualties as a whole in the Units in your Veterinary Charge.

H.Q.
9th Div
21/9/15

[signature] Major A.V.C.
9th Div

Secret

V.O.
Train

During operations please arrange to take command of the H.Q. of the Section A.V.C. at E.3. a 9 b during the absence of the O.C. with a party at Veterinary Collecting Station.

The H.Q. of the Section will remain open as a collecting Station for injured animals. No evacuations however will take place without instructions from the O.C. or myself.

H.Q.
9th Divn
21/9/15

[signature] Major
A.D.V.S.
9th Divn

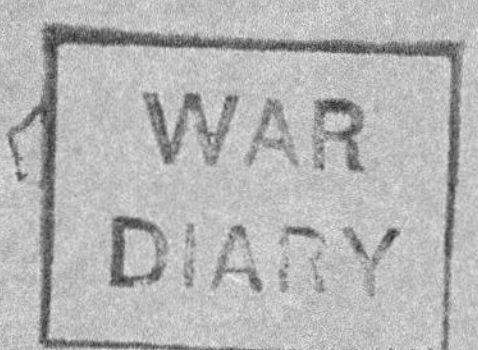

A. D. V. S.

9th DIVISION

NOVEMBER 1915

H.Q. 9th Div:
A.D.V.S.
Vol: 7

121
7656

Nov 15.

Army Form C. 2118.

Instructions regarding War Diaries and Intelligence Summaries are contained in F. S. Regs., Part II. and the Staff Manual respectively. Title pages will be prepared in manuscript.

WAR DIARY

or

~~INTELLIGENCE SUMMARY.~~

(Erase heading not required.)

Hour, Date, Place	Summary of Events and Information	Remarks and references to Appendices
V Corps 2nd Army area.		
November. 5th 1915	Weekly conference of Veterinary Officers.	HHA
6.	D.D.V.S. 2nd Army visited this Office and inspected the 21st Mobile Veterinary Section of this Division and 1. R.A. unit	HHA
12.	Weekly conference of Veterinary Officers	HHA
19	Weekly conference of Veterinary Officers	HHA
26	Weekly conference of Veterinary Officers	HHA
30.	Usual daily routine throughout the month nothing of importance to note.	HHA

1/12/15.

HH Ainsl[illegible] Major
A.D.V.S.
9th Scottish Div

(73989) W4141—463. 400,000. 9/14. H.&J.Ltd. Forms/C. 2118/10.

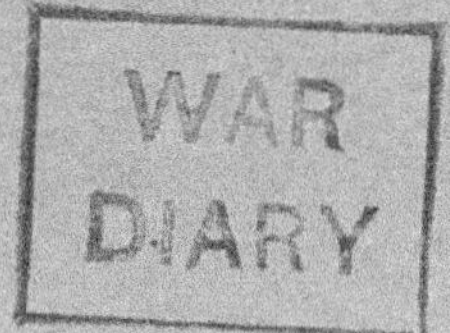

A. D. V. S.

9th DIVISION

DECEMBER 1915

Instructions regarding War Diaries and Intelligence Summaries are contained in F. S. Regs., Part II. and the Staff Manual respectively. Title pages will be prepared in manuscript.

WAR DIARY
or
INTELLIGENCE SUMMARY.
(Erase heading not required.)

Army Form C. 2118.

Hour, Date, Place	Summary of Events and Information	Remarks and references to Appendices
December 3rd 1915.	Weekly conference of Veterinary Officers	[initials]
" 10th "	Weekly conference of Veterinary Officers	[initials]
" 17 "	Weekly conference of Veterinary Officers	[initials]
" 19 "	Sunday Gas attack at 5 a.m. Smoke Helmets for Horses were not used. Horses & Mules were practically unaffected even in the Front Lines, although a few Horses were slightly off their morning feed as far back as 6000 yards from enemies lines, where men were sick & vomiting from the effect of the Gas. No irritation of the eyes or respiratory organs was noticed amongst Horses or Mules	[initials]
" 24.	Weekly conference of Veterinary Officers	[initials]
" 28.	3 Suspected cases of Mange reported. 2 in 51st B'de. R.F.A and 1 in 50th B'de R.F.A (a Remount) These 3 cases evacuated to L of C. & all necessary action taken	[initials]
" 31.	Weekly Conference of Veterinary Officers	[initials]

[signature] Major
A.D.V.S. [illegible]

2/1/16

Army Form C. 2118.

WAR DIARY
or
INTELLIGENCE SUMMARY.
(*Erase heading not required.*)

Instructions regarding War Diaries and Intelligence Summaries are contained in F. S. Regs., Part II. and the Staff Manual respectively. Title pages will be prepared in manuscript.

Hour, Date, Place	Summary of Events and Information	Remarks and references to Appendices
January 2nd 1916	One case of Suspected Mange reported in the 90th Co. R.E. evacuated to L of C and all necessary action taken.	[illegible initials]
" 7th "	Weekly conference of Veterinary Officers	[illegible initials]
" 14th "	Weekly conference of Veterinary Officers	[illegible initials]
" 21st "	Weekly conference of Veterinary Officers.	[illegible initials]
	D.D.V.S. 2nd Army visited Office and addressed Officers with reference to "Intra-dermo palpebral Mallein Test"	[illegible initials]
" 27th "	Left Merris for new area. Opened Office at Nieppe.	[illegible initials]
		[illegible signature] Major A.D.V.S. 9th Divn 2.2.16.

(73989) W4141—463. 400,000. 9/14. H.&J.Ltd. Forms/C. 2118/10.

Instructions regarding War Diaries and Intelligence Summaries are contained in F. S. Regs., Part II. and the Staff Manual respectively. Title pages will be prepared in manuscript.

WAR DIARY
~~or~~
~~INTELLIGENCE~~ SUMMARY.
(*Erase heading not required.*)

Army Form C. 2118.

Hour, Date, Place	Summary of Events and Information	Remarks and references to Appendices
February 1st 1916.	Intra-dermo Palpebral Malleinisation of Horses & Mules of Division with Mallein Dilute commenced.	[illegible]
" 2nd "	Arrival of Lt J. Conner A.V.C. placed on Strength of Division and duties alloted. Replacing Lt F. J. Stewart A.V.C. left for England 26/1/16 to report to D.G.A.V.S. on 28/1/16 on expiration of his agreement.	[illegible]
" 4th "	Weekly Conference of Veterinary Officers	[illegible]
" 11th "	Weekly conference of Veterinary Officers	[illegible]
" 13th "	Left Nieppe for Steenwerck arrived mid-day and opened new Office.	[illegible]
" 18th "	Weekly conference of Veterinary Officers	[illegible]
" 19th "	One mule in 53rd B'de R.F.A. Amm. Col. re-acted to Mallein Test. Animal destroyed and reaction confirmed by Post Mortem Examination.	[illegible]
" 25th "	Weekly conference of Veterinary Officers. Office inspected by D.D.V.S. 2nd Army.	[illegible]
" 29th "	22. Cases of Suspected Mange evacuated to L of C during the month. All necessary action taken to prevent probable spread of disease.	[illegible]

[illegible] A.D.V.S. 2nd Divn. 1/3/16

(73989) W4141—463. 400,000. 9/14. H.&J.Ltd. Forms/C. 2118/10.

Army Form C. 2118.

Instructions regarding War Diaries and Intelligence Summaries are contained in F. S. Regs., Part II. and the Staff Manual respectively. Title pages will be prepared in manuscript.

WAR DIARY
~~or~~
~~INTELLIGENCE~~ SUMMARY.

(*Erase heading not required.*)

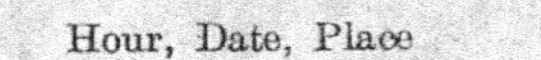

Hour, Date, Place	Summary of Events and Information	Remarks and references to Appendices
March. 3rd 1916.	Weekly conference of Veterinary. Officers.	
" 10th "	Weekly conference of Veterinary. Officers.	
	Intra-dermo palpebral. Malleinisation of Horses and Mules in Division completed. Total number of Re-actors (one)	
" 11th "	D. D. V. S. 2nd Army inspected this Office.	
" 17th "	Weekly conference of Veterinary Officers.	
" 24th "	Weekly conference of Veterinary Officers	
" 31st "	Weekly conference of Veterinary Officers	
	27 Cases of Suspected Mange evacuated to L of C during the month. All necessary action taken to prevent probable spread of the disease.	
		2/4/16 [signature] A.D.V.S. 9th Divn

(73989) W4141—463. 400,000. 9/14. H.&J.Ltd. Forms/C. 2118/10.

9th Div

Army Form C. 2118.

A DVS Vol 12

Instructions regarding War Diaries and Intelligence Summaries are contained in F. S. Regs., Part II. and the Staff Manual respectively. Title pages will be prepared in manuscript.

WAR DIARY
or
~~INTELLIGENCE SUMMARY.~~

(Erase heading not required.)

Hour, Date, Place	Summary of Events and Information	Remarks and references to Appendices
April 7th 1916	Weekly conference of Veterinary Officers.	[illegible]
" 14th	Weekly conference of Veterinary Officers.	[illegible]
" 21st	Weekly conference of Veterinary Officers	[illegible]
" 25th	1 Horse of the 11th R.S. (27th Infy Bde) evacuated to L of C. re-acted to Mallein Test at Receiving Vety Hospital. In-contacts 13 Horses and 23 Mules in this Unit re-malleined and passed the Test.	[illegible]
" 28th	Weekly conference of Veterinary Officers	[illegible]
	13 Cases Suspected Mange evacuated to L of C during the month. All necessary action taken to prevent probable spread of disease.	[illegible]

[illegible] Major
ADVS 9th Div

1/5/16

(73989) W4141—463. 400,000. 9/14. H.&J.Ltd. Forms/C. 2118/10.

ADVS
9th Div
Vol 13

Army Form C. 2118

Instructions regarding War Diaries and Intelligence Summaries are contained in F. S. Regs., Part II. and the Staff Manual respectively. Title Pages will be prepared in manuscript.

WAR DIARY

or

~~INTELLIGENCE SUMMARY~~

(Erase heading not required.)

Place	Date	Hour	Summary of Events and Information	Remarks and references to Appendices
May	5th	1916	Weekly Conference of Veterinary Officers.	HHW
"	12		Weekly Conference of Veterinary Officers	HHW
"	19	"	Weekly Conference of Veterinary Officers	HHW
"	26	"	Weekly Conference of Veterinary Officers.	HHW
"	30	"	Left STEENWERCK reopened at MERRISS mid-day.	HHW
"	31	"	9 Cases suspected Mange evacuated to Los 6 during the month - All necessary action taken to prevent probable spread of disease.	HHW

HHWood Major A.D.V.S.
9th Division
2.6.16

1875 Wt. W593/826 1,000,000 4/15 J.B.C. & A. A.D.S.S./Forms/C. 2118.

A.D.V.S.
[illegible] 7 1916
No. [illegible]
SCOTTISH DIVISION

O i/c A.V.C. Section
[illegible] Base

Herewith War Diary of
A.D.V.S. 9th Division
for June 1916

[illegible signature] Major A.D.V.S.
9th Divn.

Instructions regarding War Diaries and Intelligence Summaries are contained in F. S. Regs., Part II. and the Staff Manual respectively. Title Pages will be prepared in manuscript.

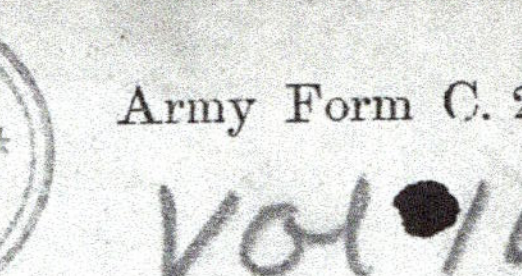

WAR DIARY
or
~~INTELLIGENCE SUMMARY~~

(Erase heading not required.)

Army Form C. 2118

Vol 14.

Place	Date	Hour	Summary of Events and Information	Remarks and references to Appendices
In the Field	1.6.16		A.D.V.S. Office closed at MERRISS 2nd Army Area & reopened at BOMY 1st Army Area.	HHW
	2.6.16		Weekly Conference of Veterinary Officers	HHW
	10.6.16		" " " "	HHW
	15.6.16		A.D.V.S. Office closed at BOMY & reopened at VAUX EN AMIENOIS 4th Army Area	HHW
	16.6.16		Weekly Conference of Veterinary Officers	HHW
	18.6.16		A.D.V.S. attended a Conference at Office of D.D.V.S. 4th Army in connection with expected active operations.	HHW
	23.6.16		A.D.V.S. Office closed at VAUX & reopened at CORBIE	HHW
	"		Weekly Conference of Veterinary Officers — Expected active operations discussed.	HHW
	24.6.16		A.D.V.S. Office closed at CORBIE & reopened at CHIPILLY	HHW
	27.6.16		" " " CHIPILLY " " " ETINEHEM	HHW
	30.6.16		Weekly Conference of Veterinary Officers	HHW
			9 Cases of Suspected Mange evacuated to L of C during the month. All necessary action taken to prevent probable spread of Disease	HHW

HHWeir Major A.D.V.S.
9th Division

1875 Wt. W593/826 1,000,000 4/15 J.B.C. & A. A.D.S.S./Forms/C. 2118.

Instructions regarding War Diaries and Intelligence Summaries are contained in F. S. Regs., Part II. and the Staff Manual respectively. Title Pages will be prepared in manuscript.

WAR DIARY
or
~~INTELLIGENCE SUMMARY~~
(Erase heading not required.)

Army Form C. 2118

9 July Vol 15

(1)

Place	Date	Hour	Summary of Events and Information	Remarks and references to Appendices
Fourth Army	Area		XIII Corps L 16. b. 3.2. Sheet 62D	
"	1st	7 a.m.	Advanced Veterinary Collecting Station posted at K 34 b. 3. 6. in touch with main body of horses during	HAH
"	"		active operations. Difficulties being experienced in watering Animals owing to the very large number of	
			Horses & Mules in the vicinity. Animals losing condition on that account. Action taken.	HAH
"	4th		Weekly conference of Veterinary Officers.	HAH
"	"		Horses & Mules of R.A. units doing a great deal of hard work, long days & nights on hilly roads	
			Many animals on Ammunition Duties doing an average of 40 miles a day. Mostly suffering in	
			condition. Stable management in general is bad in R.A. units, but good in D.A.C. Action taken	HAH
"	9th	4 P.m.	Advanced Collecting Station with Remount & complete M.V.S. advanced to K 6 d Sheet 62D	HAH
			Wagon Lines R.A. D.A.C. & Infty also advanced	HAH
			Horses of R.A. still losing condition, the result of bad stable management & unequal distribution of	
			work, which is said to be unavoidable. Action taken	HAH
	18th		54 Animals Poisoned with Gas Shells on night of 17th 18th. See append. V1083	HAH
	20th	6 P.m.	Moved to MEAULTE	HAH
	23rd	2 PM	Moved to PONT REMY	HAH
	25th	2 PM	Moved to BRUAY First Army Area IV Corps	HAH

1875 Wt. W593/826 1,000,000 4/15 J.B.C. & A. A.D.S.S./Forms/C. 2118.

Instructions regarding War Diaries and Intelligence Summaries are contained in F. S. Regs., Part II. and the Staff Manual respectively. Title Pages will be prepared in manuscript.

WAR DIARY
or
INTELLIGENCE SUMMARY
(Erase heading not required.)

Army Form C. 2118

(2) Place	Date	Hour	Summary of Events and Information	Remarks and references to Appendices
First Army Area			IV Corps	
Bruay	31st July		Divisional Artillery remained in Action in Fourth Army Area XIII Corps until 29th.	
			Total Casualties in Horses + Mules from shell fire during active Operations — 173	
			of which 80 died (Killed), 27 destroyed (incurable), 45 evacuated to L of C, + 21 retained	
			in Divn for treatment.	WHW
			Total Casualties in Horses + Mules from Gas Shells on 17th 18th — see appdx. V1083	
			— 54 — of which 1 died, 6 destroyed, 19 (Convalescent) evacuated to L of C, 28 retained	
			for treatment in Divn, all of which have recovered + returned to Duty.	WHW

W H ... Major
A.D.V.S.
9th Divn

1875 Wt. W593/826 1,000,000 4/15 J.B.C. & A. A.D.S.S./Forms/C. 2118.

Instructions regarding War Diaries and Intelligence Summaries are contained in F. S. Regs., Part II. and the Staff Manual respectively. Title Pages will be prepared in manuscript.

WAR DIARY
or
INTELLIGENCE SUMMARY
(Erase heading not required.)

Army Form C. 2118

Place	Date	Hour	Summary of Events and Information	Remarks and references to Appendices
		1	Report by A.D.V.S. on the effect of a bombardment by asphyxiating gas shells on animals of the 7th (Scottish) Division 17/18 7/1916	
			The Gas Shells were encountered by part of the first line transport of 2 Inf Bdes & a Field Coy R.E in a narrow valley between MONTAUBAN & LONGUEVAL about midnight on the 17th/18th inst.	
			The animals remained in the valley until daybreak, as, owing to casualties amongst officers & other ranks & the blocking of the road it was impossible to move. Beyond sluggishness & slight occasional coughing the animals showed no alarming symptoms on the march back to camp, about seven miles distant, until about 8 o/c same morning after reaching camp, when the following symptoms were observed. —	
			Symptoms (1) Acute cases. Very laboured breathing, nostrils dilated & exuding a white frothy discharge, mucous membrane of nose & eyes deeply injected, head held low, fore legs spread wide apart, with very appearance of acute distress somewhat like South African Horse Sickness. Colicy pains & frequent micturition. Pulse frequent, irregular & not easily perceptible. Temp 102–103. One horse showing above symptoms died in about 2 hours after reaching camp & 2 others in extremis were destroyed before mid day.	
			2 Sub Acute Cases. Symptoms similar to those described above but distress less marked & the discharge from nostrils of a different nature, a yellow mucoid discharge becoming purulent after 12 hours. Also there were frequent fits of painful coughing, especially when the animals lay down, or were moved about.	

1875 Wt. W593/826 1,000,000 4/15 J.B.C. & A. A.D.S.S./Forms/C. 2118.

Instructions regarding War Diaries and Intelligence Summaries are contained in F. S. Regs., Part II. and the Staff Manual respectively. Title Pages will be prepared in manuscript.

WAR DIARY
or
INTELLIGENCE SUMMARY
(Erase heading not required.)

Army Form C. 2118

Place	Date	Hour	Summary of Events and Information	Remarks and references to Appendices
			The milder cases appear to recover to some extent in 24 to 48 hours but still exude a purulent discharge from the nostrils, & when moved breathing becomes distressed & cough painful. Temp at this stage is normal but pulse remains weak.	
			These mild cases also feed well & have lost practically no condition.	
		2		
			"In continuation of my report on the effects of Gas Shells upon Animals of this Division I conferred with the Gas Officer of this Division, a medical Officer, on his return from the trenches. He informs me that the Gas which the enemy has been using is "K" Gas, & is practically harmless unless in a confined space or pocket, such as the valley in which our animals encountered the fumes. He knows a case in which an Officer rode through the fumes in the open, without harmful results. The Gas Shells used were "whiz bangs", & it is estimated that about a thousand shells were fired into the valley between MONTAUBAN & LONGUEVAL on the night of the 17th 18th inst: The shells were put in with a rapidity almost equal to that of a machine Gun.	
			HQ 9th Div. 24. 7. 16 Signed W. H. Nicol Major ADVS 9th (Scottish) Div.	

1875 Wt. W593/826 1,000,000 4/15 J.B.C. & A. A.D.S.S./Forms/C. 2118.

Instructions regarding War Diaries and Intelligence Summaries are contained in F. S. Regs., Part II. and the Staff Manual respectively. Title Pages will be prepared in manuscript.

WAR DIARY
or
~~INTELLIGENCE SUMMARY~~
(Erase heading not required.)

Army Form C. 2118

9

Vol 16

Place	Date	Hour	Summary of Events and Information	Remarks and references to Appendices
First Army Area August			First Army IV Corps	
	4th		Conference of Veterinary Officers in Office of A.D.V.S.	HHM
	6th		A.D.V.S attended Conference at Office of D.D.V.S First Army 4C	HHM
"	11th		Conference of Veterinary Officers	HHM
"	15th		A.D.V.S office moved to CAMBLAIN L'ABBE.	HHM
"	18th		Conference of Veterinary Officers.	HHM
"	25th		— " — " —	HHM
"	31st		D.V.S. Inspection of 2nd Mobile Veterinary Section.	HHM
"			46 Cases of Suspected Mange have been evacuated to [illegible] during the month.	
			All necessary action taken to prevent probable spread of disease	HHM

HHM [illegible] Major A.D.V.S. 9th Div

1875 Wt. W593/826 1,000,000 4/15 J.B.C. & A. A.D.S.S./Forms/C. 2118.

Instructions *regarding* War Diaries and Intelligence Summaries are contained in F. S. Regs., Part II. and the Staff Manual respectively. Title Pages will be prepared in manuscript.

WAR DIARY
or
INTELLIGENCE SUMMARY
(Erase heading not required.)

Army Form C. 2118

Vol 17

Place	Date	Hour	Summary of Events and Information	Remarks and references to Appendices
IV Corps Area			First Army	
September	1st		Weekly Conference of Veterinary Officers.	
	3rd		A.D.V.S. attended Conference of A.Ds V.S. at First Army H.Q.	
	8th		Weekly Conference of Veterinary Officers.	
	11th		Reorganisation of Divisional Artillery.	
	15th		Weekly Conference of Veterinary Officers	
	22nd		Weekly Conference of Veterinary Officers.	
	26th		A.D.V.S. Office closed at CAMBLAIN L'ABBE and reopened same day at LE CAUROY (Third Army Rest Area) XVII Corps.	
			21st Mobile Veterinary Section left FRESNICOURT and moved to PENIN.	
	27th		Capt W H Power assumed duties of A.D.V.S. during Major Nicol's leave of absence to Scotland.	

W. H. Power. Capt A.V.C
for Major A.D.V.S.
9th (Scottish) Division

1875 Wt. W593/826 1,000,000 4/15 J.B.C. & A. A.D.S.S./Forms/C. 2118.

Instructions regarding War Diaries and Intelligence Summaries are contained in F. S. Regs., Part II. and the Staff Manual respectively. Title Pages will be prepared in manuscript.

A.D.V.S. No. V1293 2/11/16 9th SCOTTISH DIVISION

WAR DIARY or ~~INTELLIGENCE SUMMARY~~ of A.D.V.S. 9th (Scottish) Division

(Erase heading not required.)

Army Form C. 2118. Vol. 18

Place	Date	Hour	Summary of Events and Information	Remarks and references to Appendices
			Third Army Training Area	
Oct.	2nd 1916		Operation Orders for move of Division received, and issued to 21st M.V.S.	[initials]
"	4th		A.D.V.S. being recalled from leave, arrived and took over administration from Capt: Power AVC who had been acting in his absence.	[initials]
	7th		A.D.V.S.'s Office closed at LE CAUROY and reopened at BAIZIEUX III Corps Area Fourth Army	[initials]
"	8th		D.D.V.S. Fourth Army visited A.D.V.S.	[initials]
"	9th		Position for M.V.S. selected by A.D.V.S.	[initials]
"	10th		A.D.V.S. Office closed at BAIZIEUX and reopened at FRICOURT FARM.	[initials]
"	20th		Conference of Veterinary Officers	[initials]
"	25th		Upon relief Division moved out of area. A.D.V.S.' Office closed at FRICOURT FARM and reopened at MILLENCOURT.	[initials]
"	26th		D.D.V.S. Fourth Army had conference with A.D.V.S. when several important Veterinary matters were discussed	[initials]
"	28th		A.D.V.S. Office closed at MILLENCOURT and reopened at FLERS Third Army Area.	[initials]
	31st		Artillery will remain in Fourth Army Area administered by ADVS 50th Div. Suspected mange evacuations for this month 11	[initials]

[signature] Major A.D.V.S. 9th Div.

1875 Wt. W593/826 1,000,000 4/15 J.B.C. & A. A.D.S.S./Forms/C. 2118.

CONFIDENTIAL.

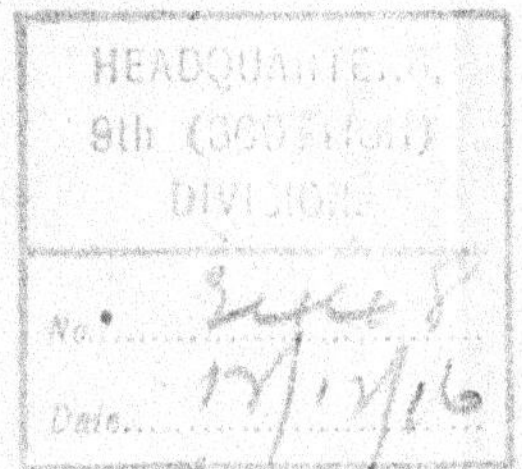

Officer in Charge,
A.G. Section,
Base.

Herewith is forwarded "War Diary" of the A.D.V.S. 9th Division for November 1916.

Major.
D.A.A & Q.M.G.
9th.(Scottish) Division.

12/12/16.

9

Instructions regarding War Diaries and Intelligence Summaries are contained in F. S. Regs., Part II. and the Staff Manual respectively. Title Pages will be prepared in manuscript.

WAR DIARY
or
~~INTELLIGENCE SUMMARY~~
(Erase heading not required.)

Army Form C. 2118

Vol 19

Place	Date	Hour	Summary of Events and Information	Remarks and references to Appendices
VI Corps Third Army Area				
	2/11/16		Weekly Conference of Veterinary Officers in this Area. R.A. remain in Fourth Army Area with V.Os attached	HAH
	3/11/16		A.D.V.S. inspected waggon lines of 26th and South African Inf. Bdes	HAH
			O.C. 21st M.V.S. proceeded on leave. Lieut Conner AVC officiates during his absence	
	6/11/16		A.D.V.S made personal inspection of Sick Lines of R.E. Coys	HAH
	7/11/16		This Office closed at FLERS and reopened same day at ROELLECOURT.	HAH
			21st M.V.S billeted also in this village. Attendance arranged for all Units.	
	9/11/16		Weekly Conference of Veterinary Officers	HAH
	13/11/16		Inspection of lines of 27th Brigade and 9th Seaforths by A.D.V.S.	HAH
	16/11/16		A.D.V.S made personal inspections of arrangements for clipping at Brigade HQs	HAH
	17/11/16		Weekly Conference of Vety: Officers.	HAH
	21/11/16		Reported on collection of 25 Animals left by 41st Div at ANVIN also on 3 which died	HAH
	22/11/16		Report sent in on "Machine" and "hand made" horse shoes	HAH
	24/11/16		Weekly Conference of Vety: Officers and inspection by ADVS of Waggon lines of incoming Units	HAH
	26/11/16		D.D. Remounts called for conference with A.D.V.S. Urgent call sent to 27th Inf Bde	HAH
	29/11/16		R.A. Units having moved into this Area A.D.V.S inspected horses of 50th Brigade R.F.A.	HAH
	30/11/16		A.D.V.S made inspection of 51st Bde R.F.A.	HAH
			1 Case only of Mange evacuated to L of C by 21st M.V.S.	

H.A. Hugo[?] Major
A.D.V.S. 9th (Scottish) Div.

1875 Wt. W593/826 1,000,000 4/15 J.B.C. & A. A.D.S.S./Forms/C. 2118.

Army Form C. 2118

WAR DIARY
or
~~INTELLIGENCE SUMMARY~~
(Erase heading not required.)

Instructions regarding War Diaries and Intelligence Summaries are contained in F. S. Regs., Part II. and the Staff Manual respectively. Title Pages will be prepared in manuscript.

A.D.V.S. 9th (Scottish) Division
DECEMBER 1916

Vol 20

Place	Date	Hour	Summary of Events and Information	Remarks and references to Appendices
VI Corps	Third Army Area			
	5/12/16		A.D.V.S Office closed at ROELLECOURT and opened at DUISANS.	[initials]
			Nothing of importance to record.	
	31/12/16		7 Cases Suspected Mange evacuated to L of C during the month and all necessary action taken to prevent probable spread of Disease.	[initials]

[signature] Major
A.D.V.S. 9th Division

1875 Wt. W593/826 1,000,000 4/15 J.B.C. & A. A.D.S.S./Forms/C. 2118.

Instructions regarding War Diaries and Intelligence Summaries are contained in F. S. Regs., Part II. and the Staff Manual respectively. Title Pages will be prepared in manuscript.

WAR DIARY
or
~~INTELLIGENCE~~ SUMMARY
(Erase heading not required.)

Army Form C. 2118

A.D.V.S.
9th (Scottish) Division.

Vol 21

Place	Date	Hour	Summary of Events and Information	Remarks and references to Appendices
	Jan.	1st 1917	VI Corps Area Third Army.	
	"	6th	Inspection of Artillery Units by D.D.V.S. Third Army.	[illegible]
	"	7th	" " " " " "	[illegible]
	"	8th	" " " " " "	[illegible]
	"	9th	" " " " " "	[illegible]
	"	12th	Weekly Conference of Veterinary Officers.	[illegible]
	"	19th	" " " "	[illegible]
	"	25th	2 cases STOMATITIS CONTAGIOSA in C/51 R.F.A. these segregated, and unit placed in "working isolation", and all necessary action taken	[illegible]
	"	26th	A.D.V.S. attended Conference at Third Army Headquarters.	[illegible]
	"	30th	21st Mobile Veterinary Section moved to AUBIGNY.	[illegible]
	"	31st	2 cases STOMATITIS CONTAGIOSA in C/51 R.F.A. doing well, outbreak considered arrested, no fresh cases have occurred.	[illegible]
			30 cases Suspected Mange evacuated to L. of C. during the month, and all necessary action taken to prevent probable spread of disease.	[illegible]

31/1/17 [illegible] Major
A.D.V.S. 9th Div.

1875 Wt. W593/826 1,000,000 4/15 J.B.C. & A. A.D.S.S./Forms/C. 2118.

Officer i/c.
A.G's Office,
Base.

Herewith War Diary of A.D.V.S.9th Division for month of January 1917. Please acknowledge receipt.

C. F. Bowman

Capt,
A/D.A.A.&.Q.M.G.
9th Division.

7/2/17.

RECEIVED

for D.A.G., G.H.Q.,
3rd ECHELON.

Army Form C. 2118

WAR DIARY
or
~~INTELLIGENCE SUMMARY~~
(Erase heading not required.)

Instructions regarding War Diaries and Intelligence Summaries are contained in F. S. Regs., Part II. and the Staff Manual respectively. Title Pages will be prepared in manuscript.

A.D.V.S.
9th Division

Vol 22

Place	Date	Hour	Summary of Events and Information	Remarks and references to Appendices
XVII Corps Area			Third Army.	
Feb.	3rd	1917	Weekly conference of Veterinary Officers	WHN
	8th		Major W.H. Nicol A.D.V.S. proceeded on leave to England. Capt. W.H. Power to officiate during his absence	WHN
	9th		Weekly conference of Veterinary Officers	WHN
	13th		Delivery of Remounts at Railhead.	WHN
	17th		Office of A.D.V.S. closed at DUISANS and opened at mid-day at ETRUN XVII Corps Area.	WHN
	21st		Major Nicol A.D.V.S. returned from leave.	WHN
	23rd		Weekly conference of Veterinary Officers	WHN
			8 cases suspected mange evacuated to L of C during the month.	

1/3/17

W.H. Nicol Major
A.D.V.S. 9th (Scottish) Division

1875 Wt. W593/826 1,000,000 4/15 J.B.C. & A. A.D.S.S./Forms/C. 2118.

Instructions regarding War Diaries and Intelligence Summaries are contained in F. S. Regs., Part II. and the Staff Manual respectively. Title Pages will be prepared in manuscript.

WAR DIARY

or

~~INTELLIGENCE SUMMARY~~

(Erase heading not required.)

Army Form C. 2118

A. D. V. S.

9th (Scottish) Division

Vol 23

A. D. V. S. No. .... Date 1/4/1917 9th (SCOTTISH) DIVISION

Place	Date	Hour	Summary of Events and Information	Remarks and references to Appendices
All 9th (Scottish) Division				
XVII Corps Area			Third Army	
March	2nd	17	Weekly Conference of Veterinary Officers	
"	6th	"	An outbreak of Mange occurred in 52nd Army Fd: Art: Bde: and SARCOPTES EQUI were found in skin scrapings taken from 4 horses. In addition, 15 suspected cases were found. All necessary action taken. Only 1 Battery affected i.e. "C." The majority of cases were found on clipping. All animals are being clipped and Battery placed in "working isolation". Pronounced cases are being evacuated, and mild cases retained and treated in Unit.	
"	10th	"	D. D. V. S. Third Army inspected C/52 in connection with Mange outbreak.	
"	12th	"	An outbreak of Mange also occurred in 50th and 51st Bdes R.F.A. SARCOPTES EQUI being found in skin scrapings taken from 1 case. Nearly all cases were found on clipping. Only 1 Battery unaffected – worst cases have been evacuated, and others dealt with in Units. Clipping of all horses is going on, as far as the military situation and other circumstances will permit. All necessary action taken.	
"	15th	"	50th and 51st Bdes R.F.A. inspected by D.D.V.S.	
"	31st	"	30 cases suspected Mange cured and returned to duty. 96 cases evacuated to Lof.C. during the month from Divisional and Attached Units	

[signature] Major
A. D. V. S. 9th (Scottish) Division

1875 Wt. W593/826 1,000,000 4/15 J.B.C. & A. A.D.S.S./Forms/C. 2118.

Instructions regarding War Diaries and Intelligence Summaries are contained in F. S. Regs., Part II. and the Staff Manual respectively. Title Pages will be prepared in manuscript.

WAR DIARY
or
~~INTELLIGENCE SUMMARY~~

(Erase heading not required.)

Army Form C. 2118

A.D.V.S.
9th (Scottish) Division

Vol 24

Place	Date	Hour	Summary of Events and Information	Remarks and references to Appendices
XVII Corps Area			Third Army	
	April	5th	Week ending April 5th. 80 Casualties amongst horses and mules in the Division and Attached Units: the majority of which were due to Debility, exposure and exhaustion caused by excessive work under most trying wintry weather conditions, particularly in R.A. Units which were much under establishment in Ld animals, and were on 3/4 rations up to the 31st of March. During this week 63 animals were evacuated to Ld C. suffering from Debility in addition to the above deaths and destructions	HH
		8th	In blood smear taken from a Ld horse in No. 2 Section 9th Div Col R.F.A. ANTHRAX bacilli were found, after microscopical examination. All precautionary measures taken	HH
		9th	Commencement of active operations	HH
		12th	Week ending this date:- 59 Deaths and Destructions and 60 Evacuations occurred from Debility Exposure, Exhaustion and Privation.	HH
		13th	All animals put on full oats ration from this date. (15th) This Office opened at HERMAVILLE	HH
		19th	Week ending this date 36 Casualties and 29 Evacuations from above causes.	HH
		21st	This Office closed at HERMAVILLE and reopened at CHELERS	HH
		25th	" " " " CHELERS " " " HERMAVILLE	HH
		30th	" " " " HERMAVILLE " " " ARRAS	HH
			Weather conditions improved and work less strenuous for horses and mules which are now improving in condition, but Divisional Artillery are still 220 Animals under strength. The majority of Casualties and Evacuations during the month were Animals which had been clipped since Jan 1 - a course which was unavoidable owing to the outbreak of mange amongst R.A. horses. 10 Cases Suspected Mange evacuated during the month	HH

[illegible] Major
~~A.D.V.S. 9th Division~~

[illegible] Major
A.D.V.S. 9th Div.
2/5/17

1875 Wt. W593/826 1,000,000 4/15 J.B.C. & A. A.D.S.S./Forms/C. 2118.

Instructions regarding War Diaries and Intelligence Summaries are contained in F. S. Regs., Part II. and the Staff Manual respectively. Title Pages will be prepared in manuscript.

WAR DIARY
or
~~INTELLIGENCE SUMMARY~~
(Erase heading not required.)

Army Form C. 2118

A. D. V. S.
9th (Scottish) Division

Vol 25

Place	Date	Hour	Summary of Events and Information	Remarks and references to Appendices
XVII Corps Area Third Army				
	May	11th	This Office closed at ARRAS and reopened at CHELERS. Veterinary Officers i/c remain in line with R.A. Units.	HHM
	"	13th	This Office closed at CHELERS and reopened at ROELLECOURT.	HHM
	"	16th	Demonstrations on use of Gas Respirators for Horses given by ADVS accompanied by Divisional Gas Officer, to Royal Artillery and other Units in front line.	HHM
	"	19th	Further demonstrations given this day to Infantry Brigades	HHM
	"	21st	Further demonstrations given to R.E. Coys and Fd. Ambces.	HHM
	"	22nd	Further demonstrations given to 9th Divisional Train A.S.C.	HHM
		31st	5 Cases Suspected Mange evacuated to L of C. during the month. Fine weather has prevailed throughout the month and all animals have improved in Condition.	HHM

HHMcof Major
A. D. V. S. 9th Division

1875 Wt. W593/826 1,000,000 4/15 J.B.C. & A. A.D.S.S./Forms/C. 2118.

9

Army Form C. 2118

Instructions regarding War Diaries and Intelligence Summaries are contained in F. S. Regs., Part II. and the Staff Manual respectively. Title Pages will be prepared in manuscript.

WAR DIARY
or
INTELLIGENCE SUMMARY
(Erase heading not required.)

June 1917. A.D.V.S. 9th Division

Vol 26

Place	Date	Hour	Summary of Events and Information	Remarks and references to Appendices
XVII Corps		Third Army		
June	2nd		This office moved from ROELLECOURT to ST NICOLAS and assumed administration of 4th and 51st Divisional Artillery, with 1 Army Field Artillery Bde.	
"	13th		moved from ST NICOLAS to ROELLECOURT after handing over 9th Div R.A. to A.D.V.S. 4th Division.	
"	18th		A.D.V.S. proceeded on 10 days leave to Scotland. Capt Power AVC officiating.	
"	19th		Major Nicol instructed to proceed to XVIII Corps as A.D.V.S. meanwhile Capt Torrance AVC. O.C. 21st M.V.S. acts as D.A.D.V.S.	
"	29th		Major Nicol returned from leave and proceeded to XVIII Corps HQ to take up his appointment.	
"	30th		A.D.V.S. XVII Corps accompanied by Capt Torrance inspected Infantry transport animals and Train.	

H. L. Torrance Capt AVC
a/ D.A.D.V.S. 9th Division

1875 Wt. W593/826 1,000,000 4/15 J.B.C. & A. A.D.S.S./Forms/C. 2118.

Instructions regarding War Diaries and Intelligence Summaries are contained in F. S. Regs., Part II. and the Staff Manual respectively. Title Pages will be prepared in manuscript.

WAR DIARY

~~or~~

~~INTELLIGENCE SUMMARY~~

(*Erase heading not required.*)

Army Form C. 2118

D.A.D.V.S., 9TH (SCOTTISH) DIVISION. No. CV 52 J. Date 2.8.17.

Vol 27

Place	Date	Hour	Summary of Events and Information	Remarks and references to Appendices
5-7-17.			Reported for duty on appointment as DADVS of the 9th Scottish Division	LHW
6-7-17.			Inspected the horses of Headquarters Units and 21st Mobile Veterinary Section	LHW
7-7-17.			Visited and inspected horses of the 27th Infantry Brigade. Attended Conference of DADVS at the Office of the ADVS. XVII CORPS. ETRUN. Inspected at the request of the ADVS VII Corps one hundred and fifty three animals at A Bty 30th Bgde. RFA.	LHW
8-7-17			Visited and inspected the animals of the 26th Infantry Bgde and 27th Field Ambulance. Visited Divisional Headquarter Units and 28th Field Ambulance.	LHW
9-7-17			Visited Divisional Headquarter Units	LHW
10-7-17			Visited and inspected horses of the 9th Divisional Train also those of the 28th Field Ambulance and the South African Field Ambulance	LHW
			Inspected horses of the 12th Field Ambulance and 90th Field Co. R E	LHW
11-7-17			Visited Mobile Veterinary Section and Divisional headquarter Units	LHW
12-7-17			Visited with the ADVS VII CORPS and inspected the horses of the 104th Coy 9th Divisional Train and 50th Bgde RFA. BOISLEAUX-AU-MONT	LHW
			Visited more military Mounted Police lines.	LHW
13-7-17			Visited the 27th Infantry Brigade and 28th Field Ambulance.	LHW
14-7-17			Visited and inspected the animals of the South African Infantry Brigade also those of the 197th M G Co. Conference ADVS Office XVII CORPS.	LHW
15-7-17			Visited Divisional headquarter Units also to ABBEVILLE with DAQMG 9th Division to distribute one hundred and forty-seven remounts	LHW
16-7-17			Distributed remounts to Divisional Units	LHW

1875 Wt. W593/826 1,000,000 4/15 J.B.C. & A. A.D.S.S./Forms/C. 2118.

Instructions regarding War Diaries and Intelligence Summaries are contained in F. S. Regs., Part II. and the Staff Manual respectively. Title Pages will be prepared in manuscript.

WAR DIARY
or
~~INTELLIGENCE SUMMARY~~

(Erase heading not required.)

D.A.D.V.S., 9TH (SCOTTISH) DIVISION. No. CV 52J Date 2.8.17

Army Form C. 2118

Place	Date	Hour	Summary of Events and Information	Remarks and references to Appendices
In the Field	17.7.17		Visited 21st M.V.S and Headquarter Units. Inspected the horses of the 106th Coy 9th Divisional Train also those of the 69th Labour Batt.n, No 1 P.B. Labour Coy and South African Field Ambulance.	J.H.W.
"	"		Visited Units Divisional headquarters.	J.H.W.
"	18.7.17		Visited 21st M.V.S and Divisional headquarter Units.	J.H.W.
"	19.7.17		Visited 64th Field Coy RE. Visited Headquarters Royal Artillery.	J.H.W.
"	20.7.17		Visited & inspected horses at 21st M.V.S. Attended Conference A.D.V.S.'s Office XVII CORPS	
"	21.7.17		Inspected horses 107 Coy 9th Divisional Train.	J.H.W.
"	"		Visited Units Headquarters of Division.	J.H.W.
"	22.7.17		Visited and inspected horses of the 26th Infantry Brigade, 26th M.G. Co. also those	
"	23.7.17		of the 197 M.G. Coy. Visited 64th Field Co. RE	J.H.W.
"	"		Visited Units divisional headquarters, also 106th Coy Divisional Train also	
"	24.7.17		Labour Battalions and South African Field Ambulance. Inspected French	
"	"		Gendarmes riding horses at AVESNES-LE-COMPTE	J.H.W.
"	"		Inspected horses for evacuation at M.V.S. Visited 63rd and 90th Field Coys RE. Met	
"	25.7.17		Artillery remounts ~~Beau~~ 10.30 P.M. (BEAUMETZ)	J.H.W.
"	"		Visited new area to meet D.A.D.V.S. 58th Division to arrange interchange of Mobile	
"	26.7.17		Veterinary Sections etc	J.H.W.
"	27.7.17		Visited 90th Field Coy RE also horse the property of Mons LESAGE CAMILLE FOSSEUX ROAD BARLY. Visited Labour Battalions and French Gendarmes' horses at AVESNES LE COMPTE	J.H.W.
"	28.7.17		Visited 90th Field Co. R.E. and Mons LESAGE CAMILLES' horse BARLY	J.H.W.
"	29.7.17		Visited Divisional headquarter Units.	J.H.W.
"	30.7.17		Inspected horses M.V.S. for evacuation. Attended entrainment of horses GOUY-EN-ARTOIS	J.H.W.
"	31.7.17		Moved to YTRES.	J.H.W.

J.H. Wright Major A.V.C.
D.A.D.V.S. 9th (Scottish) Division

1875 Wt. W593/826 1,000,000 4/15 J.B.C. & A. A.D.S.S./Forms/C. 2118.

Instructions regarding War Diaries and Intelligence Summaries are contained in F. S. Regs., Part II. and the Staff Manual respectively. Title pages will be prepared in manuscript.

WAR DIARY

~~or~~

~~INTELLIGENCE SUMMARY.~~

(Erase heading not required.)

Army Form C. 2118.

DADVS 9 D

Vol 28

Place	Date	Hour	Summary of Events and Information	Remarks and references to Appendices
In the Field	1.8.17		Inspected 20th Infantry Bgde with Veterinary Officer also the [illegible] Field [illegible] and reported to D D V S IV Corps in the evening	[illegible]
—	2.8.17		Interviewed attached Veterinary Officers 290 291 Bgdes [illegible] DAC [illegible] RA and DAC 42nd Division. Inspected H.Q. animals and [illegible]	[illegible]
—	3.8.17		South African Inf. Bgde inspected with Veterinary Officer H.Q. [illegible] Mobile Veterinary Section. Conference of Veterinary Officers	[illegible]
—	4.8.17		Attended A.D.V.S. Conference. Inspected I Section 42nd D.A.C. animals isolated with mange. [illegible] report [illegible] correspondence dealt with	[illegible]
—	5.8.17		Inspected H.Q. horses to be withdrawn also those [illegible] absorbed into the Division. Inspected Signal Co. R.E. horses also those of 11th Royal Scots 12th Royal Scots 27th Infantry Bgde BERTINCOURT	[illegible]
—	—		Visited and inspected animals 9th D.A.C. (I Section)	[illegible]
—	6.8.17		Inspected horses Divisional Train. Inspected animals Signal Co. R.E.	[illegible]
—	7.8.17		A.D.V.S. IV Corps called	
—	8.8.17		Visited 26th Infantry Bgde and 197 Machine Gun Co. also inspected I Section 42nd D.A.C.	[illegible]
—	9.8.17		Inspected horses 9th Divisional Artillery	[illegible]
—	10.8.17		Visited Signal Co. R.E. and H.Q. horses.	[illegible]
—	11.8.17		Visited M.V.S. and inspected horses for evacuation. Attended [illegible] inspection [illegible] A.B.V.H.	[illegible]
—	—		Visited and inspected 27th Infantry Bgde attended horse injured Signal Co. R.E.	[illegible]
—	12.8.17		Visited three times injured Charger C.R.A.	[illegible]
—	13.8.17		Visited South African Inf. Bde EQUANCOURT 29th Field Amb. and 64 Field Co. R.E. ROYANCOURT also 63 Field Co. R.E. NEUVILLE	[illegible]

(A7092). Wt. W12839/M1293. 750,000. 1/17. D. D. & L., Ltd. Forms/C.2118/14.

Instructions regarding War Diaries and Intelligence Summaries are contained in F. S. Regs., Part II. and the Staff Manual respectively. Title pages will be prepared in manuscript.

WAR DIARY
or
~~INTELLIGENCE SUMMARY.~~
(Erase heading not required.)

Army Form C. 2118.

Place	Date	Hour	Summary of Events and Information	Remarks and references to Appendices
[illegible]field	14.8.17		[illegible] and 197 M.G.C. [illegible]	[illegible]
– –	15.8.17		[illegible]	[illegible]
– –	16.8.17		[illegible]	[illegible]
– –	17.8.17		[illegible] 10 AM [illegible]	[illegible]
– –	18.8.17		[illegible]	[illegible]
– –	19.8.17		[illegible] Bde. [illegible]	[illegible]
– –	20.8.17		[illegible]	[illegible]
– –	21.8.17		[illegible]	[illegible]
– –	22.8.17		[illegible] MACHIE AVC [illegible] Capt TORRENCE AVC and CAPT MACHIE [illegible]	[illegible]
– –	23.8.17		[illegible] LORD HASTINGS. CAPT CAMPBELL [illegible]	[illegible]
– –	24.8.17		[illegible] CAPT TORRENCE AVC [illegible]	[illegible]
– –	25.8.17		[illegible] CORPS [illegible] LORD HASTINGS [illegible] Bde and 197 M.G.C.	[illegible]
– –	26.8.17		[illegible] LORD HASTINGS [illegible]	[illegible]

(A7092). Wt. W12839/M1293. 750,000. 1/17. D. D. & L., Ltd. Forms/C.2118/14.

Instructions regarding War Diaries and Intelligence Summaries are contained in F. S. Regs., Part II. and the Staff Manual respectively. Title pages will be prepared in manuscript.

WAR DIARY
or
INTELLIGENCE SUMMARY.
(Erase heading not required.)

Army Form C. 2118.

Place	Date	Hour	Summary of Events and Information	Remarks and references to Appendices
In the Field	27.8.17		Inspecting and selecting Brood mares from RA Units. Inspected 104 Co.	
—	—		Divisional Train and S. African Field Ambulance. Inspected 34	[illegible]
—	—		horses for evacuation.	
—	—		To [illegible] with [illegible] for MVS. To BHS inspected	
—	28.8.17		mange cases in 104 C A S C	[illegible]
—	—		Accompanied DDVS [illegible] ARMY and ADVS [illegible] CORPS during inspection	
—	29.8.17		of MVS and DDR during inspection and reallotting of surplus	
—	—		Chargers. Selecting Brood mares from 104 and HQ Divisional	
—	—		Train and MVS. Visited DHQ lines and 197 M G Co.	[illegible]
—	—		Visited and inspected CRA lines. Inspected sick lines 9th DRA	
—	30.8.17		Visited MMP lines Signals and DHQ	[illegible]

[signature] MAJOR, A. V. C.
D. A. D. V. S. 9th. (SCOTTISH) DIVISION.

D.A.D.V.S., 9TH (SCOTTISH) DIVISION.
No.
Date 1/9/1917.

(A7092). Wt. W12839/M1293. 750,000. 1/17. D. D. & L., Ltd. Forms/C.2118/14.

Army Form C. 2118.

Instructions regarding War Diaries and Intelligence Summaries are contained in F. S. Regs., Part II. and the Staff Manual respectively. Title pages will be prepared in manuscript.

WAR DIARY of D.A.D.V.S. 9th Divn
or
~~INTELLIGENCE SUMMARY.~~ September 1917

(Erase heading not required.)

Vol 29

Place	Date	Hour	Summary of Events and Information	Remarks and references to Appendices
IV Corps	Third Army Area			
	1st		DADVS attended conferences at IV and VI Corps and met M.V.S on arrival.	
	2nd		Inspected lines of DHQ Units.	
	3rd		Inspected Infantry Bdes – M.V.S and 197 M.G.C.	
	4th		Selecting Good Mares from R.A Units	
	5th		Examining surplus RA horses and mules with D.D. Remts Inspected R.A Bdes.	
	6th		Corps inspection of Brood Mares R.A and other Divisional Units at M.V.S Lines.	
	7th		Inspected surplus and sick animals for evacuation. Visited lines of S.A. Bde	
	8th		Attended Corps Conference. Inspected 27th Bde 27th Fd Ambce 106 Coy ASC Horse Lines	
	9th		Visited DHQ Units Lines and made arrangements for Veterinary attendance on and during move	
	10th		Inspected lines of 26th Bde 197 MGC, 28th Fd Ambce and horses at M.V.S for evacuation	
	11th		Visited ADVS at Corps HQ Selected horse from 27th Fd Ambce for Town Major – Closed at ACHIET LE PETIT 7.30pm	
	12th		Office reopened at POPERINGHE V Corps Fifth Army. Inspected DHQ lines and M.M.P before proceeding north	
	13th		Reported personally to A.DVS V Corps and visited Corps Horse Bath.	
	14th		Proceeded by car to 42nd DHQ and arranged transfer of attached Units.	
	15th		Inspected M.V.S at WATOU also sites of M.V.S during offensive operations, and inspected site for Advanced Post – Conferred with DADVS 42nd Divn re interchange, conference at Corps	
	16th		Visited Horse Bath and superintended dipping of horses.	
	17th		Visited and inspected DHQ horse lines. A/D.D.V.S Fifth Army visited this Office Completed V.O.D	
	18th		Office moved to forward area BRANDHOEK CAMP met Remounts (36 mules for R.A) at PROVEN	
	19th		Inspected RA Bdes of this Divn and interviewed attached Officers	
	20th		Visited transport lines of 2 Inf: Bdes, and inspected Advanced Post.	
	21st		Inspected D.A.C Lines and other Divisional Units	
	22nd		Visited M.V.S Corps HQ and lines of Fd Ambces RE.	
	23rd		DADVS proceeded on leave and Capt Doyle AVC assumed his duties.	
	24th		Moved to WINNEZEELE M.V.S. to site near D.H.Q.	
	27th		Moved to ARNEKE M.V.S. to field requisitioned by O/c.	

J M Doyle Capt AVC
for Major AVC
DADVS 9th Division.

D.A.D.V.S. 9TH (SCOTTISH) DIVISION. No ... Date ...

(A7092). Wt. W12839/M1293. 750,000. 1/17. D. D. & L., Ltd. Forms/C.2118/14

Instructions regarding War Diaries and Intelligence Summaries are contained in F. S. Regs., Part II. and the Staff Manual respectively. Title pages will be prepared in manuscript.

WAR DIARY
or
~~INTELLIGENCE SUMMARY.~~
(Erase heading not required.)

Army Form C. 2118.

D.A.D.V.S.
9th DIVISION.
OCTOBER 1917

Vol 30

Place	Date	Hour	Summary of Events and Information	Remarks and references to Appendices
In the Field	6-10-17		Returned from Leave and visited 21st M.V.S	[initials]
– – –	7-10-17		Inspected lines of Divl Signal Co RE, Received instructions to proceed to V CORPS during absence in hospital of Col GLASSE	[initials]
– – –	8-10-17		Proceeded to V CORPS – vice Col GLASSE to hospital	[initials]
– – –	9-10-17		Returned from CORPS. Office moved to BRAKE CAMP. Inspected 197 M.G.C. and H.Q. CRA and CRE	[initials]
– – –	10-10-17		Inspected MVS sites – Visited 2/1st London MVS and 104 Co ASC, Visited Corps	[initials]
– – –	11-10-17		Inspected SA Bde and MGC, Three Field Ambulances, Signal Co RE. Visited Corps and 21st MVS	[initials]
– – –	12-10-17		Selected site for Adv Coll Post (H4 a Central Sheet 28). Inspected A.B.C Btys 50 Bde	[initials]
– – –	–		XVIII CORPS conference.	[initials]
– – –	13-10-17		Inspected 51st Bde RFA and Advanced Coll Post	[initials]
– – –	14-10-17		Visited Signal Co RE and DHQ lines 197 M G Co	[initials]
– – –	15-10-17		9th DAC inspected	[initials]
– – –	16-10-17		Inspected 26th Infantry Bde	[initials]
– – –	17-10-17		Inspected 27th Infy Bde and Signal Co RE. Visited MVS 2/1 London and 21st	[initials]
– – –	18-10-17		Visited South African Bde and 2/1st London Divn. Brig General Moore	[initials]
– – –	19-10-17		inspected re-inforcements 2/1 London MVS also the MV Sections	[initials]
– – –	20-10-17		Conference at CORPS. Visited Signal Co RE examined two Shoeing Smiths	[initials]
– – –	–		Inspected 105, 106 & 107 Cos ASC	[initials]
– – –	21-10-17		Visited DHQ and Signals. Inspected two horses of 41st Bde RFA in forward area suspected of STOMATITIS CONTAGIOSA (negative)	[initials]
– – –	22-10-17			
– – –	23-10-17		Visited ADVS XVIII CORPS and 21st MVS. Arrangements made for move and inspecting horses.	[initials]
– – –	–		Inspected the horses of Signal Co RE and DHQ	[initials]
– – –	24-10-17		DIVISION moved to WORMHOUDT AREA.	[initials]
– – –	25-10-17			
– – –	26-10-17		MOVED to MALO LES BAINS	[initials]

Continued

Instructions regarding War Diaries and Intelligence Summaries are contained in F. S. Regs., Part II. and the Staff Manual respectively. Title pages will be prepared in manuscript.

WAR DIARY
or
~~INTELLIGENCE SUMMARY.~~

(Erase heading not required.)

Army Form C. 2118.

DADVS
9th DIVISION
OCTOBER 1917

Place	Date	Hour	Summary of Events and Information	Remarks and references to Appendices
In the Field	27-10-17		Visited HQ lines also attended all day animals wounded at 28th Field	
– – –	– – –		Ambulance and Signal Co RE	JHW
– – –	28-10-17		Collected and arranged urgent demand for remounts to replace bomb	
– – –	– – –		casualties. Attend CRE lines midnight examined & dressed bomb wound cases	JHW JHW
– – –	29-10-17		Visited CRE lines and arranged for collection of float case.	JHW
– – –	– – –		moved to St IDESBALD	JHW
– – –	30-10-17		Visited HQ Units n MP, CRE Selected new site for MVS	JHW
– – –	31-10-17		Inspected 50th Bde RFA also Signal Co horses at LA PANNE	JHW
– – –	– – –		Interviewed AREA COMMANDANT re MVS site	

DHQ
3. 11. 1917.

J H Wright
.... MAJOR, A. V. C.
D. A. D. V. S. 9th. (SCOTTISH) DIVISION.

(A7092). Wt. W12839/M1293. 750,000. 1/17. D. D. & L., Ltd. Forms/C.2118 14.

Instructions regarding War Diaries and Intelligence Summaries are contained in F. S. Regs., Part II. and the Staff Manual respectively. Title pages will be prepared in manuscript.

WAR DIARY
or
~~INTELLIGENCE SUMMARY.~~

(Erase heading not required.)

Army Form C. 2118.

Vol 31

Place	Date	Hour	Summary of Events and Information	Remarks and references to Appendices
In the Field	1-11-17		Proceeded with DAQMG to CALAIS to draw Remounts	AHW
"	2-11-17		Returned morning from Remount Depot. Visited HQ Units	AHW
"	3-11-17		Attended Conference at XV Corps. Visited MVS and South African F Amb	AHW
"	4-11-17		Inspected RA Units of 50th Bde. Interviewed Sgt King against whom an adverse report had been made.	AHW
"			Inspected 51st Bde RFA and 104 Coy ASC HQ and CRE	AHW
"	5-11-17		Inspected the horses of the 50th & 51st Bdes RFA with ADVS XV Corps	AHW
"	6-11-17		Inspected 4th Regt South African Bde, 26th Infantry Bde 64th & 90 Field Co RE	AHW
"	7-11-17		Visited South African Field Ambce HQ lines, CRE, SA Section DAC, 104, 105, 107	AHW
"	8-11-17		Coy Divisional Train	
"			Conference of Veterinary Officers Inspected B Echelon and Remounts in 51st	
"	9-11-17		Bde RFA also 51st Bde HQ lines and South African Field Ambce	AHW
"			Conference at XV Corps, Visited lines of Signal Co RE	AHW
"	10-11-17		Visited 50th Bde RFA re fitters for water troughs. B Echelon DAC and CRE	AHW
"	11-11-17		Visited ADVS XV Corps. 9th Scottish Rifles 11th Royal Scotts KOSB 27th M G Coy	
"	12-11-17		and 106 Coy ASC at BRAY DUNES. LEFFRINKOUCKE and MALO LES BAINS	AHW
"	13-11-17		Visited and inspected horses HQ 50th Bde Signal Co RE and South African Field Amb	AHW
"	14-11-17		Inspected Influenza and Pneumonia cases in 50th Bde RFA also the horses of Signal Co RE and South African Field Ambce	AHW
"	15-11-17		Visited and inspected horses Signal Co RE HQ and SA Field Ambulance	AHW
"	16-11-17		Conference of Veterinary Officers. Consulted with ADVS XV Corps on telephone reference use of Ambulance for Pneumonia cases. Inspected Signal Coy horses prior to departure on move.	AHW
"	17-11-17		Attended Conference at XV Corps. Visited DAC and conferred with VO i/c	AHW
"	18-11-17		Moved to HUCQUELIERS Area	AHW

(A7092). Wt. W12839/M1293. 750,000. 1/17. D. D. & L., Ltd. Forms/C.2118/14.

Instructions regarding War Diaries and Intelligence Summaries are contained in F. S. Regs., Part II. and the Staff Manual respectively. Title pages will be prepared in manuscript.

WAR DIARY
or
~~INTELLIGENCE SUMMARY.~~
(Erase heading not required.)

Army Form C. 2118.

Place	Date	Hour	Summary of Events and Information	Remarks and references to Appendices
In the Field	19.11.17		Units en route.	JHW
—	20.11.17		Units en route.	JHW
—	21.11.17		Proceeded 7.30AM to CAMPAGNE, WARDRECQUES, and HEURINGHEM to investigate Influenza cases thence to X Corps to report, also inspected horses A & S Hdrs and 107 Coy Divisional Train on the march.	JHW
—	—		Inspected stables and animals of Divisional H Q Units	JHW
—	22.11.17		Visited horses H Q Units	JHW
—	23.11.17		Visited A.D.V.S X Corps and proceeded to HEURINGHEM with A.D.V.S also to 23 Veterinary Hospital ST OMER	JHW
—	24.11.17		Inspected horses Signal Co. RE at PREURES M M P and Divl. H Q	JHW
—	25.11.17		Inspected 26th Infantry Bde excepting two battalions. 63rd Field Co. R.E	JHW
—	26.11.17		Examined M M P horses.	JHW
—	27.11.17		Visited 28th Field Ambce at SEHEN, 197 M G Co. at PREURES. Signal Co. R.E PREURES also Divisional H Q Units.	JHW
—	28.11.17		Inspected horses 6th Black Watch, 7th Seaforth, 21st MVS and 105 Coy Divisional Train.	JHW
—	29.11.17		Visited A.D.V.S X Corps also 21st M V S. Visited H Q lines.	JHW
—	30.11.17		Visited and inspected S A Infy Bde and 107 Coy 9th Divisional Train.	JHW

J.H. Wright

(A7092). Wt. W12839/M1293. 750,000. 1/17. D. D. & L., Ltd. Forms/C.2118 14.

Instructions regarding War Diaries and Intelligence Summaries are contained in F. S. Regs., Part II. and the Staff Manual respectively. Title pages will be prepared in manuscript.

WAR DIARY of D.A.D.V.S. or ~~INTELLIGENCE SUMMARY.~~ 9th (Scottish) Division

(Erase heading not required.)

Army Form C. 2118.

Vol 32

Place	Date	Hour	Summary of Events and Information	Remarks and references to Appendices
In the Field	1.12.17		X CORPS Second Army area. Visited Divisional Headquarters Units.	LHW
– – –	2.12.17		Moved to HAUTE ALLAINES C 29 b Sheet 62C.	LHW
– – –	3.12.17		Visited Headquarters Units.	LHW
– – –	4.12.17		Visited VII CORPS to interview A.D.V.S. Visited 28th Field Ambulance. ADVS VII CORPS called. Division transferred to III CORPS	LHW
– – –	5.12.17		Visited ADVS III CORPS and arranged location for 21st M.V.S. Inspected M.M.P horses and H.Q. lines	LHW
– – –	6.12.17		Moved to LIERAMONT. Visited ADVS III CORPS accompanied him to 21st M.V.S and three companies of the Divisional Train. Inspected new standings and horses of D.H.Q.	LHW
– – –	7.12.17		Visited H.Q. horse lines. Inspected animals for evacuation at 21st M.V.S. Inspected animals of the 197 M.G. Coy and 10th Argyll & Sutherland Hghrs.	LHW
– – –	8.12.17		Conference A.D.V.S. III CORPS. Visited 21st M.V.S. Signal Co. R.E. and M.M.P horses. Inspected H.Q. Units and conferred with Capt. MACKIE AVC and attached	LHW
– – –	9.12.17		V.O's of 12th Division. Compiled instructions for frost and treatment of wounds. Inspected 28th Field Ambulance 27th Infantry Bde. Inspected 27th Field	LHW
– – –	10.12.17		Ambulance and D.H.Q. lines.	LHW
– – –	11.12.17		Superintended detraining and distribution of Remounts. Visited three Field Coys. R.E. and inspected 21st M.V.S.	LHW
– – –	12.12.17		Inspected 50 and 51st Bdes R.F.A. and Pioneers. Inspected horses for evacuation at 21st M.V.S.	LHW
– – –	13.12.17		Visited C.R.A. horse lines, M.M.P and H.Q. also 21st M.V.S. Visited 104 Coy A.S.C. 9th Seaforth Hghrs and South African Field Ambulance	LHW
– – –	14.12.17		Visited 21st M.V.S. inspecting horses for evacuation.	LHW
– – –	15.12.17		Visited III CORPS 21st M.V.S. Visited 27th and 28th Field Ambulances	LHW
– – –	16.12.17		Visited 9th Divisional Artillery. To 21st M.V.S. with A.D.V.S. VII CORPS inspecting Ophthalmia cases. Visited M.M.P. horses	LHW

(A7092). Wt. W12839/M1293. 750,000. 1/17. D. D. & L., Ltd. Forms/C.2118/14.

D.A.D.V.S.
9TH
(SCOTTISH) DIVISION.
No
Date 2/1/18

Instructions regarding War Diaries and Intelligence Summaries are contained in F. S. Regs., Part II. and the Staff Manual respectively. Title pages will be prepared in manuscript.

WAR DIARY of D.A.D.V.S. 9th (Scottish) Division
or
~~INTELLIGENCE SUMMARY.~~
(Erase heading not required.)

Army Form C. 2118.

Place	Date	Hour	Summary of Events and Information	Remarks and references to Appendices
In the Field	17.12.17		Visited B Btty 50 Bde RFA also HQ horse lines.	LHW
—	18.12.17		Division moved to SOREL. Inspected 50th Bde RFA, 26th Infantry Bde and South African Bde.	LHW
—	19.12.17		Inspected horses of 27th Infantry Bde. 27th Field Ambulance DHQ and Signal Co RE	LHW
—	20.12.17		Inspected DHQ lines. Horses for evacuation in MVS. Inspected suspicious skin cases in 104 Coy ASC.	LHW
—	21.12.17		Departmental work in Office. Inspected HQ lines CRA CRE and Signals.	LHW
—	22.12.17		Conference at VII CORPS. Visited HQ MMP and Signal Co RE lines	LHW
—	23.12.17		Inspected 51st Bde RFA and evacuated 4 MVS debility cases.	LHW
—	24.12.17		Inspected Signals & HQ Units. Inspected suspicious skin disease cases of 104 and 107 Coys Divisional Train. Visited Ordnance re iron rations.	LHW
—	25.12.17		Departmental work in Office and inspected CRE lines.	LHW
—	26.12.17		Inspected 9th Divisional Signal Co. 27th and 28th Field Ambulances	LHW
—	27.12.17		Inspected HQ lines. 27th Field Ambulance 63rd and 64th Field Co RE 9th Seaforth Hghrs and 197 MGCoy.	LHW
—	28.12.17		Visited Divisional HQ Units and conferred with VO i/c 53rd Bde RFA re mange. Visited MVS.	LHW
—	29.12.17		Inspected C Btty 51 Bde RFA with VO i/c. Conference at VII CORPS. Arranged issue (to replace casualties) of surplus animals in MVS	LHW
—	30.12.17		Visited HQ and Signal lines. Proceeded to MVS with Adjt RE and OC 21st MVS. Inspected 27th Field Ambulance.	LHW
—	31.12.17		Inspected 27th Infantry Bde 51st Bde RFA. 8th Black Watch, DD Cattle Section and Signals.	

L. Knight
MAJOR, A.V.C.
D.A.D.V.S. 9th. (SCOTTISH) DIVISION.

(A7092). Wt. W12839/M1293. 750,000. 1/17. D. D. & L., Ltd. Forms/C.2118/14.

D.A.D.V.S.
9th Division

Instructions regarding War Diaries and Intelligence Summaries are contained in F. S. Regs., Part II, and the Staff Manual respectively. Title pages will be prepared in manuscript.

WAR DIARY
or
~~INTELLIGENCE SUMMARY.~~
(Erase heading not required.)

January 1918

DADVS 9D
Vol 33

Army Form C. 2118.

Place	Date	Hour	Summary of Events and Information	Remarks and references to Appendices
In the Field	1-1-18		Inspected the horses of C and D Batterys 50th Bde RFA, also those of Div' HQ lines.	HW
—	2-1-18		Met Remounts at Railhead, distributing same to Units. Visited 21st MVS	HW
—	3-1-18		Inspection of the horses of the 50th Bde with ADVS VII Corps.	HW
—	4-1-18		Inspection of the horses of the 51 Bde RFA with ADVS VII Corps. Inf Bdes with GOC	HW
—	5-1-18		Conference at VII Corps. Inspected horses of 21st MVS and 28th Field Ambulance	HW
—	6-1-18		Visited all Headquarter Units. Inspected Divisional Train with ADVS VII Corps. Conference with GOC and Transport Officers 6 PM re protection of lines from Bombs	HW
—	7-1-18		Inspected Signal Co RE and HQ animals.	HW
—	8-1-18		Visited MVS. 27th Field Ambulance and Div' Amm Column.	HW
—	9-1-18		Visited VII Corps Reinforcement Camp HQ horses lines and Signal Co	HW
—	10-1-18		Visited and inspected the animals of the 63rd 64th 90th Field Co's RE and 9th Seaforths (Pioneers)	HW
—	11-1-18		Met Remounts at Railhead, distributing same to Units. Visited MVS	HW
—	12-1-18		Conference at Corps. Visited VII Corps Reinforcement Camp and HQ Units	HW
—	13-1-18		Visited and inspected animals of 27th and 28th Field Ambulances.	HW
—	14-1-18		Visited 26th and 27th Infantry Bdes, DD Cable Section also 21st MVS.	HW
—	15-1-18		Inspected horses with skin disease in C Btty 51st Bde RFA. Visited MVS	HW
—	16-1-18		Visited MVS. Inspected horses C Btty 51st Bde RFA. Visited 27th Field Amb'ce	HW
—	17-1-18		Visited HQ Units also VII Corps Reinforcement and Training Camp.	HW
—	18-1-18		Division HQ moved to NURLU. Visited MVS. HQ lines and Signal Co RE and attached Unit DD Cable Section VII Corps	HW
—	19-1-18		Visited and inspected animals 28th Field Amb'ce and 197 Machine Gun Co.	HW
—	20-1-18		Visited 27th Field Ambulance, VII Corps Ref and Training Camp, MMP, Signals Co RE, DD Cable Section Co. 63rd 64th 90th Field Co's RE 9th Seaforth Pioneers, also 21st MVS and HQ lines	HW

(A7092). Wt. W12839/M1293. 750,000. 1/17. D. D. & L., Ltd. Forms/C.2118 14

Instructions regarding War Diaries and Intelligence Summaries are contained in F. S. Regs., Part II. and the Staff Manual respectively. Title pages will be prepared in manuscript.

WAR DIARY
or
INTELLIGENCE SUMMARY.
(Erase heading not required.)

Army Form C. 2118.

D.A.D.V.S. 9TH (SCOTTISH) DIVISION. No. .... Date ....

Place	Date	Hour	Summary of Events and Information	Remarks and references to Appendices
In the Field	21.1.18		Inspected the horses of the C Btty 51st Bde RFA. Horses for evacuation at 21 MVS. Visited and inspected horses of 107 Coy Divisional Train. Inspected AVC Sergts Veterinary Wallets and issued new instruments.	JHW
"	22.1.18		Inspected the horses of the 50th Bde RFA. Visited and inspected horses 104 Coy Div Train. Visited 21st MVS.	JHW
"	23.1.18		Visited and inspected A Btty 50th Bde RFA, VII Corps Reinforcement Camp, Signal Coy RE and VII Corps DD Cable Section. Visited and inspected horses 105 Coy Divisional Train.	JHW
"	24.1.18		Inspected horses of MMP, 51st Bde RFA, 9th Scottish Rifles, 106 Coy Divl Train. Visited 21st MVS.	JHW
"	25.1.18		Weekly Conference of Veterinary Officers. Visited 21st MVS.	JHW
"	26.1.18		Visited 27th and 28th Field Ambulances, DD Cable Section, Signal Coy, MVS.	JHW
"	27.1.18		Visited MVS, DAC, South African Field Ambulance, HQ lines. Conferred with DADVS of relieving Division (39th) and accompanied him to MVS.	JHW
"	28.1.18		Arranged details of changes after move with Corps [illegible] AVC. Visited MVS. Accompanied GOC on inspection of 27th and South African Infy Bdes.	JHW
"	29.1.18		Inspected animals of SAA Section DAC and visited MVS, MMP, VII Corps R and T Camp, Signal Coy RE and 27th Field Ambulance.	JHW
"	30.1.18		Obtained and distributed ninety five remounts. Visited MVS and sick horse DHQ lines.	JHW
"	31.1.18		Visited HQ lines, Signal Coy RE, MVS and VII Corps HQ.	JHW

J H Wright
MAJOR, A.V.C.
D.A.D.V.S. 9th (SCOTTISH) DIVISION.

(A7092). Wt. W12839/M1293. 750,000. 1/17. D. D. & L., Ltd. Forms/C.2118/14

D.A.D.V.S.,
9TH
(SCOTTISH) DIVISION.

No.

Date 2. 3. 18.

A

9th Division

Beg to attach
War Diary for
February 1918.

[signature]

MAJOR, A.V.C.
D.A.D.V.S. 9th, (SCOTTISH) DIVISION.

D.A.D.V.S

9th Division

DADVS 9D

February

Vol 34

Army Form C. 2118.

WAR DIARY

or

~~INTELLIGENCE SUMMARY.~~

(*Erase heading not required.*)

Instructions regarding War Diaries and Intelligence Summaries are contained in F. S. Regs., Part II. and the Staff Manual respectively. Title pages will be prepared in manuscript.

Place	Date	Hour	Summary of Events and Information	Remarks and references to Appendices
In the Field	1.2.18		Visited H Q Units. Inspected horses for evacuation at 21st M V S	AHW
"	2.2.18		moved to MERICOURT-SUR-SOMME	AHW
"	3.2.18		Proceeded on leave to UK	AHW
"	4.2.18		On leave to UK from 4.2.18 to 18.2.18.	AHW
"	19.2.18		Returned from leave to UK. Visited and inspected horses in 21st MVS	AHW
"	20.2.18		Inspected the horses of the 50 & 51st Bdes RFA.	AHW
"	21.2.18		Visited H Q Units also 21st MVS inspected horses for evacuation Inspected	
"	" "		animals 7th Seaforth Highlanders	AHW
"	22.2.18		Conference VII Corps. Visited Headquarter Units	AHW
"	23.2.18		Inspected animals of the 10th DLI	AHW
"	24.2.18		Visited and inspected animals of the 26th and 28th M G Cos and proposed	
"	" "		Mobile Veterinary Section site.	AHW
"	25.2.18		Visited H Q Units also inspected horses for evacuation at 21st MVS	AHW
"	26.2.18		Visited H Q Units met A DVS VII Corps at proposed site for M V S and	
"	" "		accompanied him during inspection of C Bty 51st Bde RFA, 10th DLI.	AHW
"	27.2.18		Visited and inspected animals 26th M G Coy and those of the	
"	" "		South African Field Ambulance. Visited 9th D A C	AHW
"	28.2.18		Visited 61 Labour Group. 80 Labour Group H Q and VII Corps School Visited	
"	" "		and inspected horses for evacuation at 21st M V S.	AHW

A H Wright

DADVS 14 MARCH

9th Division

DADVS 9 D

Vol 36

Army Form C. 2118.

WAR DIARY
or
INTELLIGENCE SUMMARY.

(Erase heading not required.)

Instructions regarding War Diaries and Intelligence Summaries are contained in F. S. Regs., Part II. and the Staff Manual respectively. Title pages will be prepared in manuscript.

Place	Date	Hour	Summary of Events and Information	Remarks and references to Appendices
In the Field	1.3.18		Division moved to HAUTE ALLAINES. Selected site for 21st Mobile Vet'y Section	AHW
"	2.3.18		Conference VII CORPS. Visited Headquarters horse lines, Signal Co. and M.M.P.	AHW
"	3.3.18		Visited and inspected the animals of the ½ hances H'Btty, 71st 4" Batty RGA also 63rd Field Co RE. Visited and inspected horses for evacuation at 21st MVS	AHW
"	4.3.18		Visited HQ Units and 21st MVS.	AHW
"	5.3.18		Visited and inspected the horses of 26th M G Co. Selected Riders for 9th Battalion M G Corps from 3rd South African Inf'y and 10th DLI transport. Inspected horses with Specific Ophthalmia at 107 Co ASC	AHW AHW
"	6.3.18		Inspected animals 104 and 105 Co ASC 27th M G Co 28th Field Ambulance	AHW
"	7.3.18		Visited and inspected suspicious skin disease cases D Btty 51 Bde RFA also inspected B Btty 50 Bde, B Btty and C Btty 51 Bde RFA for Debility. Visited Signal Co RE	AHW
"	8.3.18		Accompanied ADVS VII CORPS in his inspection of C and D Bttys 51 Bde RFA also suspicious skin disease cases D Btty 50 Bde RFA. Visited 21st MVS Divisional and Signal Co RE horse lines	AHW
"	9.3.18		Conference VII CORPS. Visited 21st MVS inspected horses for evacuation. Visited and inspected horses at 10th DLI transport with Skin disease	AHW
"	10.3.18		Visited HQ Units	AHW
"	11.3.18		Inspected animals 28th Field Ambulance also those of 27th M G Co. Inspected horses 26th M G Co also Ophthalmia cases 107 Co ASC. Inspected animals for evacuation at 21st MVS.	AHW
"	12.3.18		DIVISION moved to NURLU. Visited 21st MVS.	AHW
"	13.3.18		Visited 21st MVS also inspected horses 104 Co ASC with suspicious skin disease. Visited HQ horse lines	AHW

(A7092). Wt. W12839/M1293. 750,000. 1/17. D. D. & L., Ltd. Forms/C.2118 14.

DADVS
9th Division

Instructions regarding War Diaries and Intelligence Summaries are contained in F. S. Regs., Part II. and the Staff Manual respectively. Title pages will be prepared in manuscript.

WAR DIARY
or
~~INTELLIGENCE SUMMARY.~~
(Erase heading not required.)

MARCH

Army Form C. 2118.

Place	Date	Hour	Summary of Events and Information	Remarks and references to Appendices
In the Field	14.3.18		Inspected animals of the 27th Infantry Bde. Inspected horses for evacuation at 21st MVS. Visited Signal Co RE Inspected animals 9th Seaforth's (Pioneers)	AHW
- - -	15-3-18		Visited HQ horse lines, Conference of Veterinary Officers. Inspected horses for evacuation at 21st MVS.	AHW
- - -	16-3-18		Conference VII CORPS. Inspected horses for evacuation at 21st MVS.	AHW
- - -	17.3.18		Inspected men of MVS on parade with anti-gas box respirators and horse anti gas respirator drill. Inspected animals of 50 Bde RFA	AHW
- - -	18.3.18		Inspected animals of 51st Bde RFA also those of the SA Inf Bde. Inspected horses for evacuation at 21st MVS.	AHW
- - -	19.3.18		Inspected animals 26th Inf Bde. Visited MVS inspected horses for evacuation	AHW
- - -	20.3.18		Inspected animals 9th Battalion M G Co. and 27 Infantry Bde.	AHW
- - -	21.3.18		Visited wounded animals 51st Bde RFA and evacuating wounded. Inspected horses for evacuation at 21st MVS. DIVISION moved to MOISLANS	AHW
- - -	22.3.18		DIVISION moved to RANCOURT	AHW
- - -	23.3.18		DIVISION moved to MAURAPAS	AHW
- - -	24.3.18		Visited HQ horse lines dressed and evacuated eight animals injured by hostile bomb. Rear HQ moved to BRAY CORBIE Rd.	AHW
- - -	25.3.18		Rear HQ moved to ETINHEM. Visited 21st MVS.	AHW
- - -	26.3.18		DIVISION moved to MERICOURT L'ABBE. Visited 21st MVS.	AHW
- - -	27.3.18		Rear HQ moved to CONTAY. Visited 21st MVS Signal Co RE and inspected 26th Infantry Bde transport en route of march.	AHW
- - -	28.3.18		DIVISION moved to FRECHINCOURT	AHW
- - -	29.3.18		DIVISION moved to BERTANGLES. Visited 21st MVS.	AHW
- - -	30.3.18		Visited HQ horse lines.	AHW
- - -	31.3.18		DIVISION moved to CANDAS.	AHW

A. H. Wright Major AVC
DADVS 9th (Scottish) Division

(A7092). Wt. W12839/M1293 750,000. 1/17. D. D. & L., Ltd. Forms/C.2118/14

9th Division

21

WAR DIARY

or

~~INTELLIGENCE SUMMARY.~~

(~~Erase heading not required.~~)

Army Form C. 2118.

DADVS 9 D

APRIL 1918

Vol 36

Instructions regarding War Diaries and Intelligence Summaries are contained in F. S. Regs., Part II. and the Staff Manual respectively. Title pages will be prepared in manuscript.

Place	Date	Hour	Summary of Events and Information	Remarks and references to Appendices
In the Field	1.4.18.		DIVISION moved to SCHERPENBERG.	AHW.
	2.4.18.		Visited proposed location of 21st M.V.S. Inspected H Quarters horses also those of M.M.P.	AHW.
	3.4.18.		Visited intended Infantry Bde Transport lines. Formulated Veterinary arrangements and Veterinary Officers changes in new Area.	AHW
	4.4.18		Inspected the animals of Divisional Units entering Area. Visited M.V.S. site	AHW
	5.4.18		Visited A.D.V.S. IX CORPS and attended Headquarters transport lines.	AHW
	6.4.18		Visited 21 M.V.S. also Signal Coy R.E. Inspected animals South African Infantry Bde also 107 Coy 9th Divisional Train and horses of the M.M.P. Visited animals of Headquarter Units	AHW AHW
	7.4.18		Inspected animals of the 27th Infantry Bde also B and D Coy 9th Batt M.G. Corps	AHW
	8.4.18		Visited 21st M.V.S. inspecting animals for evacuation. Inspected animals 105th C[illegible]	AHW
	9.4.18		Inspected animals of the 26th Infantry Bde transport. Visited 21st M.V.S.	AHW
	10.4.18		Inspected animals of the 64th Field Coy R.E. and 28th Field Amb. & attached horses M.M.P.	AHW
	11.4.18		Inspected animals of the 9th Seaforths (Pioneers), 63rd and 90th Field Coy R.E.	AHW
	12.4.18		Conference of Veterinary Officers. Attended H.Q. and Signal Co R.E. horse lines	AHW
	13.4.18		Visited XXII CORPS for interview with A.D.V.S. Visited 21st M.V.S. and inspected animals for evacuation	AHW
	14.4.18		Inspected and distributed remounts from depot. Visited M.V.S. and H.Q. lines	AHW
	15.4.18		REAR HEADQUARTERS moved to ABEELE.	AHW
	16.4.18		Visited Sections 9th D.A.C. and 21st M.V.S.	AHW
	17.4.18		Attended Headquarter horse lines.	AHW
	18.4.18		Visited M.M.P. Signal Co R.E. and 21st M.V.S.	AHW
	19.4.18		DIVISION moved to HOOGRAAF. Inspected animals for evacuation at 21st M.V.S.	AHW
	20.4.18		Inspected animals of the 50th Bde R.F.A. and C Batty 51 Bde R.F.A. Attended Camo horses Signal Co R.E.	AHW
	21.4.18		Inspected animals of the three batteries 51st Bde R.F.A. also 9th Seaforth Pioneers and Headquarter horse lines.	AHW

(A7092). Wt. W12839/M1293. 750,000. 1/17. D. D. & L., Ltd. Forms/C.2118/14.

9th Division

2

APRIL. 1918

Army Form C. 2118.

WAR DIARY
or
~~INTELLIGENCE SUMMARY.~~

(*Erase heading not required.*)

Instructions regarding War Diaries and Intelligence Summaries are contained in F. S. Regs., Part II. and the Staff Manual respectively. Title pages will be prepared in manuscript.

Place	Date	Hour	Summary of Events and Information	Remarks and references to Appendices
In the Field	22.4.18		Visited and inspected the animals of the 27th 28th and South African Field Ambulances.	JHW
– –	–		Inspected animals of 9th Scottish Rifles. Inspected animals for evacuation at 21st MVS	JHW
– – –	23.4.18		Attend Headquarter Transport Lines also inspected horses 104 Coy ASC 9th Div Train	JHW
– – –	24.4.18		Visited Signal Co RE. D Batty 51st Bde RFA and 106 Coy ASC 9th Divisional Train	JHW
– – –	25.4.18		Visited 106 Coy ASC re casualties from hostile bombs. Inspected animals 1st and 4th Regt SA Infy Bde. Inspected animals for evacuation at 21st MVS.	JHW
– – –	26.4.18		HEADQUARTERS moved to POPERINGHE – ABEELE ROAD L.22 b 5.7 Sheet 27. Inspected animals 1st Section 9th DAC.	JHW
– – –	27.4.18		Inspected animals II SECTION and SAA 9th DAC. Inspected horses for evacuation at 21st MVS.	JHW
– – –	28.4.18		Visited Signal Co RE and Headquarters 26th Infantry Bde.	JHW
– – –	29.4.18		Visited 9th DAC Headquarters. DIVISION moved to K9 a 3.8 Sheet 27	JHW
– – –	30.4.18		Inspected animals of the Companies 9th Battn M G Corps. Visited Headquarter Signal Co RE and M M P horse lines. Visited 21st MVS.	JHW

9th (Scottish) Division was formed September 6th 1914. Arrived in France May 9th 1915.

J H Wright. Major AVC
DADVS.
9th (Scottish) Division.

(A7092). Wt. W12839/M1293. 750,000. 1/17. D. D. & L., Ltd. Forms/C.2118 14.

ADVS. 9
9th DIVISION

Instructions regarding War Diaries and Intelligence Summaries are contained in F. S. Regs., Part II. and the Staff Manual respectively. Title pages will be prepared in manuscript.

WAR DIARY
~~or~~
~~INTELLIGENCE SUMMARY.~~
(Erase heading not required.)

MAY 1918.

Army Form C. 2118.

Vol 37

Place	Date	Hour	Summary of Events and Information	Remarks and references to Appendices
In the Field	1.5.18.		Inspected the animals of the 9th Seaforth (Pioneers) also those of the 26th Infantry Bde.	A.H.W.
–	2.5.18.		Visited and inspected animals of the 51st Bde R.F.A.	A.H.W.
–	3.5.18		Division moved to ZEGGERS CAPPEL. Inspected Divisional Transport on the march	A.H.W.
–	4.5.18		Attended XXII CORPS for interview with A.D.V.S. Attended H.Q. and Signal Co R.E. horse lines	A.H.W.
–	5.5.18		Visited and inspected the animals of the S.A. Field Amb[ce]. Visited H.Q. & Signal horse lines	A.H.W.
–	6.5.18		Inspected animals of the 64th Field Co R.E.	A.H.W.
–	7.5.18		DIVISION moved to BLARINGHEM	A.H.W.
–	8.5.18		Visited 26th Infantry Bde 64th Field Co R.E. 28th Field Amb[ce] 105 Co A.S.C. and H.Q. Div[l] Train	A.H.W.
–	9.5.18		Visited and inspected animals 9th Bn M.G. Corps, also Signal Co R.E. Wagon Lines.	A.H.W.
–	10.5.18		Visited 21st M.V.S. and 104 Co A.S.C. also Signal Co R.E. and M.M.P.	A.H.W.
–	11.5.18		Visited and inspected the animals of the 27th South African Infantry Bde 63rd Field Co R.E. S.A. Field	
–	–		Ambulance and 107 Co A.S.C. HEURINGHEM AREA.	A.H.W.
–	12.5.18		Visited and inspected 26th Infantry Bde animals also those at Headquarters of Division.	A.H.W.
–	13.5.18		Attended H.Q. wagon lines also Signal Co R.E. H.Q. 9th Divisional Train. 9 Bn M.G. Corps and	
–	–		90 Co R.E.	A.H.W.
–	14.5.18		Attended 28th S.A. Infantry Bde. 107 Co A.S.C. S.A.A. 9th D.A.C. Distributed Remounts at Div. H.Q. Quarters	A.H.W.
–	15.5.18		President of Board testing Shoeing Smiths, two Privates 2nd R.S. Fusiliers 28 S.A. Inf Bde.	A.H.W.
–	16.5.18		Visited and inspected animals 27th Infantry Bde and Section of 27 Field Amb[ce] LUMBRES.	A.H.W.
–	17.5.18		Attended 26th Infantry Bde 28 Field Amb[ce] and S.A. Section D.A.C	A.H.W.
–	18.5.18		Visited Civilian farmers Cows injured by hostile bombs. President of Board for submitted to	
–	–		test Shoeing smiths, three Privates 9th Scottish Rifles. Visited 27th Field Ambulance	A.H.W.
–	19.5.18		Visited Civilian farmers cow wounded by bomb, attended Signal Co R.E. Visited 21st M.V.S.	A.H.W.
–	20.5.18		Visited 9th D.A.C. and S.A. Infantry Bde S.A. Field Amb[ce] and 107 Co A.S.C. Inspected Remounts	
–	–		on arrival	A.H.W.
–	21.5.18		Visited and inspected with A.D.V.S. XV CORPS 51st Bde R.F.A. Attended 9th Bn M.G. Corps	A.H.W.
–	22.5.18		Visited B Btty 51st Bde R.F.A. and evacuated debility cases.	A.H.W.
–	23.5.18		Visited D.A.D.V.S. 31st Division re interchange of Mobile Veterinary Sections, Visited 21st M.V.S.	
–	–		Visited and inspected 50th Bde R.F.A.	A.H.W.
–	24.5.18		Attended H.Q. and Signal Co R.E. Wagon lines.	A.H.W.
–	25.5.18		DIVISION moved to HONDEGHEM. Visited S.A. Field Ambulance and 21st M.V.S.	A.H.W.
–	26.5.18		Visited 21st M.V.S. also site of No 8 V.E.S. in company with O.C. 21st M.V.S. Attended M.M.P. and	
–	–		Signal Co R.E. wagon lines.	A.H.W.

(A7092). Wt. W12839/M1293. 750,000. 1/17. D. D. & L., Ltd. Forms/C.2118-14.

D.A.D.V.S. 9th Division

2

Instructions regarding War Diaries and Intelligence Summaries are contained in F. S. Regs., Part II. and the Staff Manual respectively. Title pages will be prepared in manuscript.

WAR DIARY
or
INTELLIGENCE SUMMARY.
(Erase heading not required.)

May 1918

Army Form C. 2118.

Place	Date	Hour	Summary of Events and Information	Remarks and references to Appendices
In the Field	27.5.18		Visited and inspected the animals of the 26th Infantry Bde. also horses for evacuation at the 21st M.V.S.	
"	"		Attended Divn Signal Coy R.E. Visited and inspected animals	
"	"		S.A. Composite Battn and 2nd Royal Scots Fusiliers (28 Inf Bde) also 107 Coy A.S.C.	A.H.W.
"	28.5.18		Visited and inspected animals 27th Infantry Bde. Visited 21st M.V.S. [illegible] 105 Coy A.S.C. Attended horses H.Q. Wagon Lines	A.H.W.
"	29.5.18		Visited & inspected animals 63rd 64th and 90th Field Coys R.E., also 21st M.V.S.	A.H.W.
"	30.5.18		Visited B & C Btys 50th Bde R.F.A. also those of A B & D Btys 51st Bde R.F.A.	A.H.W.
"	31.5.18		Attended Headquarters and Signal C.R.E. wagon lines. Visited and inspected animals for evacuation at 21st M.V.S.	A.H.W.

A.H. Wright Major A.V.C.
D.A.D.V.S.
9th Division

D. D. & L., London, E.C.
(A5001) Wt. W1771/M2031 750,000 5/17 Sch. 52 Forms/C2118/14

17

Army Form C. 2118.

WAR DIARY
~~or~~
~~INTELLIGENCE SUMMARY.~~
(Erase heading not required.)

Instructions regarding War Diaries and Intelligence Summaries are contained in F. S. Regs., Part II. and the Staff Manual respectively. Title pages will be prepared in manuscript.

D.A.D.V.S.
9th DIVISION.
June 1918
38

Place	Date	Hour	Summary of Events and Information	Remarks and references to Appendices
In the Field	1.6.18		Visited and inspected the animals of I and II Sections 9th DAC and 9th Bn M G Corps. Inspected animals for evacuation at 21st M.V.S. Visited civilian farmers colt with septic pneumonia following castration.	H.W.
-	2-6-18		Inspected animals 104 Co. 9th Div. Train and SAA Section 9th DAC. Visited civilian farmers colt	H.W.
-	3-6-18		Visited 50th and 51st Bdes RFA with ADVS XV CORPS. Attended animals M.M.P. Signal Co RE and inspected 21st M.V.S. and animals for evacuation.	H.W.
-	4-6-18		Visited and inspected animals A Co. 9th M G Corps 64th Field Co RE 21st M.V.S. Inspected animals 28th SA Infantry Bde. SA Field Ambulance and 5th Camerons	H.W.
-	5-6-18		Visited and inspected animals 26th and 27th Infantry Bdes also 63rd Field Co RE	H.W.
-	6-6-18		Visited 21st M.V.S. and inspected animals for evacuation. Inspected animals of 105 Co. 9th Div. Train. Inspected animals of the 28th Field Ambulance and 106 Co. 9 Div Train	H.W.
-	7-6-18		Visited 21st M.V.S. D Co. 9th Bn M G Corps and 28th SA Infantry Bde.	H.W.
-	8-6-18		Visited and inspected animals for evacuation at 21st M.V.S. Inspected animals 90th Field Co RE and 107 Co. 9th Divisional Train. Attended M.M.P. H.Q. and Signal Co R.E. wagon lines also 21st M.V.S. inspected two mules suffering from Mustard Gas	H.W.
-	9-6-18		Visited 21st M.V.S. Inspected animals 9th Seaforth Hghrs (Pioneers) and A B and C Co. 9th Bn M G Corps. Distributed Remounts to Infantry Units. Visited ADVS XV Corps	H.W.
-	10-6-18		Visited and inspected animals B.C.D Btys 51st Bde RFA. Attended H.Q. and M.M.P. transport lines.	H.W.
-	11-6-18		Attended H.Q. and Signal Co RE transport lines. Visited and inspected animals for evacuation at 21st M.V.S. ADVS XV CORPS visited 21st M.V.S.	H.W.
-	12-6-18		Visited 21st M.V.S. also attended H.Q. transport lines.	H.W.
-	13-6-18		Inspected animals A Bty Bde RFA also those of the 50th Bde RFA. Inspected animals for evacuation at 21st M.V.S. Attended H.Q. transport lines.	H.W.
-	14-6-18		Attended animals Signal Co RE and M.M.P. also animals for evacuation at 21st M.V.S.	
-	15-6-18		DIVISIONAL HEADQUARTERS moved to U6 a 3.6 Sheet 27. Visited 21st M.V.S. to meet DDVS and ADVS XV CORPS. Visited & VES with reference to site being occupied by 21st M.V.S.	H.W.

D. D. & L., London, E.C. (A8001) Wt. W1771/M2031 750,000 5/17 Sch. 52 Forms/C2118/14

Instructions regarding War Diaries and Intelligence Summaries are contained in F. S. Regs., Part II. and the Staff Manual respectively. Title pages will be prepared in manuscript.

WAR DIARY

~~or~~

INTELLIGENCE ~~SUMMARY~~.

(*Erase heading not required.*)

Army Form C. 2118.

Place	Date	Hour	Summary of Events and Information	Remarks and references to Appendices
In the Field	16.6.18		Visited and inspected animals of the 27th 28th and SA Field Ambulances.	JHW
– –	17.6.18		Visited 21st MVS also animals 26th Infantry Bde.	JHW
– –	18.6.18		Indisposed with Influenza	JHW
– –	19.6.18		D° d°	JHW
			D° d°	JHW
– –	20.6.18		Visited HQ transport lines and 21st MVS.	JHW
– –	21.6.18		Visited and inspected animals for evacuation at 21st MVS. ~~[illegible]~~ DRO for protection of animals against Mustard Gas published.	JHW
– –	22.6.18			
– –	23.6.18		Visited 21st MVS. CAPT HOBSON G.K. AVC reported for duty vice CAPT DOYLE T.M. AVC and was posted to 9th DAC.	JHW
– –	24.6.18		Visited and inspected animals C Blty 50th Bde and A Blty 51st Bde RFA. Visited MVS.	JHW
– –	25.6.18		Visited and inspected animals 28th SA Inf Bde. A Co 9th Bn M G Corps 90th Field Co RE. Visited 21st MVS	JHW
– –	26.6.18		Visited 21st MVS inspecting animals for evacuation. Inspected animals 106 Coy 9th Div Train. Attended HQ wagon lines	JHW
– –	27.6.18		Visited and inspected animals B.C.D 51st Bde RFA and D 50th Bde RFA	JHW
– –	28.6.18		Conference of Veterinary Officers. Attended HQ wagon lines and visited 21st MVS	JHW
– –	29.6.18		Visited and inspected animals A & B Bltys 50th Bde RFA also HQ and 1st and 2nd Sections 9th DAC	JHW
– –	30.6.18		Attended HQ, Signal Co RE wagon lines also inspected animals for evacuation at 21st MVS	JHW

J.H. Wright Major AVC
DADVS
9th Division

D. D. & L., London, E.C.
(A8001) Wt. W1771/M2031 750,000 5/17 Sch. 52 Forms/C2118/14

DADVS
9th DIVISION

DADVS 9 D
Vol 39

9

Instructions regarding War Diaries and Intelligence Summaries are contained in F. S. Regs., Part II. and the Staff Manual respectively. Title pages will be prepared in manuscript.

WAR DIARY
or
~~INTELLIGENCE SUMMARY.~~
(Erase heading not required.)

Army Form C. 2118.

Place	Date	Hour	Summary of Events and Information	Remarks and references to Appendices
In the Field	1.7.18		Visited and inspected the animals of the 63rd, 64th and 90th Field Coys RE	HW
"	2.7.18		Visited and inspected animals of the 9th Seaforth Hghrs (Pioneers) also those of A B and C Coys 9th Battn M G Corps. Attend M M P horse lines. Visited 21st M V S inspecting animals for evacuation	HW
"	3.7.18		Visited and inspected animals of the battalions of 26th Infantry Bde and 2 Coys 9th Bn M G Corps. Visited 21st M V S.	HW
"	4.7.18		Visited and inspected animals of the battalions of the 27th Infantry Bde also those of the S A Field Ambulance attended Signal Co R E Wagon lines	HW
"	"		Visited 21st M V S distributed Remounts to Divisional Units	HW
"	5.7.18		Visited 21st M V S Attended H Q horse lines. Conference of Veterinary Officers	HW
"	6.7.18		Visited and inspected animals of the battalions of the S A Infantry Bde	HW
"	"		attended M M P horse lines and inspected animals for evacuation 21st M V S	HW
"	7.7.18		Inspected animals of the 28th Field Ambulance and half of those of 156 Coy A S C	HW
"	"		attended box respirator and horse respirator practice at 21st M V S.	HW
"	8.7.18		Visited and inspected animals 27th Field Ambulance attended M M P horse lines	HW
"	"		Visited 21st M V S first Box respirator and horse gas mask demonstration for Units of Division	HW
"	9.7.18		Visited and inspected animals of the 104 and 107 Coy 9th Divl Train. Visited 21st M V S attended M M P horse lines	HW
"	10.7.18		Visited and inspected animals 26th Infantry Bde. Attended H Q and Signal Co R E wagon lines. Visited 21st M V S 2nd box respirator and horse gas mask demonstration for Divisional Units. Distributed Remounts to Divisional Units	HW
"	11.7.18		Visited and inspected Rides 27th Field Ambulance. Visited 21st M V S.	HW
"	12.7.18		Visited 21st M V S with A D V S XV CORPS attended H Q horse lines	HW
"	13.7.18		Attended Signal Co RE horse lines. Visited 21st M V S 3rd box respirator and horse gas mask demonstration for Divisional Units A D V S XV CORPS present. attended S A Field Ambulance.	HW
"	14.7.18		Visited 28th Field Ambulance 106 Coy 9th Divisional Train and 21st M V S	HW

D. D. & L., London, E.C.
(A8001) Wt. W1771/M2031 750,000 5/17 Sch. 52 Forms/C2118/14

Army Form C. 2118.

WAR DIARY
or
~~INTELLIGENCE SUMMARY.~~
(Erase heading not required.)

Instructions regarding War Diaries and Intelligence Summaries are contained in F. S. Regs., Part II. and the Staff Manual respectively. Title pages will be prepared in manuscript.

Place	Date	Hour	Summary of Events and Information	Remarks and references to Appendices
In the Field	15.7.18		Visited and inspected animals of the C battery 51st Bde RFA and D Btty 50th Bde RFA	AHW
"	16.7.18		Visited and inspected animals of B and D batteries 51st Bde RFA. Visited 21st MVS	AHW
"	17.7.18		Visited and inspected animals of the A and C Bttys 51st Bde RFA. Visited Signal Co RE horse lines and 21st MVS.	AHW
"	18.7.18		Scheme for central clipping of the horses of the Division submitted to ADVS XV CORPS. Visited and inspected animals for evacuation at 21st MVS. Visited and inspected animals of the 105 Co 9th Div Train. Issued Veterinary arrangements with reference to Advance or Retirement of Division.	AHW
"	19.7.18		Visited and inspected animals of the A and B Bttys 50th Bde RFA. Visited 21st MVS. Inspected animals for evacuation.	AHW
"	20.7.18		Attended HQ transport lines. Visited 21st MVS.	AHW
"	21.7.18		Visited C Btty 50th Bde RFA with ADVS XV CORPS and Corps Veterinary Evacuation Station. Visited 21st MVS	AHW
"	22.7.18		Visited and inspected animals of the 26th Infantry Bde and A Co 9th Bn M G Corps. Visited 21st MVS inspected animals for evacuation. Attended HQ MMP and Signal Co RE horse lines	AHW
"	23.7.18		Attended Conference XV Corps. Visited 21st MVS distributing Remounts to Divisional Units.	AHW
"	24.7.18		Visited and inspected animal at C battery 50th Bde RFA. Visited 21st MVS	AHW
"	25.7.18		Visited and inspected animals of B.C.D Cos 9th Bn M G Corps. Visited 5th Camerons and 8th Blk Watch wagon lines also 21st MVS.	AHW
"	26.7.18		Visited 21st MVS and HQ horse lines.	AHW
"	27.7.18		Visited 21st MVS	AHW
"	28.7.18		Visited and inspected animals 27th Infantry Bde and SA Field Ambulance. Attended MMP Signal Co RE and HQ horse lines. Visited 21st MVS	AHW
"	29.7.18		Visited C and D bttys 50th Bde RFA also 21st MVS	AHW
"	30.7.18		Visited and inspected animals 28th SA Infantry Bde	AHW
"	31.7.18		Visited and inspected animals 28th Field Ambulance. Visited 21st MVS and ADVS XV CORPS	AHW

A H Wright MAJOR, A. V. C.
D. A. D. V. S. 9th. (SCOTTISH) DIVISION.

D. D. & L., London, E.C. (A8004) Wt. W1771/M2031 750,000 5/17 Sch. 52 Forms/C2118/14

7 D.A.D.V.S. 9th DIVISION

AUGUST. 1918

Army Form C. 2118.

Instructions regarding War Diaries and Intelligence Summaries are contained in F. S. Regs., Part II. and the Staff Manual respectively. Title pages will be prepared in manuscript.

WAR DIARY
or
~~INTELLIGENCE SUMMARY.~~

(Erase heading not required.)

VIR 40

Place	Date	Hour	Summary of Events and Information	Remarks and references to Appendices
In the Field	1.8.18.		Visited 21st M.V.S. Attended H.Q. and Signal Co. R.E. transport lines	[illegible]
"	2.8.18		Visited and inspected the animals of the 64th and 90th Field Co. R.E.	[illegible]
"	3.8.18		Visited and inspected the animals of the 63rd Field Co. R.E. and 9th Seaforth Pioneers. Visited 21st M.V.S. inspected animals for evacuation	[illegible]
"			Choosing Site for Divisional Elimination Competitions for XV CORPS Show	[illegible]
"	4.8.18		Visited and inspected animals of the A Btty 50th Bde R.F.A. and C Btty	
"	5.8.18		51st Bde R.F.A. Visited 21st M.V.S.	[illegible]
"			Visited and inspected the animals of the 7th Seaforths and 5th Camerons	[illegible]
"	6.8.18		Attended Signal Co. R.E. and H.Q. transport lines. Visited 21st M.V.S.	[illegible]
"	7.8.18		Visited and inspected the animals of the C Btty 51st Bde with O.C. Bde. Attended CORPS committee re Corps Show. Visited 21st M.V.S.	[illegible]
"	8.8.18		Visited and inspected animals of the 27th Infantry Bde and 63rd Field Co. R.E. Visited 21st M.V.S.	[illegible]
"	9.8.18		Visited 21st M.V.S. H.Q. transport lines also 50th Bde R.F.A. H.Q. wagon lines	[illegible]
"	10.8.18		Attended Conference A.D.V.S. XV CORPS. Supervised elimination competition for Corps Horse Show. Visited 21st M.V.S. inspected animals for evacuation	[illegible]
"	11.8.18		Attended Special Service inter-denominational 2nd Army. Visited 21st M.V.S. and Div. H.Q. transport lines	[illegible]
"	12.8.18		Visited and inspected A B and D Coys 9th Bn M.G. Corps. Visited Signal Co. R.E. animals at Y.I.R. Visited 21st M.V.S. inspected animals for evacuation	[illegible]
"	13.8.18		Visited 21st M.V.S. Attended Signal Co. R.E. and H.Q. transport lines. Visited and inspected animals C Coy 9th Bn M.G. Corps and 7th Seaforth Highrs.	[illegible]
"	14.8.18		Visited and inspected animals 28th Field Ambulance. Visited 21st M.V.S. and attended Divisional Artillery elimination competitions for Corps Show. Attended H.Q. transport lines	[illegible]

D. D. & L., London, E.C.
(A8004) Wt. W1771/M2031 750,000 5/17 Sch. 52 Forms/C2118/14

Army Form C. 2118.

WAR DIARY
or
INTELLIGENCE SUMMARY.
(Erase heading not required.)

Instructions regarding War Diaries and Intelligence Summaries are contained in F. S. Regs., Part II. and the Staff Manual respectively. Title pages will be prepared in manuscript.

Place	Date	Hour	Summary of Events and Information	Remarks and references to Appendices
In the Field	15.8.18		Attended HQ transport lines. Visited 21st M.V.S. Attended Infantry elimination competitions for XV CORPS Show [illegible] XV CORPS. Visited 21st M.V.S.	EHW
"	16.8.18		Attended HQ transport lines. Visited and inspected animals for evacuation at 21st M.V.S. Conference of Veterinary Officers.	EHW
"	17.8.18		Visited 21st M.V.S. Attended HQ transport lines. Supervised elimination competitions for Corps Show.	EHW
"	18.8.18		Visited 21st M.V.S. Visited and inspected animals S.A.A. Section 9th D.A.C.	EHW
"	19.8.18		Visited 21st M.V.S. inspected animals for evacuation. Visited and inspected animals 27th and S.A. Field Ambulances, 26th Inf. Bde HQ transport lines and 105 Co. 9th Divisional Train.	EHW
"	20.8.18		Visited and inspected animals 6th Black Watch, 104 & 107 Co. 9th Divisional Train. Attended HQ and M.M.P. transport lines.	EHW
"	21.8.18		Attended Parade of selected [illegible] XV CORPS [illegible] Sheet 27. Visited and inspected animals for evacuation [illegible].	EHW
"	22.8.18		Visited and inspected animals of the I and II Sections 9th D.A.C., 64th and 90th Field Coy R.E. Visited 21st M.V.S. distributing Remounts to Divisional Infantry Units. DIVISION moved to P36 d 2.8 [illegible] 27.	EHW
"	23.8.18		Visited and inspected animals of the 50th Bde R.F.A. Attended HQ and M.M.P. transport lines.	EHW
"	24.8.18		Visited and inspected animals of the 51st Bde R.F.A. Attended Signal Co. R.E. transport lines. Visited 21st M.V.S. and A.D.V.S. XV CORPS.	EHW
"	25.8.18		DIVISION moved to [illegible].	EHW
"	26.8.18		Attended HQ and Signal Co. R.E. transport lines. Visited 21st M.V.S.	EHW
"	27.8.18		Visited and inspected animals of the S.A.A. Section 9th D.A.C., 106 Co. 9th Div. Train and 27th Infantry Bde. Visited and inspected animals 27th Field Ambulance.	EHW
"	28.8.18		Visited and inspected animals of the 26th Infantry Bde. Attended HQ and Signal Co. R.E. transport lines.	

D. D. & L., London, E.C.
(A8001) Wt. W1771/M2031 750,000 5/17 Sch. 52 Forms/C2118/14

Army Form C. 2118.

Instructions regarding War Diaries and Intelligence Summaries are contained in F. S. Regs., Part II. and the Staff Manual respectively. Title pages will be prepared in manuscript.

WAR DIARY
or
INTELLIGENCE SUMMARY.
(Erase heading not required.)

Place	Date	Hour	Summary of Events and Information	Remarks and references to Appendices
In the Field	29.8.18		Visited SA Infantry Bde 107 Co 9th Divisional Train and SA Field Ambulance [illegible] evacuated at LUMBRES. Visited O.C 5th MVS.	J.H.W.
"	30.8.18		Visited 64 and 90th Field Coy RE and ADVS XV CORPS. Visited 2[illegible] MVS inspected animals for evacuation and detailing [illegible] to Divisional Infantry Units	J.H.W.
"	31.8.18		Visited ADVS XV CORPS. Attended 1st and 2nd Coy RE transport [illegible]	J.H.W.

J.H. Wright Major AVC
DADVS
9th (Scottish) Division

D. D. & L., London, E.C.
(A8004) Wt. W1771/M2031 750,000 5/17 Sch. 52 Forms/C2118/14

24 September 1918

Instructions regarding War Diaries and Intelligence Summaries are contained in F. S. Regs., Part II. and the Staff Manual respectively. Title pages will be prepared in manuscript.

WAR DIARY or INTELLIGENCE SUMMARY.

(Erase heading not required.)

D.A.D.V.S 9th Division

Army Form C. 2118.

Vol 41

Place	Date	Hour	Summary of Events and Information	Remarks and references to Appendices
In the Field	1.9.18		Visited and inspected the animals of the 63rd Field Co RE	[initials]
	2.9.18		Visited and inspected the animals of the 9th Scottish Rifles 2nd Royal Scots Fusiliers and 107 Co 9th Divisional Train at LUMBRES. Visited and inspected animals for evacuation at 21st M.V.S. Attended H.Q. and M.M.P. transport lines	[initials]
	3.9.18		Visited and inspected the animals of the 26th Infantry Bde. Visited 21st M.V.S. and Signal Co RE transport lines	[initials]
	4.9.18		Visited and inspected the animals of the following Divisional Units: 27th Infantry Bde, 27th Field Ambulance, 9th Seaforth Hghrs (Pioneers). Visited and inspected animals for evacuation at 21st M.V.S.	[initials]
	5.9.18		Visited and inspected the animals of the 28th (SA) Infantry Bde, SA Field Ambulance and 107 Co 9th Divisional Train	[initials]
	6.9.18		Visited and inspected the animals of the A B and D Coys 9th B. Machine Gun Corps and 28th Field Ambulance. Attended Signal Co RE wagon lines. Visited and inspected animals for evacuation at 21st M.V.S.	[initials]
	7.9.18		Attended H.Q. and M.M.P. wagon lines. Visited and inspected stray heavy draught mare at 21st M.V.S.	[initials]
	8.9.18		Attended Signal Co RE wagon lines. Inspected and distributed remounts to the Divisional Infantry Units	[initials]
			Visited H.Q. M.M.P. and Signal Co RE transport lines	[initials]
	9.9.18		Visited 21st M.V.S. Attended Signal Co RE transport lines	[initials]
	10.9.18		Visited 2nd Royal Scots Fusiliers, 9th Scottish Rifles, 107 Co 9th Divisional	
	11.9.18		Train and H.Q. 28th Infantry Bde LUMBRES. Also 23rd Veterinary Hospital St OMER. Visited H.Q. Signal Co RE and M.M.P. transport lines. Visited 21st M.V.S. making arrangements with reference to move of the Section.	[initials]

D. D. & L., London, E.C. (A8004) Wt. W1771/M2031 750,000 5/17 Sch. 52 Forms C2118/14

Instructions regarding War Diaries and Intelligence Summaries are contained in F. S. Regs., Part II. and the Staff Manual respectively. Title pages will be prepared in manuscript.

Sept 1918

WAR DIARY
or
INTELLIGENCE SUMMARY.
(*Erase heading not required.*)

DADVS
9th Divn

Army Form C. 2118.

Place	Date	Hour	Summary of Events and Information	Remarks and references to Appendices
In the Field	12.9.18		DIVISION moved from WARDRECQUES XV CORPS to ESQUELBECQUE II CORPS. Visited ADVS II CORPS, inspecting animals 26th Infantry Bde en route.	H.W.
"	13.9.18		Visited HQ Units at 21st MVS site, Visited 64th Field Coy RE 107 Coy 9th Divl Train and 21st MVS at new location C 24 a 2.2 Sheet 27	H.W.
"	14.9.18		Visited 9th Scottish Rifles 2nd Royal Scots Fusiliers and Royal Newfoundland Battalions (28th Infantry Bde). Visited 11th 12th Royal Scots and 6th KOSB (27th Infantry Bde). Visited A Coy 9th Bn Machine Gun Corps, post mortem examination bay (LD) mare.	H.W.
"	15.9.18		Visited and inspected the animals of the 51st Bde RFA. Visited and inspected animals 76th Field Ambulance.	H.W.
"	16.9.18		Visited and inspected the animals of the 50th Bde RFA with Officer Commanding Brigade. Visited 27th Infantry Bde transport lines, 27 Field Ambulance and 106 Coy 9th Divisional Train inspecting the animals of these Units	H.W.
"	17.9.18		Visited and inspected animals 63rd Field Coy RE. Visited 21st MVS inspected animals for evacuation, attended MMP transport lines.	H.W.
"	18.9.18		Visited 21st MVS, also visited and inspected animals of the B C and D Coys Bn M G Corps attended HQ transport lines, Visited DADVS 14th DIVISION arranging move of 21st MVS to F13 d 1.9 Sheet 27.	H.W.
"	19.9.18		Visited 21st MVS, Signal Co RE and Battalions 27th Infantry Bde	H.W.
"	20.9.18		DIVISION moved from ESQUELBECQUE to COUTHOVE CHATEAU. Visited II CORPS VES, Conference Veterinary Officers. Visited ADVS II CORPS.	H.W.
"	21.9.18		Visited and inspected 21st MVS, Reconnaissance of area for site of advanced Collecting Post, Visited 107 Coy 9th Divisional Train and SAA Section, attended Signal Co RE and MMP transport lines	H.W.

D. D. & L., London, E.C.
(A8001) Wt. W1771/M2031 750,000 5/17 Sch. 52 Forms/C2118/14

3

WAR DIARY
~~INTELLIGENCE~~ SUMMARY.

Army Form C. 2118.

Instructions regarding War Diaries and Intelligence Summaries are contained in F. S. Regs., Part II. and the Staff Manual respectively. Title pages will be prepared in manuscript.

(Erase heading not required.)

Place	Date	Hour	Summary of Events and Information	Remarks and references to Appendices
In the Field	22.9.18		Attended H.Q. transport lines. Visited 21st M.V.S. and inspected animals for evacuation. Completed Veterinary arrangements for Active operations.	[illegible]
"	23.9.18		Visited 90th Field Coy. R.E. also inspected animals of [illegible] 9th Divisional Train, Attend Signal C.R.E. transport lines, Conference A.D.V.S. II CORPS.	[illegible]
"	24.9.18		Visited and inspected the animals of H.Q. and I Section 9th D.A.C. Visited 21st M.V.S. and inspected animals for evacuation.	[illegible]
"	25.9.18		Visited A.D.V.S. II CORPS re (A.T.) [illegible] M.G. Corps' Shoeing of animals. Visited and inspected the animals of the [illegible] Section 9th D.A.C. Visited Advanced Collecting Post also 21st M.V.S.	[illegible]
"	26.9.18		Visited Advanced Collecting Station also [illegible] Section 9th D.A.C. inspecting the animals. Visited 21st M.V.S.	[illegible]
"	27.9.18		DIVISION moved from COUTHOVE CHATEAU to BORDER CAMP A.30.c. Sheet 28. [illegible] move of 21st M.V.S. from F.30 a 8.8. Sheet 27 to A 23 b 6.7 Sheet 28.	[illegible]
"	28.9.18		Visited 21st M.V.S. Inspected the [illegible] [illegible] [illegible].	[illegible]
"	29.9.18		Visited Advanced H.Q. I Section 9th D.A.C. and 21st M.V.S. at new location.	[illegible]
"	30.9.18		Visited 21st M.V.S. arranging location of Advanced Collecting Post. A.D.V.S. II CORPS at the M.V.S. Attended H.Q. transport lines.	[illegible]

J. H. Wright Major A.V.C.
D.A.D.V.S.
9th (Scottish) Division
B.E.F.

D. D. & L., London, E.C.
(A8001) Wt. W1771/M2031 750,000 5/17 Sch. 52 Forms/C2118/14

19

Army Form C. 2118.

Instructions regarding War Diaries and Intelligence Summaries are contained in F. S. Regs., Part II. and the Staff Manual respectively. Title pages will be prepared in manuscript.

October 1918.

WAR DIARY or ~~INTELLIGENCE SUMMARY.~~

(*Erase heading not required.*)

DADVS 9th Divn

Vol 43

Place	Date	Hour	Summary of Events and Information	Remarks and references to Appendices
In the field	29-10-18		Took over temporarily duties of DADVS who proceeded on leave to UK.	[illegible]
do	30-10-18		Attended office	[illegible]
	31-10-18		do do	[illegible]

[illegible] Power Capt AVC for DADVS 9th Divn

D. D. & L., London, E.C. (A8001) Wt. W1771/M2031 750,000 5/17 Sch. 52 Forms C2118/14

October 1918 — 2 — D.A.D.V.S. 9th Divn

Army Form C. 2118.

Instructions regarding War Diaries and Intelligence Summaries are contained in F. S. Regs., Part II. and the Staff Manual respectively. Title pages will be prepared in manuscript.

WAR DIARY
or
INTELLIGENCE ~~SUMMARY~~.

(*Erase heading not required.*)

Place	Date	Hour	Summary of Events and Information	Remarks and references to Appendices
In the Field	16.10.18		Inspected animals for evacuation at 21st M.V.S. Selected site for Advanced Collecting Post in forward area which was located at 28/L5 a 3.7	J.A.W.
—	17.10.18		My Office and 21st M.V.S. moved to 28/L5 a 3.7. Visited Divl H.Q. and with O.C. 21st M.V.S. selected location for Advanced Collecting Post. Attend 9th Signal Co. R.E. transport lines	J.A.W.
—	18.10.18		Visited Divl H.Q. Inspected animals for evacuation at 21st M.V.S. Attended H.Q. and Signal Co. R.E. transport lines. Visited and inspected animals 28th Infantry Bde. 6th K.O.S.B. and 12th Royal Scotts (27th Infantry Bde)	J.A.W.
—	19.10.18		Visited H.Q. transport lines also inspected the animals of the 28th and 2/1 Lancs Field Ambulances.	J.A.W.
—	20.10.18		Attended H.Q. transport lines. Inspected animals for evacuation at 21st M.V.S.	J.A.W.
—	21.10.18		Selected Site for 21st M.V.S. and Advanced Collecting Post which moved to 29/H2 b 9.7 and 29/B30 c 7.8 respectively. Visited Divl H.Q. re Remounts	J.A.W.
—	22.10.18		Visited H.Q. transport lines also those of C.R.A. inspecting standings	J.A.W.
—	23.10.18		Attended at 28/L5 a 3.7 and distributed Remounts to Divisional Units. Visited A.D.V.S. II CORPS. A.D.V.S. II CORPS visited 21st M.V.S. Inspected animals for evacuation at 21st M.V.S.	J.A.W.
—	24.10.18		Visited and inspected the animals of the A.C. and D Coys 9th Bn M.G. Corps also those of the 63rd 64th and 90th Field Co's R.E. Visited Advanced Collecting Post. Inspected animals for evacuation at 21st M.V.S.	J.A.W.
—	25.10.18		Inspected animals for evacuation at 21st M.V.S. Visited and inspected the animals at the rear wagon lines of C Bty 51st Bde R.F.A. Visited Divisional Headquarters transport lines	J.A.W.
—	26.10.18		Office moved to HARLEBEKE. Attend M.M.P. transport lines	J.A.W.
—	27.10.18		Attended at Staging Camp ROLLINGHEM CAPELLE distributing Remounts to Divisional Units. Visited Newfoundland Battalion (28th Bde) and inspected two H.D. horses stated to be bad workers. Visited Advanced Collecting Post	J.A.W.
—	28.10.18		Visited and inspected the animals of B and D Battys 50th Bde R.F.A. also those of the Battys A & B 51st Bde R.F.A. Visited and inspected animals for evacuation at the 21st M.V.S. Attended Signal Co. R.E. wagon lines	J.A.W.

D. D. & L., London, E.C. (A5001) Wt. W1771/M2031 750,000 5/17 Sch. 52 Forms/C2118/14

October 1918 **WAR DIARY** ~~or~~ ~~**INTELLIGENCE SUMMARY.**~~ D.A.D.V.S. 9th Division

Army Form C. 2118.

Instructions regarding War Diaries and Intelligence Summaries are contained in F. S. Regs., Part II. and the Staff Manual respectively. Title pages will be prepared in manuscript.

(Erase heading not required.)

Place	Date	Hour	Summary of Events and Information	Remarks and references to Appendices
In the Field	1.10.18		Visited 21st M.V.S. and arranged its transfer to location to I 3 d 2.3 Sheet 28. POTIJZE.	H.W.
"	2.10.18		Office transferred to 21st M.V.S. 21st M.V.S. moved to I 3 d 2.3 Sheet 28. Advanced Collecting Post placed at location D 21 d 8.1 Sheet 28 ZONNEBEKE. Visited and inspected the animals of the 104 and 107 Coy. 9th Divisional Train. Detailed CAPT. HOBSON A.V.C. to 50th Bde R.F.A. vice CAPT. MACKIE A.V.C. sick.	H.W.
"	3.10.18		Visited and inspected the animals of the I II & S.A.A. Section 9th D.A.C. and 64th Field Coy R.E.	H.W.
"	4.10.18		Visited Q Office 9th Divn, Advanced Collecting Post also 26th 28th Infantry Bde transport lines and D Coy 9th Battalion M.G. Corps. Inspected the animals for evacuation at 21st M.V.S.	H.W.
"	5.10.18		Attended H.Q. transport lines. Conference of Veterinary Officers	H.W.
"	6.10.18		Visited H.Q. 9th Divisional Train and H.Q. 9th D.A.C. with reference to collection and distribution of Remounts	H.W.
"	7.10.18		Visited Advanced H.Q. Advanced Collecting Post. Selecting future location of 21st M.V.S.	H.W.
"	8.10.18		Conference Veterinary Officers. Inspected animals for evacuation at 21st M.V.S.	H.W.
"	9.10.18		Distributed Remounts at PROVEN to Divisional Units. Visited and inspected animals of 104, 106 and 107 Coy. 9th Divisional Train	H.W.
"	10.10.18		Visited Advanced H.Q. reference Remounts. Attended H.Q. transport lines	H.W.
"	11.10.18		Visited and inspected the animals of the following batteries A and C 50th Bde C and D 51st Bde. Attended G.O.C.'s two Chargers at BORDER CAMP A 30 Central Sheet 28	H.W.
"	12.10.18		Inspected animals for evacuation at 21st M.V.S. Visited and inspected animals 105 Coy. 9th Divisional Train	H.W.
"	13.10.18		Visited Advanced H.Q. and A.C.P. ZONNEBEKE (D 21 d 8.1 Sheet 28)	H.W.
"	14.10.18		My Office and 21st M.V.S. moved to 28/D 30 c 6.3. Reconnoitred forward area for Advanced Collecting Post and located this post at K 5 a 6.6 Sheet 28	H.W.
"	15.10.18		Office and 21st M.V.S. moved to K 6 c 4.6 Sheet 28 (SLYPSKAPPELLE). Visited Advanced H.Q. and H.Q. 9th Divisional Train	H.W.

D. D. & L., London, E.C. (A8004) Wt. W1771/M2031 750,000 5/17 Sch. 52 Forms/C2118/14

DADVS 9th Division 19 — November 1918 — VR 44

Instructions regarding War Diaries and Intelligence Summaries are contained in F. S. Regs., Part II. and the Staff Manual respectively. Title pages will be prepared in manuscript.

WAR DIARY
or
~~INTELLIGENCE~~ SUMMARY.
(*Erase heading not required.*)

Army Form C. 2118.

Place	Date	Hour	Summary of Events and Information	Remarks and references to Appendices
In the Field	16.11.18		Returned from leave to UK, Visited the 21st MVS. 104 Coy 9th Div Train Div HQ transport lines also HD horse No 1 Coy 31st Div Train left with inhabitant JOS VANDER SNICHT RENAIX.	J.H.W.
"	17.11.18		Visited HD stabled with civilian RENAIX and arranged transfer to 21 MVS	
"	"		Attended Belgian celebration King Albert's birthday, Visited and inspected LD horse 90th Field Coy RE	J.H.W.
"	18.11.18		Inspected MMP horses, DIVISION moved to HEDEN BRAKEL	J.H.W.
"	19.11.18		Visited and inspected the animals of the 9th DAC, Visited two HD horses and one mule left by 31st Division at 616 WIELANDAELSTRAT NEDENBRAKEL. Visited 21st MVS also Signal Coy RE transport lines	J.H.W.
"	20.11.18		DIVISION moved to GRAMMONT	J.H.W.
"	21.11.18		DIVISION moved to HAL. Inspected animals 11th and 12th Royal Scots attend Div HQ transport lines	J.H.W.
"	22.11.18		DIVISION moved to MOUNT ST JEAN Inspected animals 28th Infantry Bde	J.H.W.
"	23.11.18		DIVISION moved to GISTOUX	J.H.W.
"	24.11.18		Visited ADVS II CORPS also inspected animals 9th 13th M G Corps,	J.H.W.
"	25.11.18		Visited with DAAG, 9th Division on Army Instructions the villages BORLEZ and AINEFFE re Veterinary Stores and Equipment said to have been left by the enemy. No trace found.	J.H.W.
"	26.11.18		Visited WAVRE and distributed twenty light Remounts collected from 36th DIVISION to Divisional Units	J.H.W.
"	27.11.18		DIVISION moved to BURDINNE	J.H.W.
"	28.11.18		DIVISION moved to AMPSIN	J.H.W.
"	29.11.18		DIVISION moved to FLEMELLE GRAND	J.H.W.
"	30.11.18		Inspected animals of the 28th Infantry Bde and 9th M G Corps.	J.H.W.

J.H. Wright.
MAJOR, A.V.C.
D.A.D.V.S. 9th. (SCOTTISH) DIVISION.

(A7092). Wt. W12839/M1293. 750,000. 1/17. D. D. & L., Ltd. Forms/C.2118/14

Instructions regarding War Diaries and Intelligence Summaries are contained in F. S. Regs., Part II. and the Staff Manual respectively. Title pages will be prepared in manuscript.

7

December 1918

WAR DIARY
or
~~INTELLIGENCE SUMMARY.~~
(Erase heading not required.)

DADVS 9th Divn

Army Form C. 2118.

VR 45

Place	Date	Hour	Summary of Events and Information	Remarks and references to Appendices
In the Field	1.12.18		Divisional Headquarters moved to VERVIERS. Inspected the animals of the 63rd Field Co RE	H.W.
–	2.12.18		Visited and inspected of the 28th Inf Bde headquarters, 2/1 East Lancs Field Ambulance, Headquarters of the 9th M G Corps also those of C and D Cos	H.W.
–	–		Visited ADVS II CORPS.	H.W.
–	3.12.18		Conference Divisional Veterinary Officers ADVS II CORPS visited office with	
–	4.12.18		reference to Artillery horses. Interviewed CRA with ADVS II CORPS.	
–	–		Inspected A B and D Btys 57th Bde RFA on the line of march. Arranged veterinary attendance on Divisional Units	H.W.
–	5.12.18		Visited and examined the animals in poor condition of the 50 and 51 Bde RFA with CRA. 16 unit debility and two lame evacuated to 21st MVS	H.W.
–	6.12.18		Division moved from VERVIERS to DÜREN Rhineland Germany	H.W.
–	7.12.18		Attended the entrainment of animals 28th Infantry Bde at DÜREN	H.W.
–	7.12.18		Divisional Headquarters moved from DÜREN to HORREM	H.W.
–	8.12.18		Inspected animals Divisional Headquarters Units	H.W.
–	8.12.18		Headquarters of Division moved from HORREM to RIEHL	H.W.
–	9.12.18		Visited and inspected the animals of the 26th Infantry Bde	H.W.
–	10.12.18		Visited and inspected animals 9th Signal Co RE attended to 2 horses [illegible]	
–	11.12.18		[illegible] and Headquarters transport lines	H.W.
–	–		Attended Headquarters transport lines, also inspected horses Royal	H.W.
–	12.12.18		Newfoundland Bn injured at BICKENDORF	
–	–		Visited and inspected animals 27th 28th Infantry Bdes. 50th Bde RFA	H.W.
–	13.12.18		and Divisional train on march route	H.W.
–	–		Attended M M P transport lines	H.W.
–	14.12.18		DIVISION moved to OHLIGS	H.W.
–	15.12.18		Visited Rider at RE Headquarters	
–	16.12.18		Visited and inspected the animals of the C and D Btys 51st Bde RFA	
–	17.12.18		also inspected animals of the 7th Auxiliary H T Coy returning to Unit	
–	–		from Division. Attended Headquarter transport lines	H.W.

(A7092). Wt. W12839/M1293. 750,000. 1/17. D. D. & L., Ltd. Forms/C.2118/14.

2/

Instructions regarding War Diaries and Intelligence Summaries are contained in F. S. Regs., Part II. and the Staff Manual respectively. Title pages will be prepared in manuscript.

Dec 1918

WAR DIARY or ~~INTELLIGENCE SUMMARY.~~

(Erase heading not required.)

DADVS 9th Divn

Army Form C. 2118.

Place	Date	Hour	Summary of Events and Information	Remarks and references to Appendices
In the Field	18-12-18		Visited and inspected the animals of the A and B Bttys 51st Bde RFA. Attended Divisional HQ Transport lines. ADVS II CORPS called at this office with reference to location of II VES	[illegible]
"	19-12-18		Attended MMP and HQ [illegible] transport lines. Visited and inspected the animals of the 27th Field Ambulance	[illegible]
"	20-12-18		Visited and inspected the animals of the four batteries 50th Bde RFA. Inspected also those of the 5th Camerons and 7th Seaforth Hghrs 26th Inf Bde	[illegible]
"	21-12-18		Visited and inspected the horses of the 2/1 East Lancs Field Ambulance suffering from Influenza. Inspected animals of the II R. Scots Fusiliers. Visited and inspected 21st MVS and personnel billets	[illegible]
"	22-12-18		Visited animals 2/1 East Lancs Field Ambulance also the animals of the R Newfoundland Bn and 9th Scottish Rifles	[illegible]
"	23-12-18		Visited 21st MVS. Visited and inspected animals of the [illegible] and 6th KOSB 27th Inf Bde	[illegible]
"	24-12-18		Visited and inspected mares for Breeding purposes 50th and 51st Bdes RFA also 5th Camerons and those of the 28th Field Ambulance	[illegible]
"	25-12-18		Visited animals 2/1 E Lancs Field Ambulance. Visited HQ 9th DAC 21st MVS and MMP transport lines	[illegible]
"	26-12-18		Visited 21st MVS also 2/1 East Lancs Field Ambulance	[illegible]
"	27-12-18		Visited 21st MVS. Inspected animals I and II Sections 9th DAC also those of the 106 Coy 9th Divisional Train	[illegible]
"	28-12-18		Visited animals 2/1 East Lancs Field Ambulance. Visited 21st MVS and inspected animals of 104 Coy 9th Divisional Train	[illegible]
"	29-12-18		Visited animals 63rd Field Coy RE also 107 Coy 9th Div Train 21st MVS and Signal Coy RE. Attended sick animals 2/1 East Lancs Field Ambce	[illegible]
"	30-12-18		Visited 2/1 East Lancs Field Ambulance with DDVS II Army and ADVS II CORPS. Visited 21st MVS	[illegible]
"	31-12-18		Visited and inspected horses and mules 7th Seaforth Hghrs [illegible] 9th Bn MG Corps and animals sick at 2/1 E Lancs Field Ambulance	[illegible]

[illegible] Major [illegible]
DADVS 9th (Scottish) Division
BEF

(A7092). Wt. W12839/M1293. 750,000. 1/17. D. D. & L., Ltd. Forms/C.2118/14.

9/3 D.A.D.V.S. 1449

9th Division

Instructions regarding War Diaries and Intelligence Summaries are contained in F. S. Regs., Part II. and the Staff Manual respectively. Title pages will be prepared in manuscript.

WAR DIARY
or
INTELLIGENCE SUMMARY.

(*Erase heading not required.*)

Jany 1919

Army Form C. 2118.

V8 46

Place	Date	Hour	Summary of Events and Information	Remarks and references to Appendices
Germany	1-1-19		Visited and inspected the horses with Influenza at the 2/1 Fd Amb. Visited Signal Coy [illegible] lines.	[illegible]
	2-1-19		Visited horses at 2/1 Fd Amb & 21st M.V.S.	[illegible]
	3-1-19		Attended conference ADVS 2nd Corps re demobilization of animals. Inspected animals at 2/1 Fd Amb.	[illegible]
	4-1-19		Inspected animals at 2/1 Fd Amb. Attended 21st M.V.S. with ADVS & [illegible] 2nd Corps where they selected [illegible]. Conference of Vety Officers.	[illegible]
	5-1-19		Visited 2/1 Fd Amb & No 1 Troop No 3 Squadron Traffic Control. President of Vety Board which is examining horses for demobilization [illegible] at No 1 Section D.A.C.	[illegible]
	6-1-19		Vety Board examined animals at No 1 Section DAC. Visited 2/1 Fd Amb also attended [illegible] Signal Co [illegible].	[illegible]
	7-1-19		Visited 2/1 Fd Amb to see animals with Influenza. Inspected animals for evacuation at the 21st M.V.S.	[illegible]
	8-1-19		Attended Abbatoir [illegible] in connection with horses destroyed from 2/1 Fd Amb. Visited Influenza cases at 2/1 Fd Amb. Vety Board at No [illegible] Section D.A.C.	[illegible]
	9-1-19		Inspected animals with Influenza at 2/1 [illegible]. Visited Abbatoir [illegible] & saw animals weighed which were destroyed yesterday. Vety Board at No 2 Section DAC.	[illegible]
	10-1-19		Vety Board at No 3 Section DAC. Inspected animals at 9th Div HQ & 2/1 Fd Amb. Inspected animals at [illegible] Brewery which have had Influenza.	[illegible]
	11-1-19		Vety Board at SAA Section. Attended 2/1 Fd Amb.	[illegible]
	12-1-19		Vety Board at 9th DAC HQ. Visited 21st M.V.S. and 2/1 Fd Amb.	[illegible]
	13-1-19		Vety Board at [illegible] HQ. [illegible]	[illegible]
	14-1-19		Inspected animals at 2/1 Fd Amb also 9th D.A. HQ. Vety Board at 5th [illegible]	[illegible]
	15-1-19		Attended D.H.Q. horse lines at [illegible] 9th [illegible]	[illegible]
	16-1-19		Visited 9th D.A. HQ, 2/1 Fd Amb, 21st M.V.S., [illegible] and No 1 Troop No 3 Squadron Traffic Control	[illegible]

D. D. & L., London, E.C.
(A8004) Wt. W1771/M2031 750,000 5/17 Sch. 52 Forms/C2118/14

D.A.D.V.S

9th Division

Instructions regarding War Diaries and Intelligence Summaries are contained in F. S. Regs., Part II. and the Staff Manual respectively. Title pages will be prepared in manuscript.

WAR DIARY
or
~~INTELLIGENCE SUMMARY.~~

(Erase heading not required.)

Jan 1919

Army Form C. 2118.

Place	Date	Hour	Summary of Events and Information	Remarks and references to Appendices
Germany	17-1-19		Vety Board at [illegible] Coy R.E. [illegible] R.E. and 28 [illegible]	[illegible]
	18-1-19		Vety Board at 9th [illegible] & [illegible] T.M.B	[illegible]
	19-1-19		Vety Board at 27 Bde H.Q. [illegible] and [illegible]	[illegible]
	20-1-19		Vety Board at 63 Fd Coy R.E., 28 Inf Bde H.Q. & [illegible] Scot Rifles	[illegible]
	21-1-19		Vety Boards at [illegible] R.S.F. [illegible] 1st [illegible] [illegible]	[illegible]
	22-1-19		Vety Boards at 9th Signal Coy R.E., 9th Div [illegible], [illegible] 3 Corps Signal Coy & [illegible]	[illegible]
	23-1-19		Vety Bd at 1/9th [illegible] [illegible]	[illegible]
	24-1-19		Vety Bd at [illegible] [illegible] 50 Bde R.F.A., A/50 & B/50 Bde R.F.A. Visited 2/1 Fd [illegible] (Remounts)	[illegible]
	25-1-19		Vety Board at 9th Seaforths & C/50 Bde R.F.A.	[illegible]
	26-1-19		Inspected [illegible] animals 9th D.A.H.Q. [illegible]	[illegible]
	27-1-19		Vety Board at D/50 Bde, B/51 Bde & A/51 Bde R.F.A.	[illegible]
	28-1-19		Vety Board at A/51 Bde D/51 Bde & C/51 Bde R.F.A. also [illegible] 51 Bde R.F.A.	[illegible]
	29-1-19		Vety Board at 28th A.F.A. Bde [illegible] and 65 Bty 28 A.F.A. Bde	[illegible]
	30-1-19		Vety Board at A/[illegible] Batty & H.Q. 28 A.F.A. Bde	[illegible]
	31-1-19		Vety Board at 106 & 107 Bty [illegible]	[illegible]

A H Wright Major R.A.V.C.
D.A.D.V.S. 9th Division

D. D. & L., London, E.C.
(A8001) Wt. W1771/M2031 750,000 5/17 Sch. 52 Forms/C2118/14

D.A.D.V.S. 9th Division

Instructions regarding War Diaries and Intelligence Summaries are contained in F. S. Regs., Part II. and the Staff Manual respectively. Title pages will be prepared in manuscript.

31

WAR DIARY
or
INTELLIGENCE SUMMARY.
(Erase heading not required.)

February 1919.

Army Form C. 2118.

Vol 41

Place	Date	Hour	Summary of Events and Information	Remarks and references to Appendices
In the Field	1-2-19		Visited and examined the animals at the 105 Coy 9th Divisional Train also part of those of the 104th Coy A.S.C. (preliminary steps to demobilization of horses)	S.H.W.
-	2.2.19		Inspected and examined the remaining animals of 104th Coy 9th Div Train also those of the 21st Mobile Vet Section	S.H.W.
-	3.2.19		Visited Traffic Control Squadron 21st M.V.S. and 2/1 East Lancs Field Ambulance	S.H.W.
-	4.2.19		Visited 21st M.V.S. inspected and examined animals from Div. Units not grouped when Units were visited. Malleined animals 9th Div H.Q. and M.M.P.	S.H.W.
-	5.2.19		Inspected animals malleined at the 9th Div H.Q. and M.M.P. Visited 2/1 East Lancs Field Ambulance	S.H.W.
-	6.2.19		Visited and inspected animals I Section 9th D.A.C. and 21st M.V.S.	S.H.W.
-	7.2.19		Visited and inspected animals 9th Div Signal C.R.E.	S.H.W.
-	8.2.19		Inoculated animals grouped Y and Z by Remount Board with Mallein H.Q. and I Section 9th D.A.C.	S.H.W.
-	9.2.19		Inspected animals malleined I Section and H.Q. 9th D.A.C. Visited 21st M.V.S.	S.H.W.
-	10.2.19		Visited and malleined animals II Section 9th D.A.C. attended III T.C. Squad.	S.H.W.

(A9175) Wt W2358/P360 600,000 12/17 D. D. & L. Sch. 52a. Forms/C2118/15.

WAR DIARY
or
INTELLIGENCE SUMMARY.
(Erase heading not required.)

Army Form C. 2118.

Instructions regarding War Diaries and Intelligence Summaries are contained in F. S. Regs., Part II. and the Staff Manual respectively. Title pages will be prepared in manuscript.

Place	Date	Hour	Summary of Events and Information	Remarks and references to Appendices
In the Field	10.2.19		Attended 9th Div Signal Co RE. Visited 21st MVS.	HW
"	11.2.19		Inspected animals mallеined II Section 9th DAC. Visited 21st MVS	
"	"		Mallеined animals C Batty 51st Bde RFA	HW
"	12.2.19		Visited and inspected animals 105 Coy 9th Div Train 64 Field Coy RE	
"	"		and I Troop III T C Squadron with Remount Board.	HW
"	13.2.19		Inspected animals 9th Divisional Signal Co RE with Remount Board	HW
"	14.2.19		Mallеined animals 9th Div Signal Co RE A P Cable Section I Troop III Squadron	
"	"		T C (Corps Troops) also animals at Reception Camp CRE HQ and 9th Div Train	
"	"		Headquarters mallеined animals 27th Field Ambulance	HW
"	15.2.19		Inspected animals mallеined with following Units Signal Co RE	
"	"		HQ CRE HQ 9th Div Train AP Cable Section I Troop III T C Squadron	
"	"		(Corps Troops) and Reception Camp mallеined animals 9th Div [illegible]	HW
"	16.2.19		Visited 21st MVS Inspected animals mallеined 9th Div Trench Mor Btty	HW
"	17.2.19		Visited 21st MVS.	HW
"	18.2.19		Proceeded to II Corps to act for ADVS II Corps while he on leave	
"	"		to UK. Capt Power AVC acting DADVS in my absence	HW

(A9175) Wt W2355/P360 600,000 12/17 D. D. & L. Sch. 52a. Forms/C2118/15.

Army Form C. 2118.

Instructions regarding War Diaries and Intelligence Summaries are contained in F. S. Regs., Part II. and the Staff Manual respectively. Title pages will be prepared in manuscript.

WAR DIARY
or
INTELLIGENCE SUMMARY.
(Erase heading not required.)

Place	Date	Hour	Summary of Events and Information	Remarks and references to Appendices
Ohligs	19.2.19		Inspected animals H.Q. 9th Div. signal coy. 27th Fd Amb.	W.K.P
	20.2.19		" " 26th Inf Bgde.	W.K.P
	21.2.19		" " 27th Inf Bgde.	W.K.P
	22.2.19		Visited 5th Camerons & 90 R.E.S.	W.K.P
	23		" 26th Inf Bgde.	W.K.P
	24		Inspected animals H.Q. 9th Div. sig. coy. 106 Coy. A.S.C.	W.K.P
	25		" " 9th Batt. M.G. Corps.	W.K.P
	26		" " 27th Inf. Bgde.	W.K.P
	27		" 26th Inf Bgde.	W.K.P
	28		Visited 21st M.V.S. & 104 Coy A.S.C.	W.K.P
	~~29~~			

W.K. Power Capt. for
MAJOR, A.V.C.
D.A.D.V.S. 9th. (SCOTTISH) DIVISION

(A9175) Wt W2358/P360 600,000 12/17 D. D. & L. Sch. 52a. Forms/C2118/15.

D.D.V.S. Lowland Divn 15 March 1919 LOWLAND DVN Vol 13

Army Form C. 2118.

Instructions regarding War Diaries and Intelligence Summaries are contained in F. S. Regs., Part II. and the Staff Manual respectively. Title pages will be prepared in manuscript.

WAR DIARY
or
INTELLIGENCE SUMMARY.

(*Erase heading not required.*)

Place	Date	Hour	Summary of Events and Information	Remarks and references to Appendices
Ohligs	1-3-19		Visited 2nd Corps acting ADVS [illegible]	AHW
	2-3-19		do do [illegible] do	AHW
	3-3-19		do do [illegible] DDVS [illegible]	AHW
	4-3-19		Acting ADVS [illegible]	AHW
	5-3-19		Acting ADVS 2nd Corps	AHW
	6-3-19		do do [illegible]	AHW
	7-3-19		Acting ADVS [illegible] at the DDVS office	AHW
	8-3-19		Acting ADVS [illegible]	AHW
	9-3-19		Acting ADVS 2nd Corps HQ [illegible]	AHW
	10-3-19		Acting ADVS Inspected stables [illegible]	AHW
	11-3-19		Acting ADVS Inspected [illegible] in process of construction at [illegible] BERG GLADBACH [illegible]	AHW
	12-3-19		Visited [illegible] with DDVS [illegible] BERG GLADBACH	AHW
	13-3-19		Acting ADVS 2nd Corps	AHW
	14-3-19		do do Visited Corps HQ [illegible]	AHW
	15-3-19		do do Visited [illegible]	AHW
	16-3-19		do do [illegible]	AHW
	17-3-19		do do Visited & inspected [illegible]	AHW
	18-3-19		Returned to Lowland Divn [illegible]	AHW
	19-3-19		Visited [illegible]	AHW

D. D. & L., London, E.C. (A8004) Wt. W1771/M2031 750,000 5/17 Sch. 52 Forms/C2118/14

DADVS Lowland Div — March 1919 — (2)

Instructions regarding War Diaries and Intelligence Summaries are contained in F. S. Regs., Part II. and the Staff Manual respectively. Title pages will be prepared in manuscript.

WAR DIARY
or
INTELLIGENCE SUMMARY.
(*Erase heading not required.*)

Army Form C. 2118.

Place	Date	Hour	Summary of Events and Information	Remarks and references to Appendices
OHLIGS GERMANY	20-3-19		Visited ADVS office [illegible] Inspected [illegible] on the DDVS instructions visited No 2 VES. Distributed [illegible]	[illegible]
	21-3-19		Visited ADVS office. Inspected [illegible]	[illegible]
	22-3-19		Inspected [illegible]	[illegible]
	23-3-19		Inspected Signal Coy animals. Attended ADVS office	[illegible]
	24-3-19		Inspected animals at 8th SR & 4 RSF [illegible] Visited ADV office	[illegible]
	25-3-19		Visited 21 MVS & ADVS office	[illegible]
	26-3-19		[illegible] inspected animals [illegible] Attended ADVS office [illegible]	[illegible]
	27-3-19		Attended ADVS office. Inspected the animals of the 20 Bde RGA also horses No 3 Squadron Traffic Control	[illegible]
	28-3-19		Attended ADVS office. Inspected animals at DHQ & No 3 Squad Traffic Control	[illegible]
	29-3-19		Visited 28 AFA Bde to see Capt [illegible] also 21 MVS. Attended ADVS [illegible] office	[illegible]
	30-3-19		Left DHQ for dispersal. Capt Power takes over duties of DADVS temporarily	[illegible]
	31-3-19		Administrative work.	[illegible]

W. W. Power Capt. RAVC
A/DADVS Lowland Div.

D. D. & L., London, E.C.
(A8001) Wt. W1771/M2031 750,000 5/17 Sch. 52 Forms/C2118/14

12

Instructions regarding War Diaries and Intelligence Summaries are contained in F. S. Regs., Part II. and the Staff Manual respectively. Title pages will be prepared in manuscript.

WAR DIARY
or
~~INTELLIGENCE~~ ~~SUMMARY.~~

(Erase heading not required.)

Army Form C. 2118.

Vol 14

Place	Date	Hour	Summary of Events and Information	Remarks and references to Appendices
OHLIGS	1-4-19 to 15-4-19		During these dates there was no D.A.D.V.S. of this Division. The [illegible] officer who was acting D.A.D.V.S. apparently did not keep a diary [illegible] so far as I can ascertain nothing [illegible]	[illegible]
"	16-4-19		Reported myself for duty as D.A.D.V.S. to A.D.V.S. Corps.	[illegible]
"	17-4-19		Went to [illegible] saw A.D.V.S. and discussed with him various matters in connection with the Veterinary Services of the Corps and Division. Went to [illegible] and inspected that unit.	[illegible]
"	18-4-19		Attended to cases under treatment at D.A.C. [illegible] and went to [illegible] and inspected animals there awaiting evacuation.	[illegible]
"	19-4-19		Held conference with Veterinary Officers in the Division [illegible] various matters in connection with their duties, [illegible]	[illegible]
"	20-4-19		Normal routine	[illegible]
"	21-4-19		Attended to cases under treatment at D.H.Q. Inspected animals of [illegible]	[illegible]
"	22-4-19		Went to SOLINGEN and met Captain Graham R.A.V.C. and inspected the following units which he was in charge of: 5[illegible] Bde. R.F.A. [illegible] traffic control	[illegible]
"	23-4-19		Attended to cases under treatment at D.H.Q. Went to M.V.S. Inspected with Captain Clay R.A.V.C. D and C Batteries [illegible] Bde. R.F.A. of which units he was in Veterinary charge	[illegible]
"	24-4-19		Went to M.V.S. and inspected animals awaiting evacuation.	[illegible]
"	25-4-19		Went to M.V.S. and inspected with Capt. [illegible] R.A.V.C. [illegible] Batteries [illegible] Bde. R.F.A., of which units he was in Veterinary charge of.	[illegible]

D. D. & L., London, E.C.
(A8004) Wt. W1771/M2031 750,000 5/17 Sch. 52 Forms C2118/14

Instructions regarding War Diaries and Intelligence Summaries are contained in F. S. Regs., Part II. and the Staff Manual respectively. Title pages will be prepared in manuscript.

WAR DIARY
or
~~INTELLIGENCE SUMMARY.~~
(Erase heading not required.)

D.A.D.V.S.,
LOWLAND DIVISION.
No. ....
Date 1 5 19

Army Form C. 2118.

Place	Date	Hour	Summary of Events and Information	Remarks and references to Appendices
[illegible]	6-4-19		Met Captain J. W. [illegible] ... in Veterinary charge of D.A.C., [illegible] R.G.A., 107 Coy R.A.S.C., [illegible] ... Lancashire Field Ambulance.	J.H.T.
"	27-4-19		[illegible]	J.H.T.
"	28-4-19		Met with D.A.D.V.S. [illegible] ... R.F.A. [illegible] ... Field Ambulance ... [illegible]	J.H.T.
"	29-4-19		Met Captain J. [illegible] R.A.V.C. [illegible] ... in Veterinary charge ... R.E., [illegible] ... of the 16 H.L.I. (Pioneers) [illegible]	J.H.T.
"	30-4-19		[illegible] ... Interviewed O.C. Div. Train [illegible] ... smith.	J.H.T.

30-4-19

J. H. Taylor
Major R.A.V.C.
D.A.D.V.S. Lowland Division

D. D. & L., London, E.C.
(A8001) Wt. W1771/M2031 750,000 5/17 Sch. 52 Forms/C2118/14

Instructions regarding War Diaries and Intelligence Summaries are contained in F. S. Regs., Part II. and the Staff Manual respectively. Title pages will be prepared in manuscript.

WAR DIARY
or
~~INTELLIGENCE~~ SUMMARY.
(*Erase heading not required.*)

Army Form C. 2118.

Place	Date	Hour	Summary of Events and Information	Remarks and references to Appendices
Ohligs	16.5.19		Inspected all the animals at DHQ. Inspected animals at 9th [illegible], called upon 10% 50 Bde R.F.A. re a case of ulcerative cellulitis. Called at 28 Fd Amb & 90 Fd Coy R.E. Inspected the transport lines of the 51st H.L.I. reported to Staff Capt re the condition.	J.H.N.
	17.5.19		Normal routine. Went to M.V.S.	J.H.N.
	18.5.19		Normal routine. Went to M.V.S.	J.H.N.
	19.5.19		Acting A.D.V.S. 2nd Corps. Went to 2 V.E.S.	J.H.N.
	20.5.19		Acting A.D.V.S. went to Corps to attend to correspondence	J.H.N.
	21.5.19		Went to M.V.S. & A.D.V.S. office. Called & inspected Horse Dips in course of construction	J.H.N.
	22.5.19		Normal routine. Went [illegible] 9th [illegible]	J.H.N.
	23.5.19		Visited 2nd M.V.S. Corps	J.H.N.
[illegible]	24.5.19		Inspected animals at DHQ. Prepared administrative instructions in case of move	J.H.N.
	25.5.19		Normal routine	J.H.N.
	26.5.19		Went to A.D.V.S. office also inspected the wagon lines of the [illegible]. Selected new site for 2 V.E.S. in case of forward move.	J.H.N.
	27.5.19		Inspected animals of the 1st & 3rd Infantry Bdes also 9th [illegible]	J.H.N.
	28.5.19		Inspected animals for evacuation at M.V.S. Went to A.D.V.S. office & V.E.S.	J.H.N.
	29.5.19		Went to M.V.S. & inspected animals sent in for evacuation from 8/50 Bde R.F.A. Went to HOHSCHEID & met O.C. 2 V.E.S.	J.H.N.
	30.5.19		Went to A.D.V.S. office 2nd Corps.	J.H.N.
	31.5.19		Inspected animals at DHQ & M.V.S.	

J. H. Naylor
Major
D.A.D.V.S. Lowland Div.

D. D. & L., London, E.C.
(A8004) Wt. W1771/M2031 750,000 5/17 Sch. 52 Forms/C2118/14

Instructions regarding War Diaries and Intelligence Summaries are contained in F. S. Regs., Part II. and the Staff Manual respectively. Title pages will be prepared in manuscript.

WAR DIARY
or
~~INTELLIGENCE SUMMARY.~~
(Erase heading not required.)

D.A.D.V.S., LOWLAND DIVISION. No. ...... Date 31.5.19

Army Form C. 2118.

Place	Date	Hour	Summary of Events and Information	Remarks and references to Appendices
Ohlig.	1.5.19		Inspected animals of 51st Bde R.F.A. along with ADVS 2nd Corps. Post mortem on an animal at the 10th [illegible]	J.H.D.
	2.5.19		Normal routine	J.H.D.
	3.5.19		Inspected animals for evacuation at 21st M.V.S. Visited 9th [illegible]	J.H.D.
	4.5.19		Normal routine	J.H.D.
	5.5.19		Met an R.E. officer at 21st M.V.S. to make arrangements for a hut for sleeping accomodation for personnel. Visited wagon lines at D.H.Q. and 1st King's Regt.	J.H.D.
	6.5.19		Inspected animals of the D.A.C. along with ADVS	J.H.D.
	7.5.19		Inspected along with 10% the animals of the 28th A. Fd. Bde in quarantine at [illegible]. Inspected animals at the 9th M.G.C. ready for transfer to Animal Collecting Camp.	J.H.D.
	8.5.19		Inspected animals for evacuation to Collecting Camp. Visited 21st M.V.S.	J.H.D.
	9.5.19		Inspected animals at D.H.Q., also M.M.P. & Traffic Control. Visited 9th M.G.C. wagon lines.	J.H.D.
	10.5.19		Normal Routine. Visited M.V.S.	J.H.D.
	11.5.19		Normal routine. Visited M.V.S.	J.H.D.
	12.5.19		Went with ADVS to inspect animals at M.V.S. Inspected the animals at the 9th M.G.C.	J.H.D.
	13.5.19		Went with D.D.R. Rhine Army to inspect [illegible] at [illegible]	J.H.D.
	14.5.19		Visited M.V.S. & interviewed the new O.C.	
	15.5.19		Inspected [illegible] at the 9th [illegible]. Went to 9th M.G.C. wagon lines.	J.H.D.

D. D. & L., London, E.C. (A8001) Wt. W1771/M2031 750,000 5/17 Sch. 52 Forms/C2118/14

Instructions regarding War Diaries and Intelligence Summaries are contained in F. S. Regs., Part II. and the Staff Manual respectively. Title Pages will be prepared in manuscript.

June 1919

WAR DIARY or INTELLIGENCE SUMMARY

(Erase heading not required.)

D.A.D.V.S., LOWLAND DIVISION.
No.............
Date.............

Army Form C. 2118

Place	Date	Hour	Summary of Events and Information	Remarks and references to Appendices
1-6-19	1-6-19		Inspected animals at 9th [illegible]	J.N.D.
OHLIGS	2-6-19		Attended A.D.V.S. office	J.N.D.
	3-6-19		Kings Birthday. General holiday	J.N.D.
	4-6-19		Attended A.D.V.S. office	J.N.D.
	5-6-19		Attended 2nd M.V.S. Normal Routine at office	J.N.D.
	6-6-19		Normal Routine. Visited 2nd M.V.S. & 9th [illegible]	J.N.D.
	7-6-19		Normal Routine.	J.N.D.
	8-6-19		Normal Routine.	J.N.D.
	9-6-19		Normal Routine.	J.N.D.
	10-6-19		Went with A.D.V.S. to inspect animals of [illegible] Inf Bde, [illegible] 6th 2d Coy R.E. Made out report re these units & sent it to Div. Q. Inspected animals at the 9th [illegible]	J.N.D.
	11-6-19		Inspected animals along with 70% of the 3rd Inf Bde [illegible] made out report & forwarded to Div. Q.	J.N.D.
	12-6-19		Went with A.D.V.S. to inspect the animals of [illegible] Inf Bde, [illegible] & 90 2d Coy R.E.	J.N.D.
	13-6-19		Normal Routine. Visited 2nd M.V.S.	J.N.D.
	14-6-19		Normal Routine. [illegible]	J.N.D.
	15-6-19		Proceeded on leave. [illegible] acting for me.	J.N.D.
	16-6-19		Attended the horse lines of 16th [illegible]	J.N.D.
	17-6-19		Normal Routine. Visited 16th H.L.I. & [illegible]	J.N.D.
	18-6-19		Attended 2nd M.V.S. Inspected [illegible]	J.N.D.

1875 Wt. W593/826 1,000,000 4/15 J.B.C. & A. A.D.S.S./Forms/C. 2118.

Kum

Army Form C. 2118

D.A.D.V.S., LOWLAND DIVISION
No.........
Date.........

Instructions regarding War Diaries and Intelligence Summaries are contained in F. S. Regs., Part II. and the Staff Manual respectively. Title Pages will be prepared in manuscript.

June 1919

WAR DIARY
or
INTELLIGENCE SUMMARY
(Erase heading not required.)

Place	Date	Hour	Summary of Events and Information	Remarks and references to Appendices
OHLIGS	19.6.19		Returned from leave	J.H.T.
	20.6.19		Normal Routine	J.H.T.
	21.6.19		Normal Routine	J.H.T.
	22.6.19		Inspected animals at DHQ	J.H.T.
	23.6.19		Went to 2nd M.V.S. & 9th Signal Coy	J.H.T.
	24.6.19		Inspected animal under treatment at D.H.Q. Went with A.D.V.S. to 2nd M.V.S. Inspected animals of the 9th Bn M.G.C.	J.H.T.
	25.6.19		Normal Routine	J.H.T.
	26.6.19		Visited 9th M.G.C. Inspected animal at M.V.S. for evacuation	J.H.T.
	27.6.19		Went with ADVS to inspect animals of Divl Train	J.H.T.
	28.6.19		Inspected animals at DHQ including MMP & Traffic Control Squad	J.H.T.
	29.6.19		Inspected animals at No 1 Troop No 1 Squad Traffic Control	J.H.T.
	30.6.19		Inspected animals at No 3 Troop No 1 Squad Traffic Control, also cases under treatment at D.H.Q	J.H.T.

J. H. Taylor.
Major
D.A.D.V.S. Lowland Division

1875 Wt. W593/826 1,000,000 4/15 J.B.C. & A. A.D.S.S./Forms/C. 2118.

Instructions regarding War Diaries and Intelligence Summaries are contained in F. S. Regs., Part II. and the Staff Manual respectively. Title Pages will be prepared in manuscript.

D.A.D.V.S.,
LOWLAND DIVISION.
No.
Date 1 · 8 · 19

WAR DIARY
or
~~INTELLIGENCE~~ SUMMARY
(Erase heading not required.)

Army Form C. 2118

Place	Date	Hour	Summary of Events and Information	Remarks and references to Appendices
Germany	1-7-19		Inspected animals at the 9th [illegible] & 53rd Fd Coy R.E. Went to [illegible]	J. H. D
	2-7-19		Went with DDVS Rhine Army & ADVS 2nd Corps to inspect [illegible]	J. H. D
	3-7-19		Went with ADVS 2nd Corps to inspect the animals of the following units, 9th Bn [illegible], 53rd Fd Coy R.E., 3rd Lowland [illegible]	J. H. D
	4-7-19		General holiday for the troops	J. H. D
	5-7-19		Inspected animals at D.H.Q., [illegible] & Signal Coy	J. H. D
	6-7-19		Went to Light Division. [illegible] make arrangements with DDVS [illegible] for [illegible]	J. H. D
	7-7-19		Inspected animals at D.H.Q. Went to [illegible] animals at [illegible] for evacuation	J. H. D J. H. D
	8-7-19		Normal routine	
	9-7-19		DDVS Light Division came to make arrangements [illegible]	J. H. D
	10-7-19		D.H.Q. moves to [illegible]	J. H. D
	11-7-19		Reported in person to ADVS 4th Corps	J. H. D
	12-7-19		Visited all stables at D.H.Q. Went to [illegible]	J. H. D
	13-7-19		Normal Routine. Went to [illegible]	J. H. D
	14-7-19		Made arrangements for classifying all horses in Division	J. H. D
	15-7-19		Went with 20th Bde [illegible] to examine all animals in [illegible] 50th Bde	J. H. D
	16-7-19		Went with Remount Board to examine all animals for Remount classification. Mallein[ed] all [illegible] animals	J. H. D
	17-7-19		Went with Remount Board to classify animals at 51 [illegible] D.A.C. & D.A. H.Q.	J. H. D

1875 Wt. W593/826 1,000,000 4/15 J.B.C. & A. A.D.S.S./Forms/C. 2118.

D.A.D.V.S.
LOWLAND DIVISION.
No. (2)
Date 1 . 8 . 19

Instructions regarding War Diaries and Intelligence Summaries are contained in F. S. Regs., Part II. and the Staff Manual respectively. Title Pages will be prepared in manuscript.

WAR DIARY
or
~~INTELLIGENCE~~ SUMMARY

(Erase heading not required.)

Army Form C. 2118

Place	Date	Hour	Summary of Events and Information	Remarks and references to Appendices
Germany	18.7.19		Went with Remount Board & examined all horses & mules of 3rd Lowland Bde, 63rd Fd Coy RE, MVS & 29th Fd Amb.	J. H. T.
	19.7.19		Classified animals at DHQ & 9th Signal Coy. Visited 10th Divl Train	J. H. T.
	20.7.19		Inspected 84 animals at Niederempt previous to their departure for the Animal Collecting Camp.	J. H. T.
	21.7.19		Went with Remount Board & inspected animals at DHQ, MMP, Signal Coy & 1031 & 4 Coys Divl Train	J. H. T.
	22.7.19		Went with Remount Board to 1st Infantry Bde, 28 Fd Amb, 64 Fd Coy RE & No 2 Coy Divl Train	J. H. T.
	23.7.19		Went with Remount Board to examine animals at 2nd Inf Bde, 90 Fd Coy RE to 3 Coy Divl Train & 9th M G Corps. Nullcised animals classified 'S' in these units.	J. H. T.
	24.7.19		Went to Zeitz & examined animals at 16th R.S.I. for veterinary & Remount classification	J. H. T.
	25.7.19		Inspected MVS & animals at Signal Coy.	J. H. T.
	26.7.19		Went to Bedburg & examined animals going to Animal Collecting Camp	J. H. T.
	27.7.19		Normal Routine.	J. H. T.
	28.7.19		Inspected animals at Signal Coy & 1/8 Scot Rifles	J. H. T.
	29.7.19		Went to M.V.S & examined 32 D & D animals for evacuation.	J. H. T.
	30.7.19		Went to Signal Coy, MVS & 1/8 Scot Rifles. Arranged with DDVS for tent for MVS	J. H. T.
	31.7.19		Went to 2nd BHQ to see a horse with suspected mange	J. H. T.

J. H. Taylor.
Major
DADVS Lowland Division

1875 Wt. W593/826 1,000,000 4/15 J.B.C. & A. A.D.S.S./Forms/C. 2118.

Instructions regarding War Diaries and Intelligence Summaries are contained in F. S. Regs., Part II. and the Staff Manual respectively. Title Pages will be prepared in manuscript.

WAR DIARY
or
~~INTELLIGENCE SUMMARY~~

(Erase heading not required.)

D.A.D.V.S.
LOWLAND DIVISION
No. ....
Date 1-9-19

Army Form C. 2118

Place	Date	Hour	Summary of Events and Information	Remarks and references to Appendices
Harff	1.8.19		Went to M.V.S. Inspected animals at Signal Coy & 9th Scots Rifles	J.H.D.
	2.8.19		Normal Routine	J.H.D.
	3.8.19		Normal Routine	J.H.D.
	4.8.19		Went to Cavalry Horse Show.	J.H.D.
	5.8.19		Went to 9th Bn M.G.C. Went with V.O. to inspect animals at 5 K.O.S.	J.H.D.
	6.8.19		Went to Gommeln & examined 83 horses going to Collecting Camp.	J.H.D.
	7.8.19		Went to Gommeln & examined 106 horses going to Collecting Camp.	J.H.D.
	8.8.19		Received instructions to Mallein all animals in the Division	J.H.D.
			Malleined all animals at Signal Coy & 9th Scots Rifles	J.H.D.
	9.8.19		Examined animals malleined on the 8th inst	J.H.D.
	10.8.19		Went with V.O. 50 Bde R.F.A to mallein animals in D.A.	
	11.8.19		Went with V.O. 2nd Inf Bde Group & malleined all animals	J.H.D.
			Malleined animals at the 9th Bn M.G.	
	12.8.19		Examined animals malleined on the 11th inst	J.H.D.
	13.8.19		Went to M.V.S	J.H.D.
	14.8.19		A.D.V.S. X Corps inspected M.V.S	J.H.D.
	15.8.19		Inspected animals at Signal Coy & 9th Scots Rifles. Went to M.V.S	J.H.D.
	16.8.19		Went to Bedburg & inspected 200 animals for Collecting Camp.	J.H.D.
	17.8.19		Normal Routine	J.H.D.
	18.8.19		A.D.V.S. inspected 1st Infantry Bde & No 2 Coy Divisional Train	J.H.D.
	19.8.19		Malleined all animals at 3/51 Bde R.F.A. Held conference with V.Os.	J.H.D.
	20.8.19		Examined animals malleined on 19th. Inspected animals at Signal Coy	J.H.D.

1875 Wt. W593/826 1,000,000 4/15 J.B.C. & A. A.D.S.S./Forms/C. 2118.

Instructions regarding War Diaries and Intelligence Summaries are contained in F. S. Regs., Part II. and the Staff Manual respectively. Title Pages will be prepared in manuscript.

2

WAR DIARY
~~or~~
~~INTELLIGENCE~~ SUMMARY

(Erase heading not required.)

Army Form C. 2118

Place	Date	Hour	Summary of Events and Information	Remarks and references to Appendices
Harff	21.8.19		Went to B/50 Bde R.F.A. & 21st M.V.S	J.H.T.
	22.8.19		Went to M.V.S & took over command. O.C. on leave to U.K.	J.H.T.
	23.8.19		Went to B/51 Bde R.F.A., 63 Fd Coy R.E. & 107 Coy R.A.S.C.	J.H.T.
	24.8.19		Normal Routine	J.H.T.
	25.8.19		Went to M.V.S, 1/8 Scots Rifles, & Signal Coy	J.H.T.
	26.8.19		Went to M.V.S	J.H.T.
	27.8.19		D.V.S. Rhine Army inspected M.V.S & held conference with V.O.s	J.H.T.
	28.8.19		Went to M.V.S & B/51 Bde R.F.A. Inspected animals at D.A.C.	J.H.T.
	29.8.19		Went to Duren & inspected animals at 28 Fd Ambulance	J.H.T.
	30.8.19		Normal Routine	J.H.T.
	31.8.19		Normal Routine	J.H.T.

J. H. Taylor
Major.
Lowland Division.

1875 Wt. W593/826 1,000,000 4/15 J.B.C. & A. A.D.S.S./Forms/C. 2118.

Instructions regarding War Diaries and Intelligence Summaries are contained in F. S. Regs., Part II. and the Staff Manual respectively. Title Pages will be prepared in manuscript.

WAR DIARY
~~or~~
~~INTELLIGENCE SUMMARY~~

(Erase heading not required.)

Army Form C. 2118

Place	Date	Hour	Summary of Events and Information	Remarks and references to Appendices
Harff	1-9-19		DADVS went on leave to UK. OC 2nd [illegible] acting for him	J.H.D.
	2-9-19		Visited B/51 Bde RFA & Signal Coy	J.H.D.
	3-9-19		Went with ADVS 4th Corps to inspect animals at 51 Bde RFA	J.H.D.
	4-9-19		Normal Routine	J.H.D.
	5-9-19		Inspected animals at 63 Fd Coy RE, 3rd Inf Bde, B/51 Bde RFA and Signal Coy	J.H.D.
	6-9-19		Normal Routine	J.H.D.
	7-9-19		Inspected animals at DHQ	J.H.D.
	8-9-19		Visited 27th Fd Ambulance	J.H.D.
	9-9-19		Normal Routine	J.H.D.
	10-9-19		Examined 230 animals proceeding to Duren. Member of Shoeing Board assembled at [illegible] RASC	J.H.D.
	11-9-19		Normal Routine	J.H.D.
	12-9-19		Inspected animals at B/51 Bde RFA, Signal Coy, 63 Fd Coy RE, 107 Coy RASC & 14 RSF	J.H.D.
	13-9-19		Inspected animals at DHQ	J.H.D.
	14-9-19		Normal Routine	J.H.D.
	15-9-19		Normal Routine	J.H.D.
	16-9-19		Visited B/51 Bde RFA, Signal Coy & 27 Fd Ambulance	J.H.D.
	17-9-19		Normal Routine. DADVS returned.	J.H.D.
	18-9-19		Inspected animals at Signal Coy & [illegible]	J.H.D.
	19-9-19		Went to [illegible] & inspected animals at DHQ	J.H.D.
	20-9-19		Normal Routine	J.H.D.
	21-9-19		Normal Routine	J.H.D.
	22-9-19		ADVS 2nd Corps inspected MVS. Went to Duren & inspected animals proceeding to Remount Depot, Cologne	J.H.D.
	23-9-19		Inspected animals at B/51 Bde RFA, Signal Coy, [illegible] Coy RE, 5th [illegible]. Superintended disinfection of harness at 16th [illegible]	J.H.D.

Instructions regarding War Diaries and Intelligence Summaries are contained in F. S. Regs., Part II. and the Staff Manual respectively. Title Pages will be prepared in manuscript.

WAR DIARY
or
INTELLIGENCE SUMMARY
(Erase heading not required.)

D.A.D.V.S.
LOWLAND DIVISION
No. ....
Date 1.10.19

Army Form C. 2118

Place	Date	Hour	Summary of Events and Information	Remarks and references to Appendices
Nar H	24.9.19		Normal Routine	J.H.T.
	25.9.19		Went to M.V.S.	J.H.T.
	26.9.19		Inspected 3 sick animals at 9th Bn M.G.C.	J.H.T.
	27.9.19		Went to M.V.S., 3/61 Bde R.F.A. and Signal Coy R.E.	J.H.T.
	28.9.19		Normal Routine	J.H.T.
	29.9.19		Normal Routine	J.H.T.
	30.9.19		Inspected animals at Signal Coy R.E. & 3/51 Bde R.F.A. Superintended disinfection of saddlery & harness at D.H.Q.	J.H.T.

J. H. Taylor
Major R.A.V.C.
D.A.D.V.S. Lowland Division

1875 Wt. W593/826 1,000,000 4/15 J.B.C. & A. A.D.S.S./Forms/C. 2118.

Instructions regarding War Diaries and Intelligence Summaries are contained in F. S. Regs., Part II. and the Staff Manual respectively. Title pages will be prepared in manuscript.

WAR DIARY

~~or~~

~~INTELLIGENCE SUMMARY.~~

(Erase heading not required.)

Army Form C. 2118.

D.A.D.V.S., LOWLAND DIVISION.

No. October / 1919

Place	Date	Hour	Summary of Events and Information	Remarks and references to Appendices
Narff	1.10.19		Went to Signal Coy & examined animals proceeding to Cologne	J.H.D.
	2.10.19		Normal Routine	J.H.D.
	3.10.19		Normal Routine	J.H.D.
	4.10.19		Went to 2nd M.V.S., Signal Coy & B/51 Bde R.F.A. & inspected animals	J.H.D.
	5.10.19		Normal Routine	J.H.D.
	6.10.19		Inspected sick animal at 15th H.L.I.	J.H.D.
	7.10.19		Went to B/51 Bde. Went to Duren & arranged with O.C. Divl Train re disinfecting of harness	J.H.D.
	8.10.19		Inspected animal at Signal Coy	J.H.D.
	9.10.19		Normal Routine	J.H.D.
	10.10.19		Went to M.V.S	J.H.D.
	11.10.19		Selected riders for retention in the Rhine Army from Divl units	J.H.D.
	12.10.19		Normal Routine	J.H.D.
	13.10.19		Mallein in Cologne, 2 animals going to England	J.H.D.
	14.10.19		Examined animals mallein yesterday	J.H.D.
	15.10.19		A.D.V.S. 2nd Corps inspected animals of 50 Bde R.F.A	J.H.D.
	16.10.19		Normal Routine	J.H.D.
	17.10.19		Examined animals at Saffendorf before proceeding to Cologne	J.H.D.

D. D. & L., London, E.C.
(A8004) Wt. W1771/M2031 750,000 5/17 Sch. 52 Forms/C2.118/14

Instructions regarding War Diaries and Intelligence Summaries are contained in F. S. Regs., Part II. and the Staff Manual respectively. Title pages will be prepared in manuscript.

2

WAR DIARY ~~or~~ ~~INTELLIGENCE SUMMARY.~~

(Erase heading not required.)

Army Form C. 2118.

D.A.D.V.S., LOWLAND DIVISION.
No. October 1919.
Date........

Place	Date	Hour	Summary of Events and Information	Remarks and references to Appendices
Harff	18.10.19		Normal Routine	J. N. T.
	19.10.19		Normal Routine	J. N. T.
	20.10.19		Selected animals from Divl Train to be transferred to 50 Bde R.F.A.	J. N. T.
	21.10.19		Inspected sick animal at Dormagen. Inspected animals at [illegible]	J. N. T.
	22.10.19		Went to 18/51 Bde R.F.A.	J. N. T.
	23.10.19		Normal Routine	J. N. T.
	24.10.19		Lowland D.H.Q. & 2nd M.V.S. disbanded. Awaiting instructions for re-posting	J. N. T.

J. N. Taylor.
Major,
D.A.D.V.S.
Lowland Division

OFFICER-IN-CHARGE RECORDS
ROYAL ARMY VETERINARY CORPS

D. D. & L., London, E.C.
(A8004) Wt. W1771/M2031 750,000 5/17 Sch. 52 Forms/C2118/14

www.ingramcontent.com/pod-product-compliance
Lightning Source LLC
Chambersburg PA
CBHW080918230426
43668CB00014B/2151
9781474507431